Don't Let *Your* Love *Go* Wrong

Print: ISBN 978-1-7375162-1-7
Ebook: 978-1-7375162-2-4

Quail Crossing Press
Tallahassee, Florida

Cover and interior book design by David Prendergast

Don't Let *Your* Love *Go* Wrong

The Extraordinary Life of Anna Forbes Liddell

Carolyn Dubard

Quail Crossing Press
Tallahassee, Florida

Dedicated

To the memory of Richard T. Hull, PhD, (1939–2021)

My friend and writing mentor

Contents

Timeline

Anna Forbes Liddell (1891–1979)

Academic Degrees: AB (1918), MA (1922), PhD (1924)

Academic Enrollments

Presbyterian Female College (1906–1908)

University of Tennessee (1908)

Barnard College (1912, 1915)*

Cornell University (1921–1923)

University of North Carolina (UNC) (1915–1918, 1923–1925)**

Employment

Solicitor of ads for the *Charlotte Observer* (1911–1912) and *New York Post* (1914)

Summer employment as secretary or bookkeeper (1915–1918)

Freelance writer (1911–1921)

Letter writer for McGraw Hill (1919)

High School Teacher in Salisbury North Carolina (1919–1921)

Professor of History and Social Science at Chowan College (1925–1926)

Associate Professor/Professor of Philosophy at Florida State College for Women (1926–1947)

Professor of Philosophy at Florida State University (1947–1962)

Department Chair of Philosophy/Philosophy and Religion (1932–1951)

Professor on WFSU–TV (1960–1962)

Achievements/Awards/Recognitions

Co-founder of the North Carolina Equal Suffrage League (1913)

Co-organizer of suffrage float—first public demonstration for woman suffrage in North Carolina (1914)

Essay prizewinner from Cornell's Sage School of Philosophy (1923)

One of two women to be awarded the first PhDs from UNC (1924)

First person to be awarded a PhD in philosophy from UNC (1924)

Graham-Keenan Fellowship in Philosophy (1924–1925)

President of the Southern Society of Philosophy and Psychology (1933)

First woman from the Southern US to speak at the World Congress of Philosophy (1934)

President of the Society for the Philosophy of Religion (1948)

FSU Lawton Distinguished Professor (1959)

Professor of first credited course on WFSU-TV (1960)

Speaker before Florida legislative committees to support the Equal Rights Amendment (1973, 1974)

Posthumous Recognition

Renovation of fountain in front of Westcott Building dedicated to Liddell (1982)

Dean Eyman Award (2006)

Anna Forbes Liddell American Fellowship fully endowed (2012)

UNC Scholarship renamed for Liddell (2016)

*In some articles, Liddell is noted as enrolled in Columbia University instead of Barnard College. However, in Liddell's time, Columbia did not admit women. Women students were enrolled in Barnard College, which was the all-women college associated with Cornell.

**Liddell attended the University of North Carolina located at Chapel Hill, North Carolina. Since, in her time, it was the only university designated as the University of North Carolina, it will be referred to simply as the University of North Carolina or UNC.

Introduction

On April 9, 1973, there was standing room only in the meeting room of the Florida House Committee on Rights in Tallahassee, Florida. The Committee was to vote on sending the Equal Rights Amendment (ERA) to the US Constitution to the House floor for a vote on ratification. The ERA stated, "Equality of rights under the law shall not be denied or abridged by the United States or by any state on account of sex." Congress had passed the ERA in 1972. Now, thirty-eight states needed to ratify the amendment for it to become law.

Anna Forbes Liddell, Professor Emerita at Florida State University, frail from her eighty-one years, was pushed forward in a wheelchair to the microphone. Wearing a purple dress and a lavender cardigan, she rose from her wheelchair to speak. A hush fell over the audience. Liddell had been slightly under four feet eleven inches tall when she was a young woman; now she stood even shorter with the hunched posture of age. Her silver hair was swept back from her deeply lined face. Her arms quivered, but her voice was strong—deep and a little raspy—as she said the ERA opponents' arguments were, "the same old arguments used against women's suffrage. I could have almost repeated the first part of that argument myself."[1]

Opponents had testified that the ERA would take women out of the home. Liddell countered, "Well, dearly beloveds, it ain't necessarily so. In the first place, there ain't enough women to go around. And in the second place, not all the men want to get married—and I don't blame them."[2] When she finished speaking, she lowered herself into her wheelchair. The audience gave her a standing ovation.

As Liddell was wheeled out of the House meeting room, an ERA opponent stopped her to say, "I enjoyed your speech, Honey, but you are so wrong." Liddell replied, "Oh, no, my dear, it's I who am sorry you're so wrong. You see, I'm right. I've been right from the very beginning. And I certainly would know, because I've been around from the very beginning."[3]

In her twenties, Liddell fought for women to have the right to vote. Next, she opened doors for women in higher education as a student and as a professor. She showed a path for professional women who followed her. Her influence on students went beyond teaching intellectually demanding courses. She provided a role model of a smart, competent woman, respected in her academic field and in the university. For women, she was a role model who looked like them; for both women and men, she was an example that challenged the idea, prevalent then, that a woman could not do a man's job. Her journey to follow her dream changed minds about the role of women and inspired generations of students to follow their own personal passions.

The following chapters show how extraordinary Anna Forbes Liddell was, what barriers she faced to follow her dream, and how her circumstances and choices shaped her into the woman she became and made possible her many contributions.

Liddell Family Tree

W.J.F. Liddell and Anna Amelia Brubaker

Children

Jeanette Liddell

Annie Liddell married Rev. David Hill

Children

Walter Liddell Hill

Arthur Hill*

David Hill*

Walter Scott Liddell married Helen Sherman (Nellie) Ogden

Children

Helen Liddell

Anna Forbes Liddell

Eva Liddell

Forbes Liddell married Myra Ravenscroft

Child

Katherine Liddell

Vinton Liddell married Jane Hall

Children

John*

Vinton

Louella Liddell married Thomas Franklin

Child

Thomas Franklin, Jr.

Maud Liddell*

Thomas Liddell*

*died before age 7

The Liddells Move South

Sixteen-year-old Anna Forbes Liddell stared at a photograph of her grandfather Walter James Forbes (W.J.F.) Liddell, which hung in the Liddell family home. He had died three years before she was born; yet she wanted to know more about him. The middle-aged man in the photo had a long beard and a stern expression that matched the family stories of a conservative, deeply religious man who was strict with his children. Next to the stern photo was one of him when he was younger. She saw a young man with a tender expression. When she looked at that photo, she was proud to be his granddaughter because she knew that he built wealth in Pennsylvania, lost it in Wisconsin, and then rebuilt it in Charlotte, North Carolina, to provide a comfortable life for his family.[1]

W.J.F. was called Walter as a child. As an adult, only the people closest to him called him Walter; everyone else and published accounts of his business and social dealings used his initials. The formality of his name suited him. He was formal, even with his children. They called him Father, not Papa or Daddy.[2]

W.J.F. was the son of Scottish immigrants, James and Isabella Forbes Liddell. In 1819, James came to the United States with his Presbyterian faith, his extraordinary skill as a machinist, and his savings, which he invested in an iron foundry in Erie, Pennsylvania. The foundry had many names over the years, but it was best known as the Erie City Ironworks. In 1821, James sent for Isabella and their three children to come to Erie from Scotland. They had three more children, including W.J.F. born in 1825.[3]

The young W.J.F. took seriously the words from his maternal grandfather, James Forbes, a schoolteacher in Scotland, who reminded him that he had more opportunities than many other people did. As such, he had a responsibly to accomplish more. W.J.F. freely lent books from his personal library to his friends. Every week, he and his friends met to listen to lectures and discuss how to improve their minds. Through his studies, W.J.F. found his father's Presbyterian faith unsatisfactory. Family stories differ whether he was so inspired at a Baptist camp meeting that he suddenly came down to the front to be baptized or whether he joined through reasoning that the Baptists were at least better than the Presbyterians, but all agree that once he became a Baptist, he was an ardent believer.[4]

It was at a Baptist church meeting that W.J.F. met and fell in love with Anna Amelia Brubaker. She was short in stature, standing only five feet tall, with blue eyes and blond hair that fell into curls all over her head. The Brubakers were Swiss German farmers who lived near Lancaster, Pennsylvania, when Anna Amelia was born. There was no school nearby. When Anna Amelia was twelve years old, her family moved to Gerard, a community near Erie. Although Gerard had a school, Anna Amelia often had to stay home to take care of her younger siblings. She became a schoolteacher, although she had only about two years of formal education. Such experience was common in those days. In 1850, fewer than half of the school-age children in the United States were in school, and many teachers were teenagers with only a grade school education. With her excellent mind, Anna Amelia educated herself through extensive reading, especially the *New-York Tribune* that she read daily. All her life, Anna Amelia regretted her lack of formal education; she vowed her children would have the opportunities she lacked.[5]

W.J.F. and Anna Amelia married on October 28, 1847, and started their family of nine children. Anna Amelia quit teaching when she married, because, in that time, only unmarried women could be schoolteachers. W.J.F. became an excellent machinist as he worked with his father in the foundry. Frugal, he saved his money and bought his own shares in the foundry. In 1864, the year after the death of W.J.F.'s father, the family moved from Erie to Madison, Wisconsin. A few years later, they moved to Milwaukee. W.J.F. started the Depere Ironworks with the sale of his interest in the Erie City Ironworks (about $100,000, which is worth about $1,753,000 in 2021 dollars).[6]

In Wisconsin, the Liddells lived the American dream. They had a large home filled with beautiful furniture. The stress of providing a comfortable life for his large family affected W.J.F.'s health and disposition. He worried about money and suffered from stomach ulcers most of his adult life. Pain showed in his face, and he was often irritable. The once inquisitive, sensitive young man grew into a man unwavering in his beliefs with a morality that was black and white with no gray areas. His children knew exactly what he expected as to their behavior. Yet at heart, W.F.J. remained a gentle man. With his strict Baptist faith, one might think he would live by the scripture that says to spare the rod is to spoil the child. But he did not. Whenever a child needed discipline, he would take the child to the bedroom and pray for a length of time that to the child must have seemed forever. Then, he would require the child to memorize bible verses. One son said he remembered the verses the rest of his life.[7]

The Liddell children knew their parents expected them to follow the church's teachings and to go to college. W.J.F. and Anna Amelia's expectation of college for all their children was extraordinary. In 1870, most people in the United States did not have a high school diploma, much less a college or university degree. There were only 582 degree-awarding higher education institutions. Of those 582 institutions, 59 percent admitted men only, 12 percent women only, and 29 percent were coeducational. Women made up only 21 percent of college enrollments.[8]

Admission to college did not guarantee a woman access to the same education as a man. Most coeducational and men-only colleges stressed liberal arts education. However, at coeducational schools, if a course enrolled more women than men, faculty and students devalued the course. Most women-only colleges trained students to become nurses or teachers. The nurses and teachers usually worked in their professions only until they married. Many people thought that the purpose of education for a woman was to produce a *true woman*, a term for a pious Christian wife and mother.[9]

Little is known about the education of Jeanette, who was W.J.F. and Anna Amelia's oldest child. In 1865, sixteen-year-old Annie (second child) entered the Female Institute of the University of Lewisburg (later became Bucknell University). At the University, men enrolled in the Male Academy and women in the Female Institute. The Academy and the Institute were essentially two single-sex schools on one campus.

Not all the Liddell children shared their parents' enthusiasm about college education. That was certainly the case with Annie. Homesick, she felt like she was in a prison. She could leave the Female Institute to go to the store only when a woman teacher accompanied her. Each week, the Institute marched all students to the Baptist Sunday service, regardless of the students' religious affiliation. Annie wrote in her diary, "They dare not trust us alone outside the gate for fear we will cast a shy glance at some of the handsome (homely) students that we are sure to find on the streets at all hours when we go down [the] street. I don't see why they are at liberty to go and come at their pleasure and we are penned up here."[10]

Annie's experience was typical. Women colleges strictly controlled interactions between the sexes. A tall picket fence enclosed the Female Institute of the University of Lewisburg. The young women wedged themselves between the thick hedge and the fence to talk with and pass notes to the young men on the other side of the fence. Even at coeducational institutions, women and men had limited opportunities to interact with each other.[11]

Annie described an occasion when she flirted with the men in a dormitory. The girls went for a walk with a teacher in the lead and the girls following. As the procession passed by a men's dormitory, Annie had her handkerchief in her hand. Another girl named Lettie told her she was flirting with the boys with her handkerchief and that she should put it away. Annie replied defiantly that she would not put it away and began waving it in the air. Lettie said, "Oh Annie Liddell, see what you have done!" Annie looked up and the boys in the dormitory were leaning out the windows waving their pillowcases. One threw out his underpants, causing the girls to laugh and the teacher to look back. Annie left Lewisburg in1868 before graduating. No reason is given in her diary for her leaving the school.[12]

Then came the first half of the 1870s, a transformative time for the Liddells—a time for terrible sorrows and great joys. In October 1870, the two youngest children, four-year-old Maud and two-year-old Tommy, died from scarlet fever in a span of two weeks. A year later, Jeannette (twenty-three years old) died from tuberculosis. Those deaths left three sons (Walter, Forbes, and Vinton) and three daughters (Annie, Eva, and Louella). After these tragedies, the Liddells fulfilled a dream and sent five of their children to college between 1872 and 1875. Annie returned to the University of Lewisburg for her senior year. She graduated and married Rev. David Jayne Hill, a University of Lewisburg graduate who taught at the University. Walter started college, likely at the University of Wisconsin. Forbes attended Lawrence University, but he soon dropped out because of his asthma. Eva started college in either Milwaukee or Madison, and Vinton enrolled at the University of Lewisburg. Only the youngest child, daughter Louella, needed a chance for a college education. Unfortunately, Walter's college career ended when the school expelled him for violating the code of conduct for a prank that seems mild today. At a party, he took a dare to swim across the lake with a keg of beer strapped to his back. For Walter, expulsion was minor compared to facing his father. W.J.F., a strict teetotaler, considered anyone who drank to be morally bankrupt and weak in character.[13]

During this pivotal time, Louella Liddell and Helen (Nellie) Ogden became friends when they were eight years old. Their friendship, important only to two little girls, was one of those chance events that would have ramifications years later. The girls usually played at the Liddell home. Twenty-year-old Walter Liddell put the girls on his shoulders and pranced around the playroom.[14] Years later, Nellie and Walter married, and they had two daughters, Helen and Anna Forbes.

James and Beulah Ogden had moved to Milwaukee from Binghamton, New York, with Nellie and two-year-old William in 1872. They moved back to Binghamton, just one year later, when the Financial Panic of 1873 shook the nation. The Financial Panic of 1873 started when the European stock market crashed and investors sold off their most speculative holdings, including bonds for American railroads. As a result, the Jay Cooke & Company, a New York bank that had invested heavily in railroads, went bankrupt. This bankruptcy started a nationwide run on banks. At least 100 banks closed. Since the railroads could not find buyers for their bonds, many went bankrupt.[15]

The Depere Ironworks sent their engines and boilers to their customers by rail. It had inventory already loaded onto boxcars at the railroad yard when the panic started and the trains stopped running. In addition, one of the foundry's largest customer accounts was the railroad industry itself. Consequently, the ironworks had inventory in half-built freight cars that the defunct railroad companies no longer needed.[16]

The Panic of 1873 triggered a six-year long economic depression. The Depere Ironworks went out of business, and the Liddells were broke by 1875. W.J.F. was fifty years old and worried how he was going to support his family. He heard about an opening for a foreman at the Mecklenburg Iron Works in Charlotte, North Carolina. He got the job and went immediately to Charlotte to work. Anna Amelia and the children stayed in Wisconsin to sell the furniture and house there. They could not afford to move much to Charlotte.[17]

It was a beautiful spring day with a stiff breeze on May 20, 1875, when W.J.F. Liddell arrived in Charlotte. That day, at least 30,000 people filled the streets of the small town of 8,000 people. The people of the surrounding Mecklenburg County and beyond had arrived for the centennial celebration of the signing of the Mecklenburg Declaration of Independence. Mecklenburg citizens asserted that two dozen patriots of Mecklenburg County declared independence from Britain by signing a Declaration of Independence on May 20, 1775. This was a full year before Thomas Jefferson drafted the Continental Congress's Declaration of Independence. Furthermore, the citizens of the county believed Jefferson used phrases from the Mecklenburg Declaration to create his own document. A house fire, however, destroyed the original Mecklenburg Declaration in 1800, according to the county citizens. The owner of the house reconstructed the wording from memory. When a Raleigh newspaper printed the reconstructed Mecklenburg document in 1819, Jefferson denounced the document as a hoax. An investigation followed. The Mecklenburg citizens stuck to their story and enjoyed their celebration every May 20. On this centennial celebration in 1875, there was a morning parade of military troops and firetrucks, followed with a picnic lunch at the fairgrounds. Afterwards, there were speeches by judges, colonels, and the governors of North Carolina, South Carolina, Virginia, Illinois, and Tennessee. Few people could hear the speeches of the dignitaries because of the noise of the crowd. The festivities ended with an evening fireworks display.[18]

Eventually, the Liddells reunited in Charlotte in 1876, a year after W.J.F. arrived in Charlotte. Yet W.J.F.'s income was not enough to support the family. They took in boarders to make ends meet, and son Vinton got a job as a typesetter with the local newspaper.[19] Their lives differed from when they had lived in Wisconsin. Then, they had lived in comfort and had been part of the highest social class. Now, they were struggling financially and had no social standing.[20]

Worried about fitting into the Charlotte community, W.J.F. sternly admonished his family not to say or do anything that might offend the people of Charlotte. The Liddells were Baptists and Republicans in a town of Presbyterians and Democrats. Worst of all, they were Yankees. Just eleven years after the Civil War, there were still bad feelings on both sides, but especially in the South. The Liddells were not only Yankees, but they had been Abolitionists. Before the Civil War, they had been part of the Underground Railroad, a network of safe pathways and houses used by fugitive slaves as they fled to Canada.[21] If captured, the fugitive slaves were returned to their Southern masters and the people who aided them arrested.

The first thing the Liddells did in Charlotte was to join the First Baptist Church, which had about 160 members. As with all small churches, there were too many jobs and too few people to do them. W.J.F. quickly became a leader in the church as a deacon and a member of the Executive Committee. The First Baptist Church strictly enforced its expectations that members not drink alcohol, dance, or attend performances at the Charlotte Opera House. The Church expelled anyone who broke those rules even once. To be reinstated, those expelled had to repent publicly.[22]

Shortly after moving to Charlotte, W.J.F. thought of how to improve the cotton press. He offered his idea to his boss, John Wilkes, but Wilkes was not interested. At that, W.J.F. started a rival company, The Liddell Company, in 1878 with financial backing from Robert McDowell. The Liddell Company made machines and machine parts for textile mills and other factories. It opened as the area was changing from an agricultural to an industrial economy. The farmers sent the cotton to Northern textile mills. Businessmen considered bringing the mill to the cotton instead. In 1880, just two years after the start of the Liddell Company, two brothers, R.M. and D.W. Oates, opened a textile mill on the outskirts of Charlotte. Soon other mills and factories opened and the demand for machinery boomed.[23]

In 1880, tragedy struck again for the Liddell family. Annie Liddell Hill died two weeks after giving birth to her third son. Her husband Rev. Hill had recently been appointed President of the University of Lewisburg; he could not do his job and raise his sons. Thus, after Annie's funeral, Anna Amelia traveled by train from Lewisburg to Charlotte with the three boys (the oldest was four years old) so the Liddells could raise them.[24]

Rev. David Hill had a distinguished career. He later served as President of the University of Rochester, and then he switched from an academic to a diplomatic career. He served as US Assistant Secretary of State from 1896 to 1903, and was appointed as US Minister to Switzerland in 1903, US Minister to Netherlands and Luxembourg in 1905, and US Ambassador to Germany from 1908 to 1911.[25]

In 1881, while Rev. Hill was still President of the University of Lewisburg, Louella Liddell enrolled in the Female Institute of the University. Vinton was also at the University, but he was expelled in the fall of 1882. After a night of drinking, he led eighteen other students to the home of William Martin, the Principal of the Male Academy. The nineteen students snuck under Mr. Martin's bedroom window and shouted out three groans. Vinton was the only student expelled for the prank. He denied to his father that he had been drinking and said that he was singled out because Hill did not want to show leniency to a relative, and, perhaps, because he had been in trouble before from similar pranks.[26]

While at the University, Louella Liddell received a letter from Nellie Ogden, her Milwaukee childhood friend. Nellie attended Mrs. Keefs's boarding school in Philadelphia. When Nellie and her roommate, Clare Notels, were settling into their room at the school, they taped pictures of their boyfriends onto the side of the chest of drawers. Clare identified one picture as that of Vinton Liddell. Nellie was startled when she heard the name Liddell. She recalled that her friend Louella had three brothers: Walter, Forbes and Vinton. Nellie asked Clare whether Vinton had a sister named Louella. Clare replied that he did and that she was attending the University of Lewisburg. Nellie wrote Louella. Louella wrote back and spent Thanksgiving with friends in Philadelphia. The girls had a wonderful reunion. The next two Christmases, Louella went to

Binghamton to see Nellie, and, on the third Christmas, Nellie went to Charlotte to see Louella. It was then that Walter began his courtship of Nellie.[27]

By 1885, the Liddells had lived in Charlotte for a decade. Most of the family had found a niche in Charlotte society, even though the community still viewed them as the Yankees. W.J.F. was a founder of the Charlotte Young Men's Christian Association. Whenever there was a civic-minded project in Charlotte, he was there. Anna Amelia helped open the first Black hospital in Charlotte. Daughter Eva played the church organ and started the first Baptist women's aid society in the state. Louella quickly became popular. She made friends easily because she always had a kind word to say to everyone.[28]

Everyone, except the oldest son Walter, integrated into Charlotte society. Walter attended the First Baptist Church, but he did not fit in with the church members as the rest of the family did. He did not follow his father's advice not to offend the people of Charlotte. He was honest about his views when asked, proclaimed himself to be a Republican, dated poor girls who worked to support themselves, and gave his seat on a bus to a Black woman who was tired. These actions were offensive to his Charlotte social crowd. He became bitter and withdrew from society. It is no wonder Walter was attracted to Nellie, who was a Yankee. In 1885, Walter asked Nellie to marry him and she said yes. They planned a wedding for February 1886. Walter explained to Nellie his unease with Charlotte society and told her that when they married she would have to be the sociable one.[29]

Parents Nellie and Walter

It was dark by 8:30 p.m. in Charlotte in the summer of 1885 when Louella Liddell came home from riding with a boy. Her oldest brother Walter scolded her, "Any girl who rides with a boy after dark has no self-respect."[1]

When Nellie Ogden in Binghamton learned about the argument between Louella and Walter, presumably from a letter from Louella, she questioned whether she should marry Walter the following February. She was twenty-one and fun loving. Walter, twelve years older at age thirty-three, was serious. His sisters agreed that he took the fun out of everything.[2]

Nellie had a right to worry. State law, not federal law, regulated the rights of a married woman. The state laws varied, but all were based on English law that the English colonists brought to America. English law treated men different from women and married women different from single women. When a woman married, she lost some rights, because she was no longer considered a separate legal individual. When she married, any real estate she owned became her husband's real estate, and her personal property became her husband's property. A married woman did not own her clothes, jewelry, books, furniture, or kitchen equipment. Neither could she own any salary she earned, nor could she enter into a contract, including making a will.[3]

In the nineteenth century, several US states modified the property rights of women. In 1848, New York passed the Married Women's Property Act that allowed a woman to own the real and personal property she brought into the marriage. North Carolina did not.[4] After marriage, Nellie would move to North Carolina where women's rights were limited more than in her home state of New York. Walter was a loving fiancé, but she wondered whether he would become overbearing after marriage. Would he scold her as he had scolded Louella?

Nellie asked Walter tough questions. He did whatever he wanted to do. Why could not Louella do what she wanted to do without censure? Nellie reminded Walter that he had taken her riding after dark. Did he view her as having no self-respect? Walter replied, "Boys seek out girls who will ride with them after dark, but they respect the girls who will not." As for her riding with him after dark, he explained that was different, because they were engaged when it happened. As his fiancée, she had a right to be with him anytime and, besides, she had begged him on that occasion to return earlier, but he did not.[5]

Nellie continued to worry. Six weeks before the wedding, Walter wrote Nellie to profess his love and calm her fears:

> If you lack faith in me, now is the time to act. I can truly say that from the moment I first knew that you loved me you have been looked upon as my wife and I have been as faithful to you as though the words that will make you so had already been pronounced. I have no idea that I can supply the place of society to you nor do I intend to try. I am not going to revolutionize your life. You will go on as you have lived, and I will accept the inevitable and try to interest myself in whatever interests you. I have no law. I never dictate to those I love. I will make your life pleasant if I can, always remembering the difference in our ages and that at your age I was as fond of gaiety as yourself. . . .When I marry, you shall know as much about my affairs as I do myself and being an

equal partner with me will be left unrestrained. . . .Assuring you of my everlasting love I am
Yours always
Walter.[6]

Walter's letter must have satisfied Nellie, because the wedding went on as planned. They married on February 25, 1886, in Binghamton, New York, in an evening church ceremony with four hundred guests followed by a reception for sixty guests. They went on a two-week honeymoon to Washington, DC, and New York City.[7]

Nellie worried about moving to Charlotte. Its dirt-packed streets turned into mud when it rained. The city had no streetcars, few sidewalks, only a handful of stores, and no public library. When she visited at Christmas, it had snowed. What stuck her as odd was that people just let the snow stay on the streets until it melted.[8]

The couple moved into the Liddell family house, which was the only house on the square on Trade Street where the Old City Hall now stands. The large two-story, gray wooden farm-style house was set back from the street behind a grove of oak trees. Extensive gardens filled the back and side yards. A single-story front porch ran about one-third the width of the house with four slender posts supporting its roof. The kitchen was a separate red brick structure behind the main house, a configuration common for a house built before the Civil War.[9]

When Walter and Nellie moved into the Liddell family home, five other people lived there: his parents, his sisters (Eva and Louella), and his nephew (Walter Hill). Walter's brothers (Vinton and Forbes) lived in Tuscaloosa, Alabama, where the Liddell Company had opened a branch. The Liddell Company had also expanded to Dallas, Texas. Walter split his time between Charlotte and Dallas, since he oversaw the Dallas Branch and was the Treasurer for the entire company. Nellie stayed in Charlotte until after the birth of their first child, Helen Katherine, on August 14, 1887. Nellie and baby Helen would go to Dallas from time to time to be with Walter, and Nellie planned to move permanently to Dallas in late 1888.[10]

Before Walter and Nellie could move to Dallas, W.J.F.'s stomach ulcers worsened. He went to Atlanta for treatment at a clinic where he had received successful treatment before, but, within a week, he died suddenly at the clinic. W.J.F.'s business partner Robert McDowell had died three years earlier. These deaths changed everything. The Liddell Company became a stock company, instead of a partnership. The Liddell family owned 49 percent of the stock. Walter took the office of President, in charge of operations, and William Chambers, representing the McDowell family, became General Manager, in charge of sales and collections. From the start, Walter Liddell and William Chambers disagreed on the direction that the company should take. Their differences smoldered under the surface for many years until a final blow-up occurred. Walter left the company in 1910, leaving William Chambers to run the company as he saw fit.[11]

* * *

Anna Forbes Liddell was born on December 6, 1891. In that time, families used the same given names for children, generation after generation, and they often used family surnames for the middle name. Forbes was the maiden name of Anna Forbes's great-grandmother. Anna Forbes shared Forbes, as a middle name, with her grandfather and an uncle and shared Anna, as a first name, with her grandmother and an aunt. From the beginning, Anna Forbes was called by both her first and middle names, forming a Southern double name. In the South, families often called children, especially girls, with a double name, and sometimes, one name was shortened to a nickname or was a masculine-sounding name, such as Mary Beth, Peggy Sue, or Billie Jean. To understand a Southern double name, one needs to know its pronunciation. The names Anna and Forbes were run together, coming out in a single breath, pronounced as Annaforbes.

Anna Forbes got her brown eyes from her mother and her short stature from both sides of her family. Nellie was only five feet tall, the same height as Anna Amelia and Eva. Even the tallest Liddell was only medium height. The family joked that instead of being called the *Liddell People*, they should be called the *Little People*.[12]

An early memory of Anna Forbes was that her family differed from the others in Charlotte—they were the Yankees. She reminisced:

> When I was six, I think it was, I had a birthday party and as usual we were arguing the question of the North versus the South. I got pretty upset and pushed a little boy off the banisters. They carried him in and laid him on the sofa. For a while I was afraid I'd killed him, but he wasn't hurt. Anyhow, after that I never had to fight the Civil War again."[13]

Anna Forbes's father Walter overcame his unease with Southern society. In 1894, he was the driving force in establishing the Oasis Temple in Charlotte, which was the first masonic temple in the Carolinas. He became a 33rd degree Scottish Rite Mason. He traveled throughout the Carolinas working for the Order. The Masons in the Carolinas called him *Daddy Liddell.* Walter led the Oasis Temple's decision to establish the Widows' Fund of Oasis Temple, which was a type of life insurance. After Walter left the Liddell company, he worked for the Widows' Fund. He was the first President of the Fund and was the Treasurer of the Fund for many years.[14] Through his masonic work, Walter forged close relationships, and he began to think of himself as a Southerner.

Eventually, both the established old Confederate families and the new industrialists accepted the *entire* Liddell family. The Liddells were friends with leaders in the business community, such as D.A. Tompkins (the mastermind behind most business deals in the area), and with prominent families, such as Myers (real estate), Oates (textiles), Cramer (textiles), Alexander (law and medicine), and Van Landingham (cotton brokerage).

Other friends were Mary Anna Morrison Jackson (the widow of the Confederate General Stonewall Jackson) and politicians, such as Robert Glenn (Governor of North Carolina from 1905 to 1909) and Cameron Morrison (Governor of North Carolina from 1921 to 1925).[15]

Like her father, Anna Forbes thought of herself as a Southerner. Anna Forbes and her sister Helen did not qualify to join the United Children of the Confederacy, but went to its annual picnics as guests of their friends. Nellie, however, kept her Northern identity. Yet that did not mean she was standoffish in Charlotte. She was active in the women's club movement that swept the nation beginning around 1880 and continued into the twentieth century. She belonged to several civic-action clubs and social clubs, such as bridge and book clubs, and held offices in the local and state societies of the National Society of the Colonial Dames of America. Nellie was a founding member of the Charlotte Women's Club, which started the Charlotte Young Women's Christian Association (YWCA). She was the first president of the Charlotte YWCA from 1902 to 1903. One project of the YWCA was the opening of a residence for young single farm women who had moved into town to work in the factories.[16]

* * *

Walter kept his promise to Nellie that she would be an equal partner in the marriage. Every month, Walter turned over his pay to Nellie after taking out an allowance for himself. He used his allowance for his daily expenses and for charity. He had a soft heart for hard-luck stories and gave money to people in trouble. When asked why he did so, he replied it was only common decency and he would like help if he were in that person's situation.[17]

Nellie stretched every dollar. She did not buy cheap goods. She bought quality goods economically. When she had a dress made, she used the best dressmaker and materials. She was an excellent dressmaker in her own right and made her daughters' dresses, skirts, and blouses in the latest New York and Paris styles using silk, crepe de chine, chiffon, georgette, and other such fabrics. Nellie saved the scraps from her sewing—bits of fabric, ribbons, and lace and placed them, neatly folded or rolled, in a trunk in the attic. Twice a year, when she was making the new season's clothes, she brought the trunk down to see if last year's scraps could be worked into this year's clothes. When Anna Forbes was seven, Nellie made her a tan sailor dress from a window shade just to see if it could be done.[18]

When Anna Forbes was ten years old, her parents built a house next door to the Liddell family home. After supper, Nellie, Walter, and the girls typically went to their library for the evening. The bookshelves had many biographies, especially of kings and queens. These biographies were Nellie's favorites. Tucked on a lower shelf was a favorite of Anna Forbes, a collection of essays (likely, *Memories and Portraits* by Robert Louis Stephenson). One of her uncles had given her the book and inscribed it as "For Anna Forbes, because she is philosophically inclined."[19] Each evening, Nellie and Walter settled in front of the library fireplace with Nellie reading or sewing, and Walter thinking and smoking. Since people did not realize the health hazards of smoking, Walter may not have connected his smoking with his lifelong struggle with asthma. Anna Forbes and Helen read, sewed, gossiped or joked around. Sometimes the girls became rambunctious, and Walter had to remind them to say away from the fire in the fireplace. Most of all, Anna Forbes loved arguing with Helen. She wrote in her diary, "All we need is to be together, we never lack something to agree (or) disagree about. I love nothing better than a fair fight with Helen."[20]

The family routine was different when Nellie was not in town. Walter came home only to eat and sleep, and, after about a week, he sent his daughters next door to be watched by his mother and sister Eva, and he left town.[21]

Nellie sometimes took her daughters with her to Binghamton to see her family. Anna Forbes felt close to Nellie's younger brother, Robert (Rob)

Morris Ogden, who was born after the Ogdens moved back to Binghamton from Milwaukee. She wrote in her journal, "Rob is my uncle, but he seems more like my brother. He is fourteen years older than I, but we are congenial and moreover I have no brothers, and therefore he has always been so much to me." In Binghamton, Rob took her rowing on the lake and let her hang around with him and his friends. When he came to Charlotte, Anna Forbes spent most of the time with him.[22] One can imagine the young girl following her uncle-brother, wanting to go where he went and to do what he did. When she decided on an academic career, she followed his career path.

Walter was thoughtful and affectionate with his daughters. Nellie said Walter was not hen-pecked—he was children-pecked. The girls usually got what they asked for. He let them boss him around and tease him about what they considered his eccentric ways, one of which was that he was not handy around the house. When he did something as simple as hanging a picture, it became a major event with everyone stopping what they were doing to help.[23]

Walter still opposed girls being out after dark. His daughters also knew he did not want them to accept expensive gifts from boys. Anna Forbes easily kept those rules, but his insistence on good posture was hard. She complained, "It may be that for a week or more you walk with your shoulders squared and head erect, but on the one unlucky day when you are too sick or tired to even attempt to hold yourself up, your Daddy will remark that you are getting more round shouldered every day and to *please* hold up. Yet he never seems to realize that six days out of seven you are as straight as an arrow, because it pleases Daddy."[24]

Nellie and Walter allowed their daughters to sip alcohol in their home. When Anna Forbes was four years old, she shocked her Sunday School teacher, Mrs. Barron, who had lectured the children, "Don't drink beer as it will make you weak." The young Anna Forbes spoke up, "You are mistaken, I have tasted beer and I am as strong as a man."[25] When Anna

Forbes took a trip to Europe at age sixteen, her father warned her to beware of the Paris men who would woo her with wine and to stick with the bourbon, which she sipped at home.[26]

Anna Forbes began smoking when she was a teenager. One day her father asked her, "Anna Forbes, are you smoking?" She replied, "Yes, Papa." He further asked, "Do you smoke first thing in the morning?" She replied, "Yes, I do." He said, "It is the best cigarette of the day, isn't it?"[27]

What bothered Nellie was Anna Forbes's loud voice. When they returned home from a social event, Nellie admonished her, "Yes, I could hear *your* voice above everybody else's." Anna Forbes tried to speak softer, but could not.[28] Her voice that could be heard above everybody else's became an asset as an adult.

Walter and Nellie with Helen and Anna Forbes attended the First Baptist Church. Years later, people would say, "Yes, Walter was a Baptist," but he was not on the church membership roll, although Nellie was. Walter considered himself a Christian more than a Baptist. He worried whether he was even a good Christian because he struggled with loving the Baptist brethren. One reason may have been the church's standards for behavior. Walter did not fully accept them. He did not drink alcohol excessively, but he drank socially and also liked to go to the Opera House. His spiritual foundation was the Masonic Scottish Rites and Rituals.[29]

When Anna Forbes was thirteen years old, she was baptized and joined the First Baptist Church. She took her faith seriously and often reflected on how she should live. Yet as a teenager, Anna Forbes went to theater plays, danced, and drank alcohol—all activities condemned by her church. Her journals and letters do not explain how she reconciled these activities with her church's teachings. By the time Anna Forbes was born, the First Baptist Church had grown to 300 members and had built a new church in the center of town. By the time she was twenty, the membership had more than tripled to 967 members.[30] As the church grew in membership, its expectations likely changed or were not as strictly enforced as in her grandfather's time.

Anna Forbes was close to her mother throughout her life, and they wrote one to three letters a month to each other. When in college, she sent the letters home in a box of dirty clothes. Her mother returned the washed clothes with a letter and sometimes enclosed a newly sewn outfit or a book being passed around the family.

As for her father, Anna Forbes felt he understood her, and whenever she had a problem, she talked it over with him. As an adult, she wrote her mother, "I admire these independent freesouled [*sic*] women, and all that, but I thank the Lord every day that I have Mr. Walter to back me up. I don't know how you feel about it, but I am mighty glad you married him."[31]

Family's Influence

It seemed to the young Anna Forbes Liddell that she could not do *anything* without someone knowing about it. She was right. In Charlotte, she had eight adults—her parents, grandmother, three aunts, and two uncles—to praise, scold, encourage, and correct her daily, and they all lived on the same city block. In addition, an aunt and uncle lived in New York City.

There were three houses on the city block where Anna Forbes Liddell grew up. In one, she lived with her parents and her sister Helen. The center house was the Liddell family home where her widowed grandmother Anna Amelia Liddell lived with her two daughters, Eva, who never married, and Louella, who lived there with her husband Tom Franklin, and their son Tom Jr. Her Uncle Vinton and Aunt Jane lived in the third house with their daughter Vinton. Anna Forbes's uncle Vinton had moved to Charlotte from Tuscaloosa, Alabama, when he married Jane Hall.

The four children—Anna Forbes, Helen, Tom Jr., and Vinton played freely on that block, going from home to home at will, but always remaining under watchful eyes. The most watchful eyes were those of Aunt Eva. She was the family caretaker of the children when their parents were not there. Anna Forbes wrote in her journal at age twelve, "often I have been left with her for months at a time. . . .I have been a great trial because of my stubborn will, and how patiently, how kind she was. . .she had great influence over my life and I love her more than any woman but my mother and sister."[1]

Eva listened in on her nieces' telephone conversations when they were teenagers. At that time, a telephone operator connected calls, and several households shared *party lines*. The pattern of rings identified each household's calls. Anyone on the phone line could pick up and hear any conversation in progress. Eva would quietly pick up the phone when it rang for the Walter Liddell house and listen. This eavesdropping made Anna Forbes angry. She wanted to yell, "Stop prying!" when her aunt quizzed her later about the call, but she did not. It took all her patience to control her temper. Sometimes, Anna Forbes talked to Eva about her suitors, but it did not matter—Eva knew about them anyway.

Eva took care of others with an air of martyrdom. She made sure that everyone knew what an imposition it was. As a young child, Anna Forbes felt sorry that everyone took advantage of Eva, but, as she got older, she understood that Eva allowed people to take advantage of her and was happy complaining about it.[2]

Perhaps Eva wore her martyrdom as a protective cloak, because she had suffered great disappointment as well as great joy in her caretaking experience even before Anna Forbes was born. In 1880, when Annie Hill died and Anna Amelia Liddell brought Annie's three sons to Charlotte, Eva took on the largest share of raising the boys. Rev. Hill and Eva wrote letters to each other regularly, so that Eva could let him know how his sons were doing. Hill's early letters express gratitude for her care of his sons, such as, "I am glad they have such a loving aunt to take their mother's place in caring for them." Sadly, the youngest of the three, David, died soon after coming to Charlotte. Arthur died in 1884 at age six; that must have felt to Eva as if she had lost her own son. Then in 1885, Eva was shocked and hurt when Hill wrote that he would remarry in 1886 and that Walter would come to live with him and his new wife. Eva had been Walter Hill's substitute mother for six years, from when he was four years old until he was ten. After Rev. Hill's remarriage, she seldom saw her nephew whom she had raised as a son. Eva Liddell's path in life was common at the time for women who did not marry. When she was not caring for family members, she volunteered in her church and civic-action clubs and socialized in book and bridge clubs.[3]

Jane Hall was already a wealthy young woman through inheritance when she married Vinton Liddell. Under the law, Jane lost control of her money when she married. Thus, with Jane's inheritance, Vinton became a wealthy man and a prominent citizen of Charlotte, becoming President of the Gingham Mill, President of the Manufacturers' Club, a Vice-President of the Elizabeth Mill, a director of the Charlotte National Bank, and a contributor to many charities. Since none of his business interests required him to be in Charlotte, Vinton and Jane stayed in Charlotte only in the winter. They built a summer home in Great Barrington, Massachusetts, that was even grander than their home in Charlotte. Anna Forbes spent several summers at their Great Barrington house as a companion for their daughter Vinton.[4]

Vinton and Jane Liddell's travels thrilled Anna Forbes with the glamor of faraway places. They traveled for months at a time in the United States and Europe, staying in suites in the finest hotels without regard to cost. They became friends with nobility such as the Countess Taveggia, whose husband was a member of the Papal Court.[5]

Vinton attended the First Baptist Church until he married, and then he attended an Episcopal church with Jane. His change of denomination was not solely for marital accord. Like his brother Walter, he did not accept the strict moral code of the First Baptist Church.

Louella and Tom Franklin introduced Anna Forbes to the world of politics and power. Tom Franklin was the mayor of Charlotte from 1907 to 1909, while he was still working for the Liddell Company as bookkeeper/secretary. Later Franklin left the Liddell Company and started an insurance company. While he was mayor, the city expanded its boundaries and received an Andrew Carnegie grant to build a public library.

Because of the Franklins, Anna Forbes associated with politicians. In July 1905, on a trip with them, she dined with North Carolina Governor Robert Broadnax Glenn and his family in Atlantic City. When the Governor came to review the soldiers camping near Charlotte the following month, he ate supper with Louella, Tom, Anna Forbes, and Helen. On October 19, 1905, Anna Forbes mingled with North Carolina Lieutenant Governor Francis D. Winston and with President and Mrs. Teddy Roosevelt when they came to Charlotte.[6] The thirteen-year-old Anna Forbes noted in her journal:

> It was dark, but the street from the station to Vance Park, where [*Roosevelt*] spoke, was lighted with festoons of electric lights as well as the usual arc lights, so it was almost as light as day. Mother, Aunt Eva, and I went down to Mrs. Jacksons [*sic*] where Mrs. Roosevelt was. I thought she was very attractive as well as handsome. Teddy was larger than I had expected. There were a number of ladies at Mrs. Jackson's. We went back to the train with Mrs. Roosevelt, and told her goodbye from there.[7]

It was a full evening. After seeing the Roosevelts off, Anna Forbes went to the Southern Manufacturers Club, where she met a congressman and mingled with Lieutenant Governor Francis D. Winston and D. A. Tompkins, one of Charlotte's prominent citizens. Afterwards, everyone went to the City Hall for a library benefit. Anna Forbes rode from the Club to the City Hall in Stuart Cramer's automobile with Lieutenant Governor Winston and Mrs. Stonewall Jackson. Cramer was a prominent textile mill engineer, who later became a mill owner and founded Cramerton, NC. Anna Forbes wrote, "I felt mighty big."[8]

Anna Amelia Liddell, however, did not welcome Tom Franklin as a son-in-law. She could not understand why, of all the men available, that her popular daughter would choose to marry him. He was good enough to work for the company, but not good enough to marry into the family. As her parents' youngest child, Louella did not feel a responsibility to take anything seriously; she was used to getting her way. She and Tom married in a simple ceremony in the Liddell family home. Anna Amelia was so against the marriage that she refused to attend. It must have been awkward when Tom moved into the Liddell family home after the ceremony. Tom and Louella lived there several years until he started his political career.[9]

Of course, the family members who lived in Charlotte interacted with Anna Forbes more than her Uncle Forbes and Aunt Myra, who lived in Greenwich Village in New York City. Yet they, too, had important influences on her. They had moved from Tuscaloosa to New York City to be closer to their daughter Katherine, who was attending Barnard College. Anna Forbes stayed with them often in New York for weeks at a time. Her visits gave her a sample of a culture very different from the conservative Southern culture of Charlotte.

The entire family lovingly laughed at the Forbes Liddells, because they laughed at themselves—at Forbes's trying to raise chickens (the experiment lasted a year), at Myra's cooking, at Katherine's desire to start a bohemian newspaper in New York after college. The Forbes Liddells were the *poor Liddells*. Forbes worked sporadically because of his asthma. Their other income was revenue from the Liddell Company. Myra worked as a social worker at a settlement house, but it is unknown whether her work was paid or volunteer. They had to be frugal, which was at odds with their unpractical natures. Forbes could have compared himself with his wealthy brother, Vinton, and been bitter; instead, he remained cheerful. Anna Forbes saw that her Uncle Forbes was happier than Uncle Vinton, who was critical of most people and situations. She learned that money could make you comfortable, but it could not make you happy.[10]

The person who influenced Anna Forbes the most besides her parents was her grandmother Anna Amelia Liddell. She was the hub of the family and the one who passed the family values on to the next generations. Her house was where the family came *home* for the holidays, even if it meant just going to the house next door. She was a member of the Women's Christian Temperance Union and was as adamant against alcohol use as her husband W.J.F. had been. Abstinence from alcohol was a cornerstone of her Christian faith. She regretted that she had done a better job of teaching her faith to her daughters than to her sons.[11] However, she held an unwavering belief in personal responsibility for one's decisions. Although she did not approve of her sons' social drinking, she held that they alone were responsible for their choices. Steadfast in her beliefs all her life, she also accepted that not everyone would believe as she did, even if it pained her so. She expressed her belief in each person's free agency when she wrote to her grandson Walter Hill upon his graduation from college, "You are now a man just beginning your life's work. All that is past will soon be as a dream to you. You are an independent being, free to make your own choices socially, religiously and politically."[12]

Anna Amelia, also active in the abolitionist movement, would have known about the American women's rights movement, which rose out of the abolitionist movement. The women's rights movement is generally marked as beginning in July 1848 with the Seneca Falls Conference. The Conference was organized quickly in a week, but the idea for it began eight years earlier at the World Anti-Slavery Conference in London. There, Lucretia Mott and Elizabeth Cady Stanton served as delegates, but as women, they had not been allowed to participate in the same way as the men. They could only watch the proceedings from a balcony and began to think that women needed to be freed as well as the slaves. In 1851, Stanton and Susan B. Anthony met and formed one of the most famous partnerships for women's rights.

After the Civil War, former abolitionists formed the American Equal Rights Association, whose mission was to secure equal rights for Black men and all women. However, the association began to focus solely on suffrage for Black men, asking the women to wait. Thus, in 1869, two women's rights groups emerged: the National Woman Suffrage Association (NWSA) founded by Stanton and Anthony and the American Woman Suffrage Association (AWSA) founded by Lucy Stone, Henry Blackwell, and Julia Ward Howe. The NWSA, which only allowed women to join, focused solely on a federal amendment for woman suffrage. It was more conservative than the AWSA, which wanted to also to include the rights of working women, limitation on the power of churches, and reform of marriage laws.

The NWSA showed its single focus when the actions of member Victoria Woodhull stirred up controversy. The charismatic Woodhull had a lofty goal of running for President of the United States. She wanted the NWSA to form its own political party and support her political ambitions. Woodhull also promoted free love; she married her second husband while still legally married to her first husband. She was open about sexuality, asserting her rights to love anyone she chose and to change her mind daily about whom she loved. Anthony did not approve of sexual relations outside of marriage and thought that Woodhull with her political ambitions and her views on sexuality distracted the NWSA from its focus on suffrage. Anthony eventually prevailed, getting Woodhull ejected from the NWSA. The NWSA and the AWSA worked separately for women's rights until 1890, when they joined to form the National American Woman Suffrage Association.[13]

The Liddell family's view on women's rights aligned with those of Anthony.[14] They wanted the vote for women, while maintaining the conventional idea that sexual relations should be reserved for marriage. Anna Forbes adopted the family's views on women's rights, in addition to her grandmother's beliefs in people's responsibility for their choices, the value of education, and the importance of family. Anna Forbes may not have realized how much her grandmother influenced her. She absorbed these values with no effort on her part and without her even noticing, exactly as one does not notice the air one breathes.

However, Anna Forbes knew how much her grandmother's garden meant to her. The garden was her favorite place to play as a child. She remembered:

> No where [*sic*] else in the world are violets as fresh and dainty, roses as sweet, and irises as delicate to me. The old lilac bushes, the hollyhocks, the tulips, the cornflowers, poppies, and larkspurs, they seem less gorgeous in any other garden. Each flower meant my grandmother to me. I remembered how she planted it or else how tenderly she cared for it. I learned to know my grandmother by growing up in her garden.[15]

Anna Forbes let her imagination go wild in that garden. She recalled, "I thought every flower had a fairy concealed within it, and that this fairy made the bud open, unfold, and finally wither. The fairy was named for the blossom it inhabited and dressed to represent that flower. I used to hold conversations with the flowers while I was gathering them in bunches."[16] Anna Forbes brought her young cousin Vinton into her garden fairyland, telling her, "fairy stories of the months and seasons, of the winds and rain and shadow and sunlight, of the trees and flowers."[17] On summer afternoons, Anna Forbes took a cushion and several books, usually poetry, and climbed way up into the top branches of the pear tree in the garden, "away from the world of people into the world of fairies," reading and dreaming of her life when she grew up.[18]

Anna Forbes also invented games to amuse herself. She lay on the cool grass, watched the clouds float by in the sky, and imagined. She picked up a stone and imagined that it was magical and could grant wishes. She wished for the stone to shrink her and her grandmother's cat to the size of insects. As tiny creatures of her imagination, they wandered through the dense forest formed by tall blades of grass and rode a seedpod boat to faraway lands on the rushing stream spewing out of a water hose. What if that were not really a June bug, but a Green Knight on a mission to save a damsel in distress? They joined him in his quest. She wished them to faraway places she had read about in her books. What if the land of China was made of porcelain and inhabited by blue people like those on the Blue Willow dinnerware? Of course, they would get in trouble—chased by giant birds or Blue Willow men with pigtails, trapped in deep pits, captured by giants. It was up to her to get them out of danger using diversions and creative MacGyver-like solutions.[19]

Anna Forbes sketched in her mind plots of love stories and psychological mysteries that she would later write in her journal. She wrote two kinds of love stories, scripting out potential life choices. The first kind had the traditional theme: girl and boy fall in love, a misunderstanding drives the lovers apart, and then the lovers reunite for a happy ending. The second kind was actually an anti-love story. The girl forsakes all romantic love and follows her heart's desire for a career as a writer. She becomes famous for her writing, but she wonders if she made the right choice. Her mysteries started with the murder already committed, so there was no blood and gore. She described the clever detective using his insight and knowledge of human nature to catch the killer.[20]

Four of her journals have survived. They are more than diaries—she included impressions, essays, character studies, short stories, and plays. She sometimes reread her own writings and added a note about what the older Anna Forbes thought about what the younger one had written.[21] The journals give us insights into her thoughts. She mused on the human condition even at a young age, such as this excerpt, written when she was twelve:

> This life seems a constant struggle of reaching up or out for things just beyond our reach and never being satisfied until we obtain them.
>
> When I go to pick wisteria blossoms off the vine, the prettiest are often out of reach, almost always. I must either get a chair or ladder to get them or else have somebody reach them for me. It is so with everything and everybody.[22]

Besides providing the garden that fueled Anna Forbes's vivid imagination, Anna Amelia Liddell encouraged her to read, as she did all her grandchildren. Anna Forbes learned to read at age three. By age twelve, she had read Emerson, Shakespeare, Dickens, Sir Walter Scott, and Louisa May Alcott, but her favorite stories were the fairy tales that her grandmother read to her.[23]

Anna Amelia, herself, was an avid reader. Although she read the current best sellers, she preferred the standard classics, rereading her favorites until she knew them by heart. She talked about Tolstoy with anyone who would listen. Although she never traveled outside the country, she could talk about Europe and China—the people, landmarks, history and customs—as if she had been there. She read newspapers and magazines for current events and could hold her own in conversations from the "riots in Russia to the President's last speech."[24]

Regardless of whether Anna Forbes chose marriage or a career, she knew she was expected to go to college. Of Anna Amelia's six surviving grandchildren, the educational status of five are known. Helen Liddell earned an associate degree; Walter Hill earned a bachelor's degree; Katherine and Vinton Liddell earned master's degrees; Anna Forbes Liddell earned a PhD. The schools the Liddell grandchildren attended included Bryn Mawr College, Barnard College, Cornell University, Oxford University (England), Presbyterian College (later became Queens University), St. Mary's College, University of Lewisburg (later became Bucknell University), University of North Carolina, University of Tennessee, and Yale University.[25]

Yet Anna Forbes Liddell wondered how she would use her education. She struggled throughout her youth with her choice between marriage and a career, and, as she dreamed, read, wrote, and played, that question was in the back of her imaginative mind. In her youth, she had few models of women with professional careers. There were none in her family. In the community, she could think of Miss Lillie Long, the headmistress of the Presbyterian Female College, or Dr. Annie Lowrie Alexander, the unmarried daughter of a physician who herself became a physician, but Anna Forbes was not interested in either of those paths. Her interest was in a life of writing. Her models were the women writers she read, such as Jane Austin and Louisa May Alcott.

Coming of Age (1898-1912)

Anna Forbes Liddell went to primary school (grades 1-8) at the South Graded School. It was Charlotte's first public school and was housed in the former Carolina Military Institute. The former barracks were converted to large classrooms with a large stove for heat in the center of the room. Each large classroom held up to fifty students with one teacher in charge.[1]

Anna Forbes was the type of student that teachers cannot forget—the one who is very smart and who challenges and corrects them. One day, a teacher said that she knew her students better than they knew themselves and that she could see right through them. Liddell, with her sharp wit, even as a twelve-year-old, wrote in her journal that the teacher was wrong—many students may be like panes of glass that can be seen through, but a greater number of students are like prisms that catch the light and cannot be seen through.[2]

Although very bright, Anna Forbes did not like everything she studied. She dreaded arithmetic and Latin grammar, yet loved reading and writing, especially the creative writing assignments. One imaginative story Anna Forbes wrote when she was ten years old described a conversation between a stately old maple tree and an elf. In the early evening as the moon was rising, a young elf came up from the ground and noticed that the old tree was sighing. The elf asked the tree why it was sighing. He wanted to know the story of the tree's life. The tree recounted its life from being a tiny young shoot. It told of the sorrow of the death of its leaves in autumn, the gratitude for the winter's snow that kept it warm from the wind, and the joys of spring's return when young girls danced below its branches and the sun warmed its emerging leaves. It told of summer when birds nested in its nooks and crannies, and of the return of autumn. And so it was, year after year, and the tree grew old. The old maple tree said that old age comes with joy or sorrow, sometimes both, and that was why it sighed. The elf scampered off when day broke. Because the elf was young, he quickly forgot the maple tree's story, but the tree was old and remembered all. It would have been a blessing to forget. This story shows Liddell's intellect, imagination, and wisdom expressed at an early age.[3]

After Liddell graduated from primary school in 1904, at age twelve, she went to high school at the Preparatory Department of the Presbyterian Female College (later it became Queens University) in Charlotte. At the Preparatory Department, students earned a high school diploma after two years of instruction.[4]

Anna Forbes was fortunate to have access to high school. In North Carolina in 1904, children were not required to attend school and many did not have such access. It was not until 1907 that rural high schools existed in North Carolina. In 1913, the North Carolina Compulsory Attendance Act required attendance for all children between the ages of eight and twelve for four months during the year. In 1919, the required school term was extended to six months.[5]

Most of all, Anna Forbes enjoyed being with her best friend Katherine (Kitty) Cramer, who was a year older. They drifted apart when Kitty attended the Preparatory Department and Anna Forbes was still in primary school. Once Anna Forbes enrolled at the Preparatory Department, the girls again became best friends. After school each day, they went to Kitty's house, where they talked, sang, and sewed in Kitty's bedroom under the eaves. Sometimes, they went to Kitty's music room to play the baby grand piano and sing; sometimes they just sat together in silence and dreamed.[6]

When Anna Forbes graduated from high school, she begged her parents to let her continue at the Presbyterian Female College as a college freshman and to let her live on the campus in the new dormitory. The dormitory had modern amenities of steam heat, gas and electric lighting systems, and plumbing. The bathrooms and closets were in a separate building from the bedrooms, because the designers feared that noxious gases from the bathrooms would make the young women sick.[7]

Of course, Walter and Nellie thought it was a waste of money to board at a school in Charlotte. But Anna Forbes was a strong-willed child and continued to pester them to change their minds. She reasoned that she could study better at boarding school, because home had no regular study hours. Anna Forbes had not yet learned that structure and discipline must come from within herself. Academics was the reason Anna Forbes gave for boarding; friendship was the real reason. She and Kitty had drifted apart when she was in high school and Kitty was in college. Anna Forbes wanted Kitty back as her best friend.[8]

Walter and Nellie finally relented, even though they still thought that living on the campus was foolish. Anna Forbes went to Presbyterian College as a boarding student with dreams of long talks of boyfriends, musical duets, and shared laughter with her best friend. On her first day at college, even before she could move her things into her dorm room, Kitty rushed to her, saying, "I couldn't wait any longer, just had to see you."[9] Anna Forbes felt joy from her head to her toes—her dream was coming true. Then disappointment set in. With rooms on different floors and mainly separate classes, she and Kitty rarely saw each other, except in college clubs and other activities.[10]

Anna Forbes loved being a member of the *Edelweiss* (college annual) staff and the Pierian Literary Society. She also joined the Goat Club (unknown mission), the Tom Thumb Club (a club for short girls whose motto was "Every Little Bit Helps"), the Daddy Rabbit Tennis Club, and the Gitchimanito (Git-ye-a-man-or-two) Club, which had as its occupation, "seeking the inevitable." Kitty was in all the same clubs, except for the Tom Thumb Club for which she did not qualify.[11]

However, Anna Forbes was jealous of the time Kitty spent with Bud, another sophomore. Kitty and Bud were now best friends and Anna Forbes felt unwelcome in the threesome. So, she tried to forget Kitty and make friends with other girls. She got along well with her roommate Alice. In fact, the girls conspired to break minor dorm rules. Anna Forbes wrote in her journal:

> There is a peculiar joy in breaking college rules. Out of the list of twenty-three, which hangs on our door, Alice and I have kept only five. Yet we are considered models of deportment. Our favorite stunt is burning the light after the bell rings. This requires diligence and alertness, for teachers are liable to pass at all hours of the night. To me there is nothing more exhilarating than to sit up after light bell to read or study. . . .To be in danger and to avoid that danger by stratagems, what can be more delicious?[12]

Neither Alice nor any of the other girls could replace Kitty in Anna Forbes's heart. She confided her feelings to a teacher, Miss Armstrong, and broke down crying when telling the story of her and Kitty's friendship. Armstrong told Kitty how upset Anna Forbes was. With tears in her eyes, Kitty came to see Anna Forbes and said with trembling lips, "I'm sorry, I didn't understand." Anna Forbes was so touched that she could not speak at first, but finally whispered, "It is all right, Kitty." Yet the distance between them remained. Later in the school year, Anna Forbes and Kitty had a heart-to-heart talk. Kitty explained that after Armstrong talked with her, she avoided Anna Forbes, because she was ashamed. Anna Forbes felt that their talk helped.[13]

In her first year of boarding, Anna Forbes had received the structure and discipline she said she craved and was looking forward to going home for the summer break. She wrote in her journal:

> All winter I have gotten up by bells and gone to bed by bells. Worked by bells, eaten by bells, and even played by bells.
>
> In four weeks I shall be able to go lie down on the cool sweet grass and idly watch the clouds sail by above me and know that I may lie there indefinitely and still no bells will interrupt my reverie.
>
> But the bells are useful nevertheless. Perhaps I have not learned many things at my year at boarding school, but this one thing I have learned well—the value of fifteen minutes. I used to think that fifteen minutes was of no value. This year I have dressed nearly every morning in that time. I know now that fifteen minutes spent in reading, or in dressing is time to do well any one of the above named deeds and all of them after a fashion.[14]

After the summer break, Anna Forbes returned to college content with her friendship with Kitty. Her contentment was short-lived. The Junior Class, under the leadership of Kitty as class President, started a conflict with Anna Forbes's Sophomore Class. Following college tradition, the sophomores planted a young sapling in November. The class president gave a speech about the tree and the girls sang the class song and shouted the class yell. Next, they had refreshments in the gym and celebrated. Meanwhile, the juniors pulled up the tree that the sophomores had planted. Pulling up the tree was serious. Tradition held that a class tree planted could not be uprooted. The juniors planned further mischief. They planned to bring the sophomores into a room, one at a time, to haze them. Yet before the juniors could act, the faculty intervened. They placed the sophomores in one room and the juniors in another room. The faculty went back and forth between the two rooms, talking separately to each class. The sophomores demanded that the juniors apologize. The juniors refused to do so unless the sophomores change their demand for an apology to a request for an apology. The faculty could not get either class to budge from its position. Several days later, the sophomores skipped morning assembly, with approval from the faculty, and replanted their tree. Just a few hours later, the tree was uprooted again. The faculty mediated again, but it took several days to reach a resolution. The entire student body silently watched Kitty, holding the sapling with trembling hands, walk to the hole and replant the tree. The tree was pulled up yet again. But this time, the juniors could prove they were not responsible. Was it a sophomore wanting to stir up trouble between the classes or a senior conspiring with the juniors? When no culprit could be found, the commotion died down, but this was not the end of the matter.[15]

Anna Forbes was the Sophomore Class Historian. In January 1908, Kitty stole Anna Forbes's notes about the tree incident, which had been tucked in a German grammar book. In a letter, Anna Forbes asked Kitty for an apology and said that she had heard from others that Kitty was using their friendship to further her own ends. She wrote that she had never believed that rumor, but now she felt she had to ask Kitty about her motives. Kitty was furious when she got the letter. On a Friday afternoon, she told the juniors that Anna Forbes had said the Junior Class was not loyal to Kitty. The class members were indignant. They asked Anna Forbes to meet them the next morning. She recounted, "Bud was against me from the first. However, when I had told my story calmly and coherently three or four times without any variations, they *all* came over to my side."[16] The juniors concluded that Kitty had misconstrued Anna Forbes's words. Next, they asked whether the sophomores had confidence in Kitty's leadership of the Junior Class. The juniors would ask for Kitty's resignation if the sophomores distrusted Kitty. Torn between loyalty to her friend and loyalty to her class, Anna Forbes would not answer. The juniors called in Mary and Shorty, two other sophomore girls, and asked them the same question. They answered that they believed the juniors had been loyal, but they did not trust Kitty. The juniors dismissed the sophomores and called in Kitty, who had been waiting in the library.[17]

Anna Forbes felt uneasy. Suddenly, she realized the friendship had meant more to her than it had to Kitty. She was shaken that she had not seen that before and questioned whether Kitty had ever valued their friendship as she had.[18] Throughout her life, Anna Forbes valued her friendships and was loyal to her friends.

There may have been another reason for Anna Forbes to feel uneasy about the theft of the notes. She had looked virtuous, while Kitty had been disgraced.[19] Anna Forbes's journal does not say what happened just before the theft. How did Kitty even know the notes were in the book? Did Anna Forbes taunt her friend about what she had written?

The deep friendship between Anna Forbes and Kitty was over. However, with families entwined in social and business dealings, the girls could not avoid each other. They were cordial to each other at social events, but they were never again best friends.

Then February came. February's gloomy days reminded Anna Forbes of the story of Medea and the red-hot bronze giant. The giant had one vein along its back filled with molten brass with a nail at the bottom of the vein to hold in the fluid. When the giant went to sleep, Medea removed the nail. Anna Forbes said, "I know how that giant felt when the fluid ran out. I feel that way every February."[20]

February 1908 was especially hard, since the theft of the class history notes had happened the month before. Anna Forbes wrote, "As usual the February tiredness has come over me. I feel grumpy and cross and out of sorts with everything. School is a bore, and not worth the trouble."[21]

It was time for a change. Anna Forbes left Presbyterian College in the middle of her sophomore year.[22] In summer of 1908, Anna Forbes attended the University of Tennessee, where her Uncle Robert Ogden, her mother's brother, was a professor.[23]

* * *

Between the ages of twelve and sixteen, Anna Forbes struggled against growing up. She wrote in her journal at age sixteen:

> Someway I expected to be entirely different from the stupid 'grown-ups' who lived in houses and couldn't climb trees, and wouldn't sit on the ground on account of the ants.
>
> Last summer, a year ago nearly, I took my cushion and my books and climbed the pear tree as I had every summer since I could remember.
>
> But I was uncomfortable on the limb, and longed for the porch and a rocking chair, although I hated to admit it even to myself. Sadly, I descended from the tree and returned to the house.
>
> A strange creepy sensation stole over me and I wanted to cry. I actually preferred a rocking chair on the porch where the people were to a seat in the pear tree with the fairies. I felt that I had been changed in some way without my knowledge—some wicked witch had cast me under a spell. . . .
>
> I felt strange and a little regretful, but the road before me as far as I could see went through a county not as beautiful as I might have imagined it might be, and I would not have turned back even if I could.[24]

Later she added the following note to the above journal passage:

> Since I wrote that, I have been thinking. I have resolved never to grow up—never to be one of the stupid persons that I used to feel such a contempt for—a "grown-up." My body in time must grow old, but my mind and heart never shall, and my body won't until a long time from now.
>
> I am going back to the pear tree this summer and I will not let myself cease to love it. The fairies with whom I was so intimate years ago shall still be my friends. However, I have never [illegible] them. Fairies are a creation of the brain. I believe in them perfectly as much as I used, only I once thought they existed outside my brain, now I know they exist inside of it.[25]

That same year, Anna Forbes wrote:

> If the girl I was four years ago should look into the eyes of the girl I am now—there would be disappointment in the face of the former. For my dear little twelve-year-old self was an ambitious little girl—a little girl who thought that with a few years of work she would be able to conquer the world.
>
> She didn't believe in love, even though she had a weakness for love stories. She wanted equal rights for men and women—more freedom for her sex. . . .
>
> She was a dear little goose—even as myself now is a dear little goose—but a goose of another color.
>
> Suppose myself should say to my former self—"What is your greatest ambition."

> "To be famous, as a true noble woman and a gifted reformer and writer," she would reply with shining eyes, "and yours?"
>
> Then the fire in her eyes would change to the look of sadness and disgust as I would answer, "To be happily married."[26]

That same year, Anna Forbes wrote a short story about a woman's choice of career over marriage told from the viewpoint of Marrianne, a thirty-five-year-old writer. At a dinner party, Marrianne sat next to William Holt, a handsome, famous scientist. Anna Forbes wrote:

> [Marrianne] knew she had charmed him. She was a brilliant woman, a writer of quite a little notoriety, and possessed of both ease and tact. Never before had Marrianne so thoroughly enjoyed herself as during those two hours. Here was a man—she had thought who appreciated intellectual women, a man who would not be infatuated [illegible] mere beauty, nor contented with the emptiness of life with a woman who knew nothing except the laws of etiquette, the latest styles from Paris, and the best way to play bridge.[27]

In the story, the hostess asked Marianne to entertain by playing the piano and singing. After Marianne finished singing, she saw William talking with Dorothy Hunt, a beautiful young woman. He was "bending low to speak to her and was holding her doll-like hands in his own." Marrianne wanted to either scream or kill Dorothy, but pretended the rest of the evening that she was having a good time. When she got home, she scolded herself, "You ought to be contented. You gladly gave up all hopes of love and marriage years ago when you first began writing, then you said nothing was too great to sacrifice for a career." Anna Forbes ended the story with, "but moralizing gave her little comfort and finally she broke down in sobs. I know she murmured [unreadable], 'I offered up my chance for love for the sake of fame, and now I would only too gladly give all my little honor and glory for love—but it is too late.'"[28] In this story, Anna Forbes depicted her call for a career as a writer, but she concluded that she would later regret that decision.

* * *

By age fourteen Anna Forbes had given up her dreams of a career and was a romantic, looking for her *one true love*. In January 1906, mid-year of her senior high school year at Presbyterian College, Aunt Louella asked her to come to supper at Anna Amelia Liddell's. Louella wanted Anna Forbes to entertain Billy Hardison, the teenage son of a school friend of Louella. The Hardisons were visiting Charlotte from Wadesboro, a town about fifty miles away. Billy was over a foot taller than Anna Forbes. As she gazed up into his blue eyes, her entire body trembled. Instantly, she knew he was the man she was destined to love.[29]

The relationship got off to a fast start. Whenever Billy came to Charlotte, he brought Anna Forbes flowers and chocolates and they went for drives in the country. She showed him off to the Charlotte crowd. He was her date at a Presbyterian College reception. They wrote letters and cards to each other during the months he did not visit.[30]

While Anna Forbes was falling in love with Billy, her friends had also fallen in love. She wondered whether she and her friends were truly in love with their boyfriends, or were they in love with this new experience of romantic love? She developed a love test and reasoned that a girl in love with love would answer "Yes" to all three questions. Was she just as happy when Billy was present as when he was absent? Her answer was "Yes." Did she fantasize about minor details that were not unique to him? She wrote what she loved about him—"the way his hair curled above his temple so that it tempts me to run my fingers through it, the serious expression of his blue eyes, the queer little droop of the corners of his kissable mouth, the lazy swing of his shoulders as he walks, and his easy grace in dancing."

These characteristics were not unique to Billy, so the answer was "Yes." Did she think he was perfect? Billy was sensitive to a fault, a little conceited, not a good student, and a flirt. Yet when she looked at him, she could not see these defects. Thus, the answer was "Yes." Based on her love test, Anna Forbes concluded she was behaving as a girl who was in love with love.[31]

In the summer of 1907, Billy suddenly stopped writing to Anna Forbes. Each day, she waited anxiously for the postman, and was disappointed. When Virginia Stanback, a Charlotte friend, told her cattily that Billy was dating Bessie Dockery from Wadesboro, the words stung, but Anna Forbes did not admit her feelings to Virginia, because she believed Virginia was trying to be hurtful. Privately, though, she agonized in her journal, "But oh Billy dear, you are my only suitor I've got and I haven't got you I am afraid."[32] The silence from Billy stopped in late January 1908, when Anna Forbes received two postcards from him.

It was customary at the time for a young woman in Liddell's social class to be a debutante for up to three years. To announce the beginning of the debutante time, a family friend or relative hosted an afternoon tea in honor of the new debutante to introduce her to society, after which there were three years of picnics, baseball games, bridge games, dances, and theater plays. Young couples announced marriage engagements by the end of the third year.

Anna Forbes's sister Helen would have started her debutante time soon after she graduated from St. Mary's College in 1907 with a degree similar to an AA degree today. At the end of 1912, Helen was an unmarried kindergarten teacher. She did not want a career; the traditional life for women was fine with her, but she wanted it on her terms. At the time, she was dating Dexter McBride, but she was in no hurry to marry and settle down.[33]

Anna Forbes had her first debutante party, hosted by her aunts Eva Liddell and Louella Franklin, in November 1910. As she entered her debutante time, she questioned Billy's devotion to her. Often, over the past few years, he had seemed devoted to her. Yet, sometimes she did not hear from him for months at a time. She began to have doubts. In January 1911, Anna Forbes got out the bundle of letters and cards Billy had sent over the past five years and carefully read each one with tears in her eyes, looking for a sign that he loved her as she loved him. She saw only friendship in his letters. She had thought about him almost every day.[34]

Three months later, on a Tuesday, Anna Forbes got a letter from Billy. He wanted to see her on Thursday. Most of that Thursday morning they sat in the porch swing and talked about meaningless things that they usually discussed. In the afternoon, they borrowed a car from Lucy Bland and went riding for hours. Anna Forbes recounted, "Nothing much was said, and yet I felt, that he was as glad as I that we were together one more time." She did not tell him how she felt about him. After supper at the Bland's house, everyone got into the car to take Billy to the train station. She wanted to have a private goodbye with him, but it did not happen. Billy took her hand, they said a few trite goodbye words and then he was gone.[35]

A few days later, she took her first steps toward a professional career with the help of Preston Allen, a casual friend. They saw a touring production of the play "The King's Game" with the lead played by James K. Hackett, a famous actor. The next day, they went to the Selwyn Hotel under the pretense of seeing D.A. Tompkins, but they really wanted to meet with Hackett. Allen had the idea that Anna Forbes could interview him and submit the interview to the *Charlotte Observer*.

Tompkins was the person who could make their plan happen. He had come to Charlotte in 1881 and became the leading industrialist in the Carolinas. He helped to build over 350 cotton and cotton oils mills and 150 electrical plants in North and South Carolina. He bought the *Charlotte Observer* and, through his editorials, became the voice of industry for the region. He was a business partner with the Liddells and a close family friend. He often joined in Liddell family occasions, such as singing carols on Christmas Eve.[36]

After Allen and Anna Forbes explained their plan to Tompkins; he arranged a meeting with Hackett, who said that the play got poor reviews, because it was a satire so subtle that the public and critics misunderstood it. They took the play literally and thought it was a melodrama. Hackett told them funny stories about his many stage experiences. Anna Forbes wrote the interview, Allen edited it, and the *Charlotte Observer* printed it. Next, the newspaper printed her book reviews. At last, she was a published writer. Next, she got a full-time job soliciting ads for *Charlotte Observer*. She was not reporting on news, but at least she was in the writing/publishing business.[37]

It was another year of debutante parties before Anna Forbes had a serious boyfriend. In summer of 1912, Anna Forbes dated Winder Harris, an up-and-coming Charlotte newspaperman. Harris was lame and used crutches. At summer's end, they talked of marriage before parting in the fall, when he went to Baltimore to have an operation to correct his lameness, and she moved to New York City to attend Barnard College for a semester. It is unknown what she studied in college, but it was likely journalism since she had an interest in newspaper reporting. When Winder returned from Baltimore, he told her that he could not marry her, because the operation had been unsuccessful. He refused to marry with his disability. Anna Forbes was heart-broken; she went back to her obsession with Billy.[38] At the end of 1912, Anna Forbes had only six months left to be a debutante. Winder had just ended the engagement. She hoped Billy would become a serious suitor. In December 1912, the month she turned twenty-one, she stood on the cusp of adulthood with possibilities. Would she marry? Perhaps. If she did not marry, then she would have a career as a writer.

Suffrage Work (1913-1914)

Anna Forbes Liddell began her public advocacy for woman suffrage in May 1913, while visiting her Uncle Forbes and Aunt Myra in New York City. There, she was at the hub of suffrage activity for the nation, since the National American Woman suffrage Association (NAWSA) had its headquarters in the city. In 1910, the NAWSA had held a peaceful suffrage parade along Fifth Avenue, starting where the Avenue emerges from Greenwich Village's Washington Square. The parade got so much positive publicity that the NAWSA held parades in subsequent years. No one knows with certainty the number of marchers in the May 6, 1912, New York parade—estimates range from 8,000 to 20,000. Most of the marchers walked, while the older women rode in carriages decorated with flowers. Besides parades, the NAWSA advanced suffrage through polite conversations with men in power. Its policy, led by its president Dr. Anna Howard Shaw, remained strictly nonpartisan and nonaggressive. Shaw, a physician, was a charismatic orator, which likely came from her also being one of the first women in the United States to be ordained as a Methodist minister.[1]

Shaw and most of the NAWSA members considered themselves *suffragists*, to differentiate themselves from the English *suffragettes*, who smashed windows, destroyed letters in mailboxes, and went on hunger strikes. Yet by the beginning of 1913, dissent was growing within the ranks of NAWSA concerning focus and methods. Alice Paul was the leader of the dissidents. Paul was raised as a Quaker in New Jersey. When she studied in Europe, she joined the English suffragettes and was arrested during a protest where windows were smashed. While jailed, she went on a hunger strike and was force-fed. When she returned to the United States in 1910, she advocated for the NAWSA to use aggressive and partisan methods. The dissidents wanted to blame whichever political party was in power. They also urged passage of an amendment to the US Constitution instead of only changing state laws, which was the NAWSA's policy. The state-by-state progress had been slow. By 1913, only California, Colorado, Idaho, Utah, Washington, and Wyoming had granted women the right to vote.[2]

The NAWSA allowed Paul and her followers to organize a suffrage parade to be held in Washington, DC, on March 3, 1913, which was the day before the inauguration of President Woodrow Wilson. Planning the parade was a logistics nightmare. Lodging in the city was scarce because of the inauguration the next day. A rumor circulated that college boys planned to release mice to scare the marchers. One controversy was the parade color scheme. The historical black-and-white photographs of the parade do not show the vivid parade colors. Paul had ordered items in the colors of purple, white, and green, which were the colors of the English suffragettes. Shaw and others absolutely refused to march with those colors. They wanted the American suffragist colors of yellow and white. Thus, both color schemes were used with some sections decked out in purple, white, and green and others in yellow and white. The most serious controversy was the participation of Black women. Paul, with her Quaker background, supported a racially integrated parade. However, the sentiment for white supremacy was high in the capital then. There were ongoing legal proceedings against a Black man accused of the rape of a white woman in the city. In addition, Southern White suffragists told Paul that they would not march if Black women marched. Paul tried to avoid the issue—she wanted to allow Black marchers, but with no one noticing.[3]

The day of the parade was sunny and clear, yet cold. The parade route ran from the Peace Monument in front of the Capital to the marble steps of Continental Hall, where a grand pageant would be performed when the last marcher arrived. Instructed to look out for college boys with mice, Boy Scout troops stood all along the parade route. Inez Milholland, a New York labor lawyer, wrapped in a long white billowing cape and riding a white horse, led the parade down Pennsylvania Avenue. Behind her were bands, mounted brigades, floats, and over 5,000 marchers. First in the procession came women from foreign countries that already recognized woman suffrage. Next came the *Pioneers* who had worked for suffrage for many years. Then came the working women grouped by occupation, including teachers, doctors, nurses, farmers, pharmacists, actresses, and librarians. Women wore their uniforms or work clothes—nurses marched in their nurses' uniforms and college women in their academic gowns. Next came marchers grouped by state of residence. Celebrity marchers included Helen Keller and Nellie Bly. The last group of marchers were men who supported woman suffrage.[4]

Ida B. Wells, a prominent Black journalist and activist, traveled from Chicago to Washington, DC, to march. When she, along with sixty other Black women, tried to join the section for Illinois women, they were turned away and told to move to the back of the parade as to not to upset the White Southern marchers. Wells refused, saying, "Either I go with you or not at all. I am not taking this stand because I personally wish for recognition. I am doing it for the future benefit of my whole race." To defuse the situation, she left. However, she soon returned and slipped into the Illinois section to march with her state. Students and alumni of Howard University (a historically Black university) joined in the section for college women.[5]

The parade was calm for the first few blocks, but soon spectators, mainly the men in town for the inauguration, ran into the street, blocking the marchers' progress. In some spots, the marchers could only pass single file. Some spectators yelled obscenities at the women and shoved and tripped them. Others spat on the marchers. They yelled 'Henpecko' and "Where are your skirts?" at the marching men. The police did little to protect the marchers. Some even joined in harassing them. The boy scouts did not see any mice, but they were exhausted by using wooden shafts to hold back grown men from the parade route. For six hours, marchers pushed through the spectators, skirmishes broke out, and over one hundred marchers were injured. Ambulances had trouble moving through the mass of people to reach the injured. Finally, the police chief appealed to the federal government, which sent the cavalry from nearby Fort Myer to restore order. With cavalry horses pushing back the spectators, the last of the parade proceeded to Continental Hall.[6]

The pageant participants waiting at Centennial Hall had wondered what took the marchers so long. When the bedraggled marchers finally reached the Hall, they were angry. They despaired that the parade had been a failure. Helen Keller was scheduled to speak, but she had become so frightened that she left. The next day, the newspapers across the nation graphically reported on the parade. The mistreatment of the marchers and the lack of police protection outraged people. Eventually, Congress held hearings with over 150 witnesses. Shaw and Paul were ecstatic. The publicity had done far more to help the suffrage cause than if the parade had gone smoothly.[7]

On May 3, 1913, two months after the Washington, DC, parade, a suffrage parade was held in New York City. That one was orderly with over 1,000 police officers stationed along the route to restrain spectators behind the lines to protect the 10,000 marchers.[8] Liddell likely marched in this parade, since we know she was in New York on that day. The day before the 1913 parade, she had been an usher at a suffrage rally at the Metropolitan Opera, where former President Theodore Roosevelt spoke in support of woman suffrage. Her aunt and uncle's apartment was only two blocks off the parade route and about fourteen blocks from the start of the parade. At age 81, she reminisced, "When I was visiting an aunt in New York, I was a marching suffragette. . . .I think it was in May. . . .It was a long walk up Fifth Avenue on a bright and beautiful day. A very pretty parade as well as big and impressive."[9]

Soon afterwards, Liddell and her friend, Suzanne Bynum, returned to Charlotte excited about suffrage. At the same time, Laura Reilley returned to Charlotte after a trip in the West also excited about suffrage. Other North Carolina women thought it was time for the state to do something about suffrage. In July 1913, seven women in Morgantown formed a suffrage league. Other leagues popped up in Greensboro and Greenville. On October 10, 1913, Anna Forbes Liddell and Suzanne Bynum organized a meeting in Charlotte to form the Charlotte Equal Suffrage League. Four other women attended the meeting in the Bynum home: Anne Abbott, Mary Bynum (Suzanne's mother), Mary Belle Palmer, and Laura Reilley. Liddell chaired the meeting and Susanne Bynum acted as secretary.[10] The Charlotte League asked the men of the town to support woman suffrage. There were only five men in the entire town who publicly gave their support: Clarence Kuester, David Owens, W.T. Shore, T.W. Wade and Dr. W.M. Vines (pastor of the First Baptist Church). Laura Reilley said people treated her differently after she stated her opinion publicly. She recounted, "Heretofore, I had felt myself a very respected citizen of the town but after I came out for suffrage, I could notice the loafers and others at Independence Square begin to nudge each other as I passed."[11]

The Charlotte League differed from the leagues formed the previous summer. At the first meeting, Reilley proposed that it have a statewide focus with headquarters in Charlotte. The league adopted the motion. At the second meeting on Saturday, November 1, 1913, Lila Valentine, President of the Virginia Suffrage League, spoke. Liddell chaired the meeting. Valentine outlined the benefits of woman suffrage to both men and women. Yet, she criticized the militant tactics used in England. Bynum read congratulatory messages from around the state. The members kept the officers elected at the earlier meeting, which were Anna Forbes Liddell as President and Susanne Bynum as Secretary. On the following Monday,

Liddell and Bynum accompanied Valentine to Winston-Salem, where she spoke. There, they recruited fifty-six people for the statewide league and returned to Charlotte excited.[12]

On November 23, 1913, the seven members of the Charlotte League incorporated the Equal Suffrage League of North Carolina, Inc. Incorporation allowed the organization to own property and receive donations. Directors were the presidents of the local leagues. Officers were Barbara Bynum Henderson (President), Laura Reilley (Vice-President), Gertrude Weil (Vice-President), Mrs. Malcolm Platt (Vice-president), Mrs. David Stern (Treasurer), Anna Forbes Liddell (Recording Secretary) and Suzanne Bynum (Corresponding Secretary). Chief Justice of the North Carolina Supreme Court Walter Clark, Archibald Henderson, Wade Harris, and E.K. Graham made up an advisory committee. The Equal Suffrage, League of North Carolina (ESL) affiliated with the National American Woman Suffrage Association with a 1913 charter of 210 women and men.[13] The officers, selected from across the state, were women who lived traditional lives. No one could accuse them of being militant feminists. This was important, since suffrage was unpopular in North Carolina and was thought to be a threat to the way of life in the South.

Politics had stopped the efforts of an earlier suffrage league. In 1894, forty-five women and men organized an Equal Suffrage League in Asheville. Initially, there was much support for suffrage, but the support eroded after the election of 1896, when Populist and Republican candidates defeated Democratic Party incumbents. In response to the loss, the Democratic Party aligned with White supremacists, since Black voters generally voted for Populist and Republican candidates. The Democratic Party roused up fear of *Negro Domination*. This fear of Blacks with power also included the idea that Black men could not control their sexual urges and would attack White women. This fear diminished support for woman suffrage because most people thought Black women would vote at a higher rate than White women. Thus, woman suffrage would double the Black vote but not the White vote, because White women were considered too refined to want to participate in political matters. Nonetheless, the League got a woman suffrage bill filed for the 1897 North Carolina General Assembly, but the legislators did not take the bill seriously. They sent it to the Committee on Insane Asylums.[14]

The racial tension increased. In 1898, North Carolina election officials threw out many ballots cast by Black voters. Other Black citizens did not vote because of the threat of violence if they voted. Tension was especially high in Wilmington, which had a biracial city government and many Black-owned businesses, including a newspaper. Two days after the 1898 election, hundreds of white supremacists violently overturned the newly elected city officials in Wilmington. The mob murdered at least ten Black men and injured many others. Some accounts of the event cite even more Black men murdered and injured. Depending on the decade and the viewpoint of the speaker, this event has been called a race riot, an insurrection, a massacre, or a coup d'état. In 1898, white supremacists called it the *Revolution of 1898*. The phrase "Remember the Revolution of 1898" was a rallying cry for opposition to woman suffrage for decades. The phrase was coded wording to scare White voters with the thought that if women voted, Black citizens would take over control of the state.[15]

The Democratic Party regained control of the state in the 1898 election and quickly worked to disenfranchise Black voters. In 1900, North Carolina passed a literacy test as a requirement for voting. Beginning in 1902, the literacy test initially applied only to Black men, since there was an exception through 1907 for any voter whose father or grandfather was eligible to vote in 1867 when White men were the only voters. Violence and the threat of violence discouraged Black men from voting. On election days, White men wearing red shirts (The Red Shirts) and carrying rifles rode on horses through Black neighborhoods and near the polling places to intimidate Black voters. They did this during the daytime and did not hide their faces.[16]

By the time the Equal Suffrage League was formed in 1913, the industrialists had joined incumbent politicians in opposition to woman suffrage. They believed women were more moral than men and would vote for labor reform and clean-up of government corruption, especially the corruption involving railroads. Workers in the textile industry, mostly women and children, worked, under harsh conditions, up to twelve hours a day, six days a week. In 1902, North Carolina had passed a child labor law prohibiting children under the age of twelve from working unless they were children of widows. The industrialists worried that women would vote for laws that provided minimum wages, better working conditions, and further restrictions on child labor.[17]

The suffrage issue divided the alcohol prohibitionists. In 1908, North Carolina became the first state to outlaw alcohol consumption. Some North Carolina Women Christian Temperance Union (WCTU) members thought that woman suffrage was crucial for prohibition to become national law. Others thought it would increase the number of Black voters regardless of gender and that Black men would vote against prohibition.[18]

The North Carolina suffragists were not unified as to why women should vote. They came to the cause from many paths. Some, especially those in the WCTU, wanted the vote to make family life safe for women and children, while keeping the traditional role of women. Others viewed the vote as an inherent right and envisioned a *new woman* who would take part in public life as an equal with men. Some North Carolina women supported suffrage because they wanted to serve on local school boards. By state law, school board members must be qualified voters. Since women were not qualified voters, they could not be school board members. Sadly, not all suffragists desired universal suffrage. In many places, but especially in the South, the suffrage movement was for White women only. Many wanted the vote only for middle and upper class White women with other women disenfranchised through a literacy test or intimidation.[19]

The Southern suffragists were a generation behind the Northern suffragists. Many women gained the leadership skills necessary for advocacy through club leadership. It was not until the last two decades of the nineteenth century that Southern women had organized local social and civic clubs. And it was not until 1900 that they organized the local clubs into statewide clubs. There were separate clubs for White and Black women. The two clubs sometimes worked together on a project. However, Black women often found such arrangements unsatisfactory, because White women assumed leadership and treated the Black women as little sisters who needed guidance. Because of the racial segregation, the Equal Suffrage League admitted only White women. Black North Carolina women, however, did not form a club that advocated only for woman suffrage. Their advocacy for woman suffrage was done within the North Carolina Federation of Colored Women Clubs (NCFCWC), which worked for equal rights for Blacks in many areas. Lack of woman suffrage was only one injustice that North Carolina Black women fought. Black women focused on better education for their children and for the voting rights of all Black citizens regardless of gender, instead of the single issue of woman suffrage.[20]

The North Carolina anti-suffragists also organized. Some anti-suffrage arguments contradicted each other. One example: a wife would vote the same as her husband versus women might have different views as their husband, causing discord in the home. Another example: women are too good to want to vote versus women are irresponsible—they would vote and desert their family responsibilities. The anti-suffragists wanted the White men in power to remain in power. Women would be heard when those men listened to the women's concerns and made decisions that were in the best interest of women. Fear of loss of power and privilege was the basis of the opposition to suffrage.

Yet the biggest obstacle to suffrage was not the anti-suffragists, but the people who did not speak up because of intimidation or apathy. Twenty years after the vote was won, Laura Reilly stated, "plenty of women around here wanted to vote, but they just didn't have the nerve to say so."[21] Also, many women and men (those not in power) likely had no opinion on the suffrage question. They went about their daily life taking care of their families and, if asked if they were for or against woman suffrage, they might have just shrugged their shoulders.

Anna Forbes's family members are absent from the lists of people publically supporting woman suffrage. The letters between Anna Forbes and her mother show that Nellie supported suffrage. Why Nellie was not a member of the League remains a mystery. Perhaps Liddell family members supported suffrage, but did not want to attract attention, following W.J.F. Liddell's advice to not say anything contrary to the community's values. Although not publicly supporting Anna Forbes's suffrage work, there is no evidence that family members discouraged her. In later years, the family was proud of its suffragist.

"Votes for Women" was not the only thing on Anna Forbes's mind in 1913. Her sister Helen married Dexter McBride in a summer wedding. Helen married at age twenty-five, which was much older than the traditional age for a bride then.[22] Anna Forbes still hoped in 1913 that Billy Hardison would propose. She felt she there was time to wait for him since Helen, four years older, had just married. Surely, she dreamed of her own wedding as she went to the many bridal showers and served as maid of honor in her sister's wedding.

Later that fall, Liddell's world turned upside down when she learned Hardison was engaged to marry.[23] Devastated, she wrote the poem "My House of Dreams," in which she described roses in a corsage that she crushed unknowingly from wearing and loving them. The petals dropped, and the roses were dying. She wrote:

> I am just a bunch of roses to my lover, and even now I see my beauty fading. . . .How could I tell my lover that the pain which cut into my spirit like a knife had come into my life because of him. How could I tell him he had kissed away my very soul. I knew (that only a) [*sic*] so little joy was left for me. A little while and I should droop and wither—

I could not tell him how I feared the darkness.[24]

As in Liddell's friendship with Kitty Cramer, the relationship had never meant as much to Hardison as it had to her. Except for her brief romance with Winder Harris, her obsession with Billy had kept her from developing romantic relationships with other men.[25]

Billy married on December 24, 1913. Although Anna Forbes had worked at *The Charlotte Observer* as a free-lance reporter and a salesperson and had attended colleges, it was not until after his wedding that she showed a commitment to education and a career. A month later, in late January 1914, Liddell moved to New York City to be a writer. She explained why she did so in the following poem:

The pattern for a Charlotte girl
To follow was quite clear.
As debutante a season's whirl
Man-hunt the second year.

One, two, three out. No more.
She felt a creeping fear
The third year she must marry, or
Embark on a career.

Not there at home in Charlotte, where
The brides would show their pity.
But independent, debonair,
Depart for New York City.[26]

For her New York City job hunt, Liddell walked hesitantly into Rollo Ogden's office at the *New York Evening Post* (later *The New York Post*) to ask for a job as a reporter. Ogden was a distant relative, but one whom she had never met. She had dreaded the meeting, because every year when her parents received Ogden's Christmas card, her father had made unkind remarks about him. She was relieved when he was kind to her. He, however, knew of no jobs open for reporters, but he would give her letter of introduction to his boss, the City Editor Charles Selden. Liddell then told Ogden that she had sold ads for the *Charlotte Observer*. Seeing an opportunity for her in sales, he took her to meet Emil Scholz, the Business Manager. Scholz had worked for a few months as the Business Manager for the *Charlotte Observer*. He knew Anna Forbes's father and all her friends in the newspaper office and knew exactly what she had done when she worked there. He hired her on the spot for a temporary sales job with a promise of a permanent one if it worked out. He apologized that the pay was only fifteen dollars a week. She kept a stone face, hiding her surprise—she had expected only six dollars a week![27]

The job was to last a month and was like the one back home. She worked nine to five, walking the streets of New York selling ads to her clients, primarily dry goods stores. If the distance between stores was too great to walk, the newspaper paid her streetcar fare. The highlight of her day was eating lunch at the Women Suffrage Headquarters on 34th Street, where for $0.25, she could get a hot meal and sit with other women at a long table, engaging in interesting conversations. She was a career woman on equal footing with her companions and could speak without a rebuke that she was *butting in* as often happened back home in Charlotte. One day, she ate with a young woman dressed all in black as if in deep mourning. The woman was not in mourning—that was her customary dress. The woman was the famous suffragist hiker General Rosalie Jones. She took the name *General* when she organized a hike from New York City to Albany, New York, in December 1912 to promote woman suffrage. General Jones was a leader in suffrage hikes and protests from 1912 through 1915.[28]

Anna Forbes Liddell stayed in her aunt and uncle's Greenwich Village apartment. During the day, she worked in commercial New York and, in the evenings and on weekends, she absorbed the atmosphere of Greenwich

Village. The Village was in its Golden Age (1912–1917) of bohemian activity. Nowhere else was there a greater contrast to conservative Charlotte. In the Village, longhaired men and bobbed-hair women, smoking and drinking together in basement enclaves, discussed woman suffrage, sexual emancipation, birth control, communism, workers' rights, and socialism. No topic was taboo in the Village at a time when a person could be arrested for sending birth control information through the mail and women who smoked were expected to do so privately. For decades, artists, writers, and social reformers had flocked to the Village. In 1912, several started a self-published magazine, *The Masses*, which printed material unacceptable to mainstream media, such as a poem on menstruation and a cartoon favorably depicting an unwed mother. *The Masses* attacked dogma and social norms, and cared about neither making money nor pleasing its readers. Soon Greenwich Village was the place where social reformers and aspiring writers and artists wanted to live.[29] In a letter to her sister Helen, Anna Forbes described the meetings she attended while in Greenwich Village:

> One night Aunt Myra and I went to a Feminist Meeting. There is a series going on at Cooper Union. The subject is "Breaking into the Human Race" and Mrs. Marie Jennie Howe, who was chairman, explained that women had tired of developing just their little female selves and wanted to develop their real selves. There were six short addresses, all very inspiring although some seemed rather extreme to me. I suppose I have not progressed that far yet. I have been to some Socialist meetings too.[30]

Anna Forbes had hoped the *New York Evening Post* job would lead to a job as a newspaper reporter, but that did not happen. By March, she was in Scranton, Pennsylvania, visiting her cousin Walter Hill's family.[31] By May, she was home in Charlotte in time to be one of the Charlotte suffragists on a float in the annual Mecklenburg Declaration of Independence Parade.

Floats, bands, and mounted police filled the streets of Charlotte that day. Cars pulled most of the floats, but a horse pulled the suffrage float. Suzanne Bynum recounted that no man in Charlotte who owned an automobile would lend it to them. They feared what their friends would say if they helped the suffragists. A Black man leased them his white horse and dray for $2.50. The cost for decorating the float was $7.50. This was indeed a frugal enterprise when contrasted with the float for the City of Charlotte that cost $350.[32]

Gladys Avery walked in front of the float carrying the yellow and white suffrage flag. Other women walked behind her. Then came the horse, pulling the float decked in yellow and white. The front banner displayed the title of the float, "Signing the Mecklenburg Declaration of Independence of 1914;" the side banners displayed "Votes For Women;" the back banner displayed "Taxation without Representation Is Tyranny." Anna Forbes stood on the suffrage float wearing a long white dress and a gold liberty crown. Standing with nothing nearby to grab, she had to steady herself as the float fitfully made its starts and stops along the parade route. Next to her were five young women, similarly dressed: Mary Belle Palmer, Jane Stillman, Catherine McLaughlin, Mae Simmonds, and Suzanne Bynum. Suzanne held a banner, "Equal Suffrage League of North Carolina." The suffragists carefully chose the details of the float. Juliet McNinch sat at a desk on the float and, as the float passed in front of the marker commemorating the signing of the Mecklenburg Declaration of Independence of 1775, she signed the suffragists' Mecklenburg Declaration of Independence of 1914. The seven young women on the float represented the seven original members of the Charlotte League. Despite the lack of support in the community for woman suffrage, the crowd clapped for their local young women all along the parade route. Before this date, most North Carolinians had not considered woman suffrage an important issue. Most thought of aggressive women throwing bricks when they heard the phrase *woman suffrage*. This float gave a new face to the issue. It amazed many to see genteel Southern women advocating for the vote. The Charlotte suffrage float was the first public demonstration for woman suffrage in North Carolina.[33]

The next month, Anna Forbes had an essay published in the June 4, 1914, issue of *Life* magazine. Her essay was one of eight winners (from 2,867 entries) of an essay contest on the subject of Feminism. Here is her extremely short essay:

> Feminism
>
> When the world has recognized the right of women to assume half the authority and responsibility of controlling its affairs, Universal Peace will become an established fact instead of an elusive dream. Wars, inflicting misery and death upon individual innocent people, will cease. Women labor to produce life; they know its cost too well to consent to destroy it needlessly. Every woman's child is precious to every other woman. The Brotherhood of Man may be only a beautiful ideal, but the Motherhood of Woman is an eternal truth.[34]

Liddell's essay expressed the belief, widely held at the time, in the moral superiority of women over men.

The North Carolina suffragists spread their message in local newspapers. Liddell and Bynum edited one of the best newspaper campaigns—a three-page special section on woman suffrage in the November 1, 1914, issue of the *Charlotte Observer.* The section contained photos of leading suffragists, a reading list, opinion pieces, and humor. Some articles dealt with the *rightness* of the cause. Liddell wrote an article entitled, "Which Are More Important, Home or Business Interests?" Here is an excerpt from the point of view of Woman:

> In the beginning, she says the first man and the first woman shared equally between them the labors of providing food and shelter for themselves and their young. Gradually you have taken away from me my portion of labor and added it to your own. Now I demand that you

give me again half of the work and half of the responsibility. We can not [*sic*] return to the simplicity of primitive life, but we can once more divide equally the toil and cares of life.

You think only of your business. You forget that without the home your greatest industrial development would be futile. I demand that the home be once more recognized as supreme. I demand that it be given a place in government; that its interests be no longer set aside. I am not seeking to interfere with your business, I shall not lessen your individual independence. I am merely seeking to perform that which from the beginning has been conceded to be my duty to protect and preserve the home.

Other articles included in the special section addressed concerns that suffrage would take women out of the home and create discord, such as this poem:

While you are voting Curly Locks mine
Who will wash dishes and go feed the swine?

You needn't worry about it, my dear
I shall not vote every day in the year.

The special section also included the following article written by Liddell, which highlighted the controlling tendency of many men to interrupt women when they are speaking:

The Last Words

Once upon a time a certain suffragist asked a man who happened to be married whether he did not believe in equal suffrage and he replied certainly he did not. He thought that woman's place was in the home.

"But," began the suffragist, for she knew that the man and his wife lived in a boarding house.

"Furthermore," continued the man, "no woman could devote her time to politics without neglecting her domestic duties."

"Really," began the suffragist, for she knew his wife belonged to three bridge clubs, one book club, one sewing club, and a dancing class.

"And," continued the man with the modest air of one who knows and has no fear that Solomon himself could speak more wisely, "If women vote, they will go to the Legislature. Don't you see how that will separate husband and wife?"

"But consider," once more attempted the suffragist, remembering that his wife went to the mountains every June and remained until the end of September.

"The worst effect of the whole thing, however," the man was still speaking, "would be that it would create discord between married people. Woman would wrangle with their husbands over politics, and a house divided against itself can not stand."

"Don't you think a woman should at least have the right to express her opinions?" This time the suffragist managed to get in a complete sentence, subject, predicate and all.

"The trouble with you women is that you express too many opinions." And he walked away satisfied.

All of which goes to prove that you can't argue with a woman anyhow and she will have the last word.

The special section addressed the pay inequity of women compared to men by this satire on a popular children's rhyme:

> Jack and Jill went up the hill
> To fetch a pail of water
> Jack's weekly pay was two per day
> But Jill's just one and a quarter.

This special section in the *Charlotte Observer* announced the first annual conference of the North Carolina Equal Suffrage League. The conference, held on November 9–11, 1914, in Charlotte adopted a resolution to be presented to the 1915 North Carolina Legislature. The resolution called for the amendment of the North Carolina State Constitution to give women the vote. Barbara Henderson summarized the work the League had done the previous year. She stated that the League had raised awareness of the need for suffrage through speeches, letters, meetings, and the distribution of literature. The goal was to educate the public without creating opposition.[35]

The ESL re-elected the officers elected the previous year, except for Liddell and Bynum. The League passed a rule that only one person from any local league could serve as an officer. Liddell and Bynum stepped down as Recording Secretary and Corresponding Secretary, so that Laura Reilley could remain as Vice-President. Liddell along with Bynum and Mary Henderson represented North Carolina at the National American Woman Suffrage Association held in Nashville, Tennessee, on November 12–17, 1914.[36] From this point onward, Liddell remained active in the suffrage movement, but no longer took leadership roles.

Besides, Liddell now had a new boyfriend. In 1914, she started dating Rawlinson (Rawley) Myers, a Charlotte real estate developer. Myers was of medium build and height and had blue eyes and light hair. He lived with his widowed mother in the large Myers family home. His father had made his fortune in the real estate boom that accompanied the growth of the textile industry.[37]

Anna Forbes had always known Myers. There was an eleven-year age difference between them, which mirrored the twelve-year age difference between her parents. As a child, she called him Uncle Rawley. Now as a young woman, she considered him as the "birth of Passion." She now thought of Billy Hardison as "youthful passion unreturned."[38]

Myers had an automobile, which was quite a luxury then, and the couple enjoyed riding in it. They also went to movies and plays and bantered about all kinds of subjects with Anna Forbes taking a contrary view, which she did not really hold, just for the fun of it, as she had with her sister and childhood friends. Sometimes, they legitimately had different views. Their relationship, starting as an easy friendship, had grown into a rocky courtship by the end of 1914.

A Formative Time (1915-1916)

In February 1915, Anna Forbes Liddell enrolled in the University of North Carolina in Chapel Hill. Before she left Charlotte to attend classes, she had a bitter argument with Rawley Myers. He opposed her going, likely thinking the male environment was not safe for a woman.[1]

The university was still mainly an undergraduate school for men. After the university first admitted women students in 1897, the administration excluded them from class pictures and the graduation ceremony. Women got their diplomas privately. Faculty and students followed the tone set by the administration. Mary Graves, a 1906 graduate, said, "One of the most remarkable things about being a coed is the amount of room you take up. You start toward an empty seat on the end of a bench and by the time you get there the whole row is vacant."[2]

By 1915, the university included women in the class pictures and ceremonies, but some professors and male students were still antagonistic toward the enrollment of women. Some professors said openly that their classes were too hard for women to master. Many male students still left vacant seats around the few women students and acted condescendingly toward them.[3]

The only dormitories on the campus were for men. Since the

dormitories did not have hot water, students bathed in the basement of Smith Hall or in Bynum Gymnasium. Young men dashed from the dorm to the showers wearing only towels wrapped around their waists. Whenever a woman appeared, a man would yell, "Angel on campus!" warning any young men who were naked except for a towel to hide behind a shrub.[4]

At Chapel Hill, Liddell was close to the fight over woman suffrage taking place in Raleigh, the state capital. A few North Carolina legislators had strong views on suffrage, but most did not take it seriously. Most newspapers opposed it. The *Charlotte News* said that it was "bowed down with woe" about the folly of bringing the suffrage issue to the state legislature. A *Salisbury Carolina Watchman* editorial concluded, "there is no more need for woman suffrage than there is for cow suffrage."[5]

On February 2, before classes started for the semester, Liddell attended the special woman suffrage hearing before the state General Assembly. At the hearing, Barbara Henderson's testimony pointed out that not all men are protective of women. She asked how the legislators would protect the women who are not so protected and have no power to protect themselves. She affirmed "women should not be given a social conscience by God, and deprived by man of the power to give practical expression to their convictions."[6] Laura Reilly and Dr. Anna Howard Shaw also testified. Shaw was a charismatic speaker who gave a long speech. She began with quotes of Founding Fathers such as Benjamin Franklin and Sam Adams. Next, she quoted from the documents of the Continental Congress and the US Constitution. She then used those words to show that the intent of the Founding Fathers to form a republican form of government in each state was unfulfilled, since half of the population could not elect the people who represent them in government. She further stated that the greatest men in the country have forgotten the women. Not only have the men forgotten women, they do not think of women as they think of other men. Women are referenced as to how they relate to a man—they are someone's daughter, wife, or sister. She asked for men to "think of us as they think of each other, not only as to the concerns which come within the limits of the inside of the house but those which come without."[7]

Before the special legislative hearing, Liddell went to a luncheon in honor of Shaw and, in the evening, heard her speak in the Raney Library. Afterwards, she rode back to Chapel Hill with Barbara Henderson.[8]

Although the speech by Shaw at the special hearing impressed the legislators, the 1915 General Assembly did not pass the equal suffrage bill. Adding insult to injury, a group of drunken legislators showed their contempt by destroying a United States map hanging in the suffragist headquarters depicting the status of suffrage by state.[9]

In 1915, Carrie Chapman Catt returned to the presidency of the NAWSA. She had previously been president from 1900 to 1904, but had stepped down because of the ill health of her husband. Catt, a better strategist than Shaw, kept the focus on nonpartisan, nonaggressive tactics and led the Association to work for both state-by-state suffrage laws and an amendment to the US constitution. Catt's goal was to get the federal amendment ratified by 1920. However, when Catt returned to power, Alice Paul was expelled from the NAWSA. Paul and her followers had formed the Congressional Union inside the NAWSA after the 1913 Washington Parade. They later changed the group's name to the National Woman's Party (NWP), yet still worked within the NAWSA. With Paul's expulsion, the NAWSA and the NWP became separate organizations.[10]

During Liddell's studies at UNC, she found time to advocate for suffrage by writing a letter to the editor of the *Charlotte News*. Her letter was a response to an article that asked women to influence men to vote for school bonds for public schools. Her letter, in part, follows:

> First, how can all the women of Charlotte vote through the men? A great many widows, spinsters, and let us not forget deserted wives, have no man to vote through. Second, granting for the sake of argument,

> that every woman might be represented through some man, would he allow her to control his vote? It seems to me that a man who is qualified to vote is qualified to vote as he himself sees fit and would naturally prefer to do so. And third, if a woman is capable of instructing a man how to vote, is she not also capable of casting her own ballot and giving the community the benefit of her opinion without dissipating her energies through the exercise of indirect influence?[11]

Liddell's spring semester at Chapel Hill must not have been what she wanted because, after being home for the summer in Charlotte, she moved to New York City to return to Barnard College to study journalism.[12] She had previously attended one semester at the college in the fall of 1912. Liddell again lived with her aunt and uncle in their North Greenwich Village apartment. The North Village has a grid pattern with streets running east and west and avenues running north and south. Fifth Avenue divides the streets into their east and west branches. As Liddell walked east from the apartment at 149 W. 12th Street, she hit Fifth Avenue. One block north was E. 13th Street, home to Emma Goldman, the anarchist implicated in the attempted assassination of the capitalist Henry Clay Frick in 1892. Goldman's lover, Alexander Berkman, went to prison for fourteen years for the assassination attempt. Goldman lectured on topics considered subversive, such as anarchy, atheism, and free love. She advocated for an eight-hour workday, unionization of workers, and birth control. Often arrested for what she said and wrote, she worked with the Free Speech League for the right for herself and others to express opinions publicly. The work of the Free Speech League led to the founding of the American Civil Liberties Union.[13]

Going south on Fifth Avenue, Liddell passed the Brevoot Mansion. Across from it was 23 Fifth Avenue, where Mabel Dodge, a wealthy art patron, lived on the second floor. She decorated her living room in all white, including the woodwork, wallpaper, fireplace, and rugs. White linen draperies covered the tall windows from ceiling to floor. On the walls were paintings by Marsden Hartley and Arthur B. Davies. Against this backdrop, Dodge placed silver-blue couches and chairs and filled the rooms with fresh flowers, including snapdragons and larkspur for a pop of salmon and blue interspersed among white lilies. Dressed dramatically in a long white dress with an emerald chiffon wrap, she entertained one hundred people for Wednesday night discussions on sex and politics, followed by a midnight buffet. The attendees included anarchists, socialists, union organizers, feminists, literary and visual artists, journalists, and people who could be best described as eccentrics. At these evening gatherings, people with varying ideologies discussed how to better the world. Emma Goldman and Hippolyte Havel proposed anarchy as the answer; Big Bill Haywood (the leader of the International Workers of the World) proposed unionization and the right of workers to strike; Walter Lippman and Hutchins Hapgood proposed that words alone could bring change. There were feminists, such as Margaret Sanger, advocating for birth control, and Henrietta Rodman. Rodman sued the New York public school board, because it required female teachers to report a change in their marital status, while not requiring male teachers to do so. Rodman, wearing sandals and a shapeless shift, rejected conventional dress for women. In her company were her followers, other women teachers and high school girls, who dressed similarly. Other attendees at Dodge's Wednesday night events were Max Eastman (publisher of *The Masses*); writers Floyd Dell, Frank Harris, and Djuan Barnes (writer and art critic who had both male and female lovers); Carl Van Doren; poets Amy Lowell and Edwin Arlington Robinson; artists Charles Demuth, Marsden Hartley, and John Sloan; political cartoonist Art Young; John Reed (journalist, writer for *The Masses*, and communist activist).[14]

John Reed and Bill Haywood met at Dodge's discussions. Suggestions by Haywood and Dodge prompted Reed to produce *The Pageant of the Paterson Strike* in Madison Square Garden to dramatize the five-month-long strike by silk mill workers in 1913. The strike resulted in the deaths of a bystander and a striker by the police. However, *The Masses* was the only news publication that covered the strike. The production by Reed showed the impact of Dodge's discussions. Her introductions of people to others of similar and different ideologies stimulated new ideas and collaborations. Newspaper coverage of the Wednesday night discussions contributed to the reputation of the Village as a hotbed of radical ideas.[15]

One block south of Dodge's residence, Liddell reached the beginning of Fifth Avenue and entered Washington Square through a seventy-seven-foot-high marble arch. The tree-lined Square was the center of Village life and starting point for the suffrage parades up Fifth Avenue. It is likely that Liddell marched in New York City's largest woman suffrage parade (25,000 marchers) held on October 23, 1915. South of Washington Square were ethnic neighborhoods (Italian, German, Irish, and African-American), where the sounds of native languages mingled with the sounds of the city and of children playing in the streets. Each neighborhood was close knit. There, however, was little interaction among the various ethnic neighborhoods, or between the Bohemians and the others. Exceptions were the "black and tan bars," where Blacks and Whites mingled, and the settlement houses, where immigrants from many countries received services, such as day care for children and classes for adults. Liddell helped her aunt with social work at a settlement home on days she had only a few college classes.[16]

In the winter of 1916, Liddell left Barnard College because she felt there were too many prerequisite courses for a journalism degree.[17] She stayed in the Village to write full-time and moved to Milligan Place, a group of four apartment buildings with a central courtyard on the corner of Sixth Avenue and Tenth Street. Milligan Place is on the National Historical Registry because of its place in the Village bohemian history. Today it is a desirable high rent location. Yet, in the winter of 1916, in the heart of the bohemian resurgence, it was low-rent and run-down. For her $16 monthly rent, she had two rooms and a kitchenette, with electricity and a daily housekeeper provided.[18]

Liddell lived at Milligan Place for less than two months, but the artistic residents impressed her. It was the home of Susan Glaspell and Jig Cook, along with some of the theater group who hung around them.[19] Glaspell and Cook were married, but Glaspell kept her maiden name. They moved to Milligan Place in 1915 and stayed for three years. Already a published writer in her late thirties when she came to the Village, Glaspell would win a Pulitzer Prize in 1931 for her play *Alison's House*. Glaspell and Cook acted for the Washington Street Players when it started in 1915 to promote experimental theater. After the group rejected several plays, one of which was Glaspell's, for being *too* experimental, they formed the Provincetown Players in Provincetown, Massachusetts, in the summer of 1915. The Players opened in the Village in the winter of 1917. Many of the theater people spent the summers in Provincetown and the winters in the Village. From 1915 through 1922, the Provincetown Players revolutionized American Theatre. The Players' big discovery was Eugene O'Neill, whose work was too extreme for everyone else. Although Glaspell and Cook discovered O'Neil in the summer of 1916, he was there in the Village hanging around the theater people as early as 1915.

In 1916, Liddell was twenty-four years old and living for the first time without structure provided by family or school. She was free to try out new things with no one knowing. There are only a few comments in her journals and letters to provide clues about her time here, although, in her seventies, she reminisced that this time in Greenwich Village was a formative time for her.[20] She read the bohemian magazine *The Masses* and attended John Reed's communist lectures. She defiantly smoked cigarettes in public as she hung out with Bobby Edwards, the Troubadour of the Village. Edwards was likely the first person she had met who was divorced.[21] Edwards was part of the Provincetown Players crowd. He made ukulele-like instruments from brightly painted cigar boxes and sold them to tourists who came to gawk at the Bohemians. He walked through the Village strumming his homemade ukulele and singing ballads about Village life with his reedy voice. Edwards wrote for *The Masses* and was later editor of *The Quill*, a self-published magazine that popularized Village bohemian life.[22]

Edwards introduced Liddell to the people and places in his Village world. Liddell would have met Polly Holladay, another Provincetown player. Holladay also ran Polly's Restaurant, a popular bohemian hangout featuring cheap meals and deep intellectual discussions. Polly's cook-waiter and lover, Hippolyte Havel, was an anarchist who called the customers bourgeois pigs as he slapped their meals on the table. Next to Polly's Restaurant was the Washington Square Book Shop, a popular place to thumb through the latest bohemian publications. Above Polly's Restaurant was the Liberal Club, where there were lectures, poetry readings, ragtime music (considered obscene at the time), new dances (such as the shimmy and the turkey trot), and plenty of alcohol. Helen Rodman, one founder of the Liberal Club, led the move to form this group when her ideas of free love split the membership of the uptown, more conservative Liberal Club. Many who came regularly to the Liberal Club were the same ones who attended Mabel Dodge's evenings. These three—the Liberal Club, Polly's Restaurant, and the Bookstore—became magnets for the bohemians. It was hard to see where one began and the other ended. On evenings that the Liberal Club had an event, the bohemians, including Polly and Hippolyte, would eat together at Polly's and then go upstairs to the Liberal Club.[23]

Polly's Restaurant and other places, such as The Hell Hole bar, closed at one o'clock in the morning. Then, some of the crowd would go to Romany Marie's Tavern, which stayed open until three o'clock. Bobby Edwards was a close friend of Marie, and Liddell would have likely wandered into the Tavern at least once. The smells of chorba (Moldavian and Romanian stew) and of logs burning in the fireplace filled Marie's Tavern. Although called a tavern, it served no beverage stronger than Turkish tea. After you drank your tea, Marie, dressed in flowing gypsy-styled garb, might tell your fortune from the tea leaves left in your cup. She was a Jewish immigrant from Romania who learned English by ushering at

Goldman's lectures. Her tavern became a meeting place for writers, artists, and intellectuals. At the Tavern, the writers and artists shared their day's work or stared quietly into the fireplace, holding their thoughts to themselves. Although a source of some income, the Tavern was primarily a haven for Marie's inner circle of creative persons. When journalists and tourists came in large enough numbers to disturb her creative group, she moved her tavern until outsiders found it again. Her inner circle included famous or soon-to-be famous writers, such as Theodore Dreiser, Will Durant, Floyd Dell, Eugene O'Neill, and Upton Sinclair. As young aspiring writers and artists came to Marie's, she sized them up. Did they have something important to say or were they just escaping from their childhood and responsibility? One group she nurtured; the other she told to go home.[24]

Liddell was struggling to determine what she wanted out of life; she did not yet know what she wanted to say. For weeks in the Village, she suffered from writer's block. She often sat in her apartment with a blank sheet of paper in her typewriter. The words would not come. She blamed the cold New York winter for her writer's block. Charming Milligan Place was ill-heated. The winter's air numbed her fingers and hijacked her brain. All she could think of was getting warm.[25] By March, Liddell had moved out of Milligan Place because of the cold and was living just north of Washington Square in a room at 5 Fifth Avenue. Yet, she was still cold. She wrote her Aunt Jane:

> I find my little room very bright and cheerful, but impossible to keep warm in spite of the pipe and the radiator. The air blows in like streams of ice water around my charming bow window, and the floor naturally is a bit chilly. I don't expect humming birds, however, with a two dollar coat, and the house seems so quiet and dignified and the situation is so convenient that I wear my sweater or roll up in my eider down quilt and remind myself that winter can't last more than two months longer.[26]

Finally, despite the cold, she could write, although she wondered if there was not a warm tropical island where she could live cheaply and write.

Liddell debated the bohemians at the Liberal Club over the question of how a woman can best live her life. The Village feminists generally agreed that gaining the vote would not give women equality, but they disagreed on the answers, which ranged from a communal system of child-rearing and household duties to a change in the roles where men and women shared the duties of changing diapers, preparing meals, and supporting the family financially. Economic independence, for women, necessary for equality to happen, would be elusive, as long as a woman could not control when and how often she was pregnant. Rich women could get birth control information, but reformers, such as Margaret Sanger, were jailed when they provided such information to poor women. Sanger was a nurse who had seen patients ruin their health and even die from unwanted pregnancies. She hoped that, when women no longer feared getting pregnant, they could enjoy sex, an idea that was scandalous to those who thought sex was only for producing children. The Village bohemians endorsed free love and thought that monogamy hindered a person from fully developing their full potential. Although Liddell admired the Village feminists' passion to make the world a better place and agreed that women needed equality, she disagreed with them about the need to reject almost all conventional standards. She did not agree with the feminism view that depicted women's lives, oppressed by marriage, as limited and tragic, and that called for free love and the breakdown of all social norms.[27] The greatest tragedy in her life up to this point had been her unrequited love for Billy Hardison.[28]

The Liddell women were not oppressed by their marriages, but their choices were limited by society's expectations for women, especially married women. Given the opportunity, Anna Amelia Liddell may have been a social reformer or college professor. Her daughter Annie Hill died a few weeks after giving birth to her third child. Aunt Jane lost control over the large inheritance she brought to the marriage because it became her husband's money. Aunt Myra was the only Liddell woman who was out of the house most of the day working at the settlement house. She could do so since Uncle Forbes was gone during the week and did not need her undivided attention at all times. The Liddell women channeled their energy into volunteer work in churches and clubs and had leisure time for reading and playing bridge. They were fortunate that the family had money, yet they, like most women of their time, were dependent on the men in the family. Anna Forbes Liddell wanted economic independence for women.[29]

John Reed and Bill Haywood decried the oppression of workers by insensitive industrialists and called for factories run by the workers themselves. Such talk collided with the Liddell family story of building wealth, losing it, and then rebuilding it through the values of hard work, frugality, and a strong Christian faith. Anna Forbes attended college and lived in the Village because of her family's income from the Liddell Company. Her industrialist father was a kind man who gave money to those with bad luck. Her friend D.A. Tompkins did not see himself as an oppressor, but as a benefactor who provided opportunity. Although a young woman from a farm family worked in a textile mill up to seventy-two hours a week under harsh conditions, she made more in one month at the mill than her family back home on the farm made in a year. Tompkins felt that working in mills and factories built character in children. However, he acknowledged that some people would take advantage of child labor.[30]

How did Greenwich Village influence Liddell? Her exposure to the full range of thought from conservative Charlotte to progressive—at times anarchist—Greenwich Village provided a range for her own choices. Personal responsibility for one's philosophy and actions was a value she brought to the village. It was strengthened there. She experienced the bohemian view of life, but kept the values of her childhood. She remained a strong supporter of capitalism throughout her life.

Liddell's time in the Village helped her determine which path in life she should take. Except for a few murder mysteries, her writings before the

Village had plots of 'Girl gets Boy' or 'Girl chooses between Career and Marriage.' If a woman chose a career, Liddell had questioned whether that woman would later regret her choice. After her experiences in the Village, Liddell thought that either path, marriage or career, could bring fulfillment. She sketched in her journal the plot of a play about three sisters, Constance, Vivienne, and Isabel, who go to New York to seek their fortunes. Constance wants to be a famous singer, Vivienne a famous playwright and Isabelle a famous artist. Constance gives up her dream when she marries and has a son. Vivienne (likely reminiscent of Susan Glaspell) sells her silent movie screenplays to pay the bills until her theater plays sell. Beautiful Isabelle is courted by Arthur, a wealthy man. She "is too much of an artist to give up her work, and too much of a woman to avoid being loved." Other characters are Phyllis, a married woman who has progressive ideas and does social work even though she has a husband to support her (reminiscent of Aunt Myra), and Marian, an unmarried high school physics teacher who lives a solitary life with "hidden dreams that nobody would have guessed." The plot centered on Isabelle's dilemma: should she give up her dream of being an artist and marry Arthur?[31] Constance, who gave up her singing career for marriage, tells Isabel:

> When I heard [Geraldine] Farrar sing and thought that if I had kept on working and trying, I might have stood where she stood and sing what she was singing, and then I thought about little son and his father—and I couldn't be sorry. For every one that reaches the top thousands never pass the middle and you must be sure that not success, but the struggle itself is worth the sacrifice. I wouldn't tell you what to do Isabel, I have never been satisfied with myself. I couldn't give up Pierre now—but if I were young and free as you are—you must decide for yourself.[32]

Here, the married woman would not give up her family to pursue a career, but realized that a single career woman could be happy, but the woman must decide when young. In the earlier story written when Liddell was sixteen, the career woman regretted her choice.

Back in Charlotte in the summer of 1916, Liddell sat on her front lawn drinking iced tea with Victor Stephenson, a newspaperman who worked for the *Charlotte Observer.* She told him about her experiences in New York—the *New York Evening Post,* Greenwich Village, suffrage marches, political speeches, Milligan Place, and Bobby Edwards. Stephenson later worked in New York at the *New York Evening Post* as a reporter. They likely talked about the University of North Carolina. He was an alumnus, and she had attended one semester there.[33]

Stephenson fell in love with Liddell. His letters to her have survived, but not her letters to him. He addressed her as 'Forbes Dear' or 'Soulmate' and signed the letters "L.V." standing for "Little Victor," which was her name for him. Based on his replies to her letters, he seemed unsure about how she felt about him. Sometimes, he replied as if she had encouraged romance in her letter; other times, he replied as if she had chastised him for wanting more than friendship.[34]

By summer's end, Liddell decided what she wanted to try next. Several Charlotte men who had studied philosophy at the University of North Carolina had formed a Philosopher's Club, which met on Sunday afternoons. After the meeting, some would go to Liddell's house and continue their philosophy discussions with her. She became excited about philosophy and Chapel Hill.[35]

University of North Carolina (1916-1918)

In the fall of 1916, Anna Forbes Liddell returned to the University of North Carolina at Chapel Hill (UNC) as a junior. She had a commitment to finishing her degree that she had not had earlier. As her trunk crossed the threshold of the boarding house where she would stay, she felt like Julius Caesar crossing the Rubicon. She knew she had reached a point of no return and said to herself, "Here I am, for better or for worse."[1]

There were now fourteen women students at UNC, up from eight women students two years before. She could have felt lost among the 1,000 men students, but she found a place for herself when she walked into Professor Horace Williams's Philosophy 1 class. His classes were the only ones she mentioned in her letters home. Her experiences with Williams caused her to change her major from journalism to philosophy.[2]

Williams began teaching at UNC in 1890, when it was an all-male school and he called his students *my boys*. Later, when his classes had women students, he continued to refer to his students as *my boys*. Liddell's family teased her when she went home and talked about what the *other* boys did or said. Not that she felt masculine, but that she felt she was one of Williams's special group.[3] Liddell reminisced sixty years later:

> Among ourselves we called him Horace. Through respect for established academic custom we addressed him as professor, but during the many occasions when we quoted him after class, and argued over questions he had raised, to speak of him as Professor Williams seemed as absurd as to say Professor Plato.
>
> 'We' were those who had studied with Horace Williams. It became a mark of distinction. All of his students and former students had something in common however great the differences in age might be. We constituted an unorganized fraternity and regarded ourselves as the elect. We tried to be modest, but we felt an inner superiority.[4]

Novelist Thomas Wolfe was a sophomore when Liddell was a senior. Wolfe was so strongly influenced by Williams that he modeled the character Professor Virgil Weldon in *Look Homeward Angel* after him. Wolfe said of Williams, "he communicated his own alertness, his originality, his power to think. First came Socrates, then Plato, next Hegel. After Hegel—well, it didn't matter, for after Hegel we had *him*. He was our own Old Man."[5]

Williams had studied at Yale and Harvard, where he was an excellent student. However, he did not complete his PhD program. He felt contempt for the education of most PhDs. He said, "Your PhD can tell you precisely how many hairs there are on the left hind leg of a dog and which hair is in the exact center." Williams considered that training and not education.[6]

Neither did Williams write scholarly papers. He was not a skilled writer, and the few books he wrote were unorganized. However, he excelled at teaching because he was a natural storyteller. Williams associated with ordinary men at Pickard's livery stables and the drugstore, sharing town gossip, telling stories, and discussing life. Then, he was ready to bring real-life examples to the classroom.[7]

Williams often said he was a Hegelian, because his personal philosophy aligned that that of Georg Wilhelm Friedrich Hegel who lived from 1770 to 1831. Although modern scholars may differ on what Hegel's philosophy was or whether Williams was a proper Hegelian, what is important here is what Williams taught his students about Hegel's philosophy. Hegel's dialectic process leads to knowledge through arguing and debating contradictory ideas and synthesizing them.[8] Hegel's philosophy and the dialectic method of teaching were well known in Europe and New England, but they were new to the US South. Williams used Hegel's dialectic process as his teaching method. Wolfe called Williams the "Hegel of the Cotton Patch."[9] Williams said, "To teach philosophy is to philosophize. Do it before the class and invite them to join. To philosophize is to exhibit truth in the process of intelligence. I did not ask my students to learn about Plato. I invited them into the Platonic experience. Stand upon the mountain and see what Plato saw."[10]

The following describes a typical lesson in which Williams invited the students to philosophize. Williams stood at a large window overlooking a grove of oaks as students came into the classroom to take their seats on semi-circular wooden benches. When the room quieted, he moved from the window to begin the class. The class discussion went like this:

> "Mr. Jacobs," he would ask, "what is the most important part of an ox-cart?"
> "The wheels, Professor," Jacobs would glibly reply.
> "No, not the wheels."
> "Then, Professor, it must be the body," Adams would venture.
> "No, not the body."
> "Is it the ox, Professor?" Thompson would timidly inquire.
> "No, not the ox. It's the concept of a cart, the blueprint. After the blueprint has been made, any jackleg can do the rest. The blueprint is immortal; it lasts forever. The cart soon wears out."[11]

Then, he might ask the students "which is smarter, a sheep or a goat" or "can a horse appreciate a sunset." After the discussion, he gave an example from the life of a philosopher. He often answered students' questions with a question.[12] This frustrated some students who wanted answers and facts, not questions and abstractions. One day, a student named Couch (unknown first name) interrupted:

> Professor Williams, I don't see any sense in all that. What good can it do us? I know that up is down and down is up and that minus three multiplied by minus three gives plus nine and this side of the street is the other side of the street, but what of it? I came into your class because I was told you solve the problems of life: progress and poverty, society and crime. I adhere to the absolute, but what I want is something workable.[13]

When Couch finished talking, Williams moved to the window and looked out. The students sat on the edges of the benches in anticipation. Williams moved from the window and faced Couch:

> Mr. Couch, I fear you are in the wrong room. You should be in the School of Commerce under Dean Carroll. You are inclined to be particularistic. You deal in accessories, not in principle. Some day [*sic*] Mr. Couch, you will emerge from the particular into the universal. You will discover that principle governs the accessories. The tail, Mr. Couch, follows the hide.[14]

In an article in *The Daily Tar Heel*, the campus newspaper, Liddell explained the term *concept* she learned in Williams's class. It read, in part:

> Perhaps you are one of the people who won't believe in concepts because they can't see 'em.' There are perfectly good folks who feel that way and you can pick out any number of famous men to back you up.

You might live and work and eat and sleep and acquire property and fame and never bother about concepts at all, and perhaps be just as happy. That is if you like that kind of bliss.

If you have elected Philosophy 1–2 you have passed beyond that happy state—you have heard about the concept and you are wondering in your secret soul whether you will ever achieve one, whether you perhaps have one already without recognizing it as such. You don't care what kind of concept it happens to be, a concept of the origin of the species or a concept of a biscuit. The biscuit type seems easier to investigate. But a few minutes reflection on this apparently simple subject convinces you that your mind is hardly up to the task. "What is a biscuit?" Why of course a biscuit is a biscuit, anybody know what a biscuit is, certainly you do. You have eaten your thousands of biscuits, hot, cold, big, little, soda, beaten and buttermilk. You know the color, size and shape, you can look in the cook book and read the recipe. But you can't explain how it happened to be a biscuit instead of a waffle or short cake. Oh! you can beg the question and say the cook did it, but that brings you back to the realization that the cook must have had a concept, and if you are going to arrive at a concept and not your own but the cook's concept, your last state is worse than your first.

One disconsolate senior walked from the Alumni Building to the Post Office pondering this concept business, "I don't know what I have done in the last three years, I reckon I haven't done anything, I haven't any concept."

His companion was equally mournful, "I haven't got it. I don't know what I know. I don't know anything."

Professor Williams professes that he has a number of concepts. He says

> he got most of them under his maple tree, he says he doesn't know how he did it, but they just come under that tree.
>
> This is an enlightened community, the students have evoluted [*sic*] beyond the stage of vandalism. But if the Tree of Knowledge is growing right here within our midst. . .some night a delegation from Philosophy 1–2 is liable to sally forth and steal the shoots.[15]

In Liddell's first class with Williams, she received a grade of C. If Williams had thought that she was a better student, she might have received a D, because he gave the lowest grades to his best first-time students. He thought that giving a student a good grade in his first course, even if the student had earned it, caused the student to become lazy. Later, he would give his best students Bs, but seldom As. In forty years of teaching, he only gave about a dozen As. Williams also gave low grades to students who only repeated what he said. Even if the students gave eloquent explanations of Williams's views, he gave them Ds for not providing original work. Williams's grading system crushed the spirit of some students, but spurred others to excel. It must have motivated Liddell since she earned Bs in her next courses. His teaching method—debating and questioning—was ideal for her.[16]

Although Williams taught students to question assumptions, he had a lifelong gender bias that he did not question. He wrote in his autobiography that women could be excellent students, but they could not keep the honor code. To support his stereotype, Williams gave the example of a female student who voted to punish another for being fifteen minutes late for curfew when the same evening, she had been two hours late but had not been caught. She bragged it did not matter what one did as long as nobody knew.[17] Yet, Williams did not stereotype the men students about keeping the honor code, although there were many instances of male students and male faculty acting dishonorably. Their actions reflected only on the individuals, not on the entire gender. Williams's anecdote of the actions of one female student to support his gender stereotype is an example of confirmation bias. Williams had several female students, like Liddell, who kept the honor code. However, a case that supports the group stereotype is viewed as proof of the stereotype, while a case that contradicts the stereotype is viewed as atypical. Thus, the stereotypical belief remains intact.

Liddell was aware of Williams's gender bias and thought it might cause him to discriminate in hiring. Later, when she was a student at Cornell University, another student said that he wanted to return to Chapel Hill when he graduated to be an assistant for Professor Williams. Liddell noted wistfully, "Never before have I regretted being a woman. Above all things I should like to be Prof. Williams' [*sic*] assistant in Philosophy. I have the training and other qualifications—but being a woman it would be useless even to apply."[18]

Many parents became alarmed when their children explained what they were learning in Williams's classes. He gained a statewide reputation as someone who was corrupting the youth of the state, especially concerning the fundamentalist Christianity, which was prevalent in North Carolina. Ministers from pulpits and editorials in newspapers denounced his teaching. Many considered him an atheist. Newspapers asked whether the state should spend public money for an atheist to teach at the university.[19]

Early in Williams's career, Cornelia Spencer, one of the most influential people in North Carolina, summoned him to her office at UNC. Today, we would call her an *influencer*. Although she had no official title at UNC, she had a campus office. In an age when women had little public influence, Spencer exerted significant power through her letters to politicians and to newspapers. Her letters were eloquent, yet blunt with a scolding tone, opposite of the soft voice expected of a Southern woman. Her views were conservative. She thought that slavery had been evil, but held white supremacist views, romanticizing the relationships that had existed between slaveholders and slaves. Her view on the role of women was complicated.

She held it was natural and biblically based that men dominate women and that women should accept their subservient role. Yet, she advocated for education for women so they could be better wives and mothers. She held that single women, whether never married or widowed like herself, could have public roles in society to use their talents fully. Her opinions influenced educational policy in North Carolina from elementary school through graduate school. Her condemnation could end Williams's career as a professor in the state of North Carolina.[20]

Williams recounted his conversation with Spencer:

> "I don't like what you are doing," she said.
>
> "Why, Mrs. Spencer, I am doing my best."
>
> "No, you are not. You are the Professor of Christian Philosophy. I want you to understand that we do not want any of that Yankee skepticism down here."
>
> The catalog said I was Professor of Philosophy. I had to think and be quick about it. Mrs. Spencer's son-in-law was Professor of Mathematics. I said, "If you will make Professor Love change his title to Christian Mathematics, I will change mine."
>
> Her eyes flashed. "Get out of here with your impudence."
>
> I obeyed. I had saved my official neck.[21]

Actually, Williams held a strong Christian faith. He had examined the fundamentalist Christianity of his youth and replaced it with a liberal Christian faith. He remembered vividly the day in college when he realized that Jesus was not a Methodist and that the Bible should not be interpreted literally. His adult Christian faith transcended the orthodoxy of his youth. He considered Christianity the perfect religion because its inner meaning, not its literal interpretations, aligns with the principles of philosophy. Williams taught that religion was not the relation of a person to an institution, but the relation of a person to the totality of things, that totality being God. The source of religion is beauty, which is truth spontaneously expressing itself. Nor did Williams think that philosophy and religion were incompatible with science He defined science as a body of knowledge gained through analysis. Science leads to knowledge of the world and searches for the universal that is scientific law. The universal that philosophy seeks is truth.[22]

Williams influenced thousands of students, both men and women. Many became leaders of North Carolina and beyond. One was Frank Porter Graham, who was President of UNC from 1930 to 1949 and US senator from North Carolina from 1949 to 1950. He said, "Horace Williams has made more University students intellectually conscious than any other professor in the history of the University."[23] Another student of Williams was John J. Parker, who was Judge of US Court of Appeals for the Fourth Circuit from 1925 through 1958, serving as Chief Judge from 1948 to 1958. He said, "[Williams] was the greatest intellectual and spiritual force in our State. He visualized philosophy as the synthesis of all knowledge. A great teacher, a great philosopher, a great man, he took us by the hand in the dewy and liquid morn of youth and led us up to heights, which we could not have reached without him."[24]

While Liddell focused on her studies, she still wondered whether she would marry, and if so, whether it would be to someone she already knew. She dated Rawley Myers and several university students and wondered if she would marry Victor Stephenson. Living in New York City at that time, Stephenson marched in the October 1917 suffrage parade. He wrote to Liddell, "[I] thought often of you and the first one—tried to picture your little feet tripping along with martial tread (as it were) on the same pavement I was traversing. . . .Write to me often and tell me how much you love me."[25] In another letter, Stephenson wrote, "Some day, some day, Forbesy dear. . . .I shall leave off talking and take you in my arms, undeterred by preliminary wiggles and squeals and witticisms designed to make me feel big and awkward and foolish and silly, and I shall hold you tight as tight can be, and then some more."[26]

In 1914, the powerful countries of Europe became engaged in World War I. Initially, the United States was neutral, but supplied war materials to the Allied Powers of France and Britain. Sentiment grew for the country to enter the fighting after Germany sank US merchant ships and tried to start a war between Mexico and the United States. By early 1917, the push for the United States to enter the fighting was strong. The looming entry of the United States into the war cast a shadow on Liddell's Junior Class. Many students wondered if they would even have a senior year if the country entered the war. Preparing for war had seemed impersonal to Liddell before the night of her Junior Banquet in March 1917. That night, she looked around at the students sitting at her table and realized that it was *these* irresponsible and inexperienced boys that may soon go to war. Suddenly, the war seemed real to her, and she hated it.[27]

After United States entered World War I, the University of North Carolina experienced a drop in enrollment when the older men left for war, leaving only the younger men and the women. The 1915 freshman class had 320 men; by fall 1918, only 130 remained in that class.[28]

By Liddell's senior year in the fall of 1917, she had earned the respect of the men. The college yearbook had a paragraph written about each senior student. Her paragraph stated:

> Miss Liddell was with us in our freshman year; then deserted, but returned in time to graduate with us. She is one of the first of the new regime, which has turned 'Co-Ed' into 'women students in the University.' When she came the first time, the sight of a woman on campus was an event talked of for weeks; now you can't look around without seeing several. She was also the first lady to put herself on a basis of absolute equality with the boys. She acted like a nice companionable human being and immediately was taken as such. She isn't afraid of us, as they used to be; so we no longer look with scorn

upon the Co-Eds. She talks a great deal, and is the only person in College who can absolutely tell you what Horace Williams means, when he does not know. She is a good fellow.[29]

The increase in the number of women that the yearbook author describes was modest—from eight students in 1915 to twenty-six in 1918.[30] Nonetheless, this small increase changed the UNC culture; for example, male students could no longer walk around campus wearing only towels around their waists. However, some men still felt awkward around the women, some of whom remained afraid of the men. *The Daily Tar Hill* printed a regular column named, Coediquette. Liddell wrote many, but not all, of the articles for Coediquette. One column not written by Liddell commented, in part:

> When they [women] appear on campus, all conversations among the groups nearby ceases…furtive looks are exchanged, and there is a general tension that gives way only with the retreating foot steps of the unfortunate woman. . .This is bad enough but there is something worse to come. . . .She appears an oasis in a desert of seats. On the various edges of the desert are seated the fair representatives of the stronger sex, studiously avoiding proximity to the dread being, who though she may be brilliant intellectually would gladly give her all for a drop of that milk called human kindness, which seems to be at a premium so far as she is concerned.[31]

An article written three weeks later by Liddell, referred to the above article and acknowledged the validity of the woman's experience. However, it provided a different viewpoint. It read, in part:

> Instead of feeling herself a creature set apart, she has had the very opposite experience. Naturally a girl can't loaf around the dorms and

> the drug store, go out for football or track, not to mention the many other interesting and sociable things which an Ed enjoys. She must always remain a bit of a stranger to the boys on the Hill, even her own classmates, but if she feels herself a creature set apart, isn't it her own fault?
>
> Nearly four years ago a co-ed entered the University as a special Junior, but she was just as green as any of the boys she had First History with then, the same boys she hopes to graduate with in June. One lone girl in a big section of Freshman History might be pardoned for wondering if the usher hadn't made a mistake, and the co-editor might have felt embarrassed then if something hadn't have happened within a week after her coming.
>
> She was taking her meals at Pickard's Hotel and rooming almost a block away, a lonely dark block after supper. A very nice Ed sat across from her at the table. One night he walked all the way home with her, and the co-ed felt flattered and grateful. He went with her to the porch and up the steps and in the door and on upstairs, and then the co-editor realized that he hadn't exactly been bringing her home, he lived there too. They had gone along together.
>
> After that she didn't expect the Eds to fight for the honor of sitting by her in class, she didn't even notice where they sat. She went on [*sic*] class and sat down and spoke up when her name was called or the spirit moved her to speak. If she wanted to borrow a knife, she asked the nearest person to lend her one, and if she heard somebody asking for something that she had she passed it over. She tried to go ahead quietly as any other student would and make her own place in the University.[32]

Coediquette was aptly named, because men and women were questioning the proper etiquette for interacting with each other as the old rules became outdated. At that time, it was thought to be improper for a woman to talk with a man she did not know unless a friend who knew them both made an introduction. Thus, men and women students hesitated to start conversations with each other. One Coediquette article of unknown authorship stated:

> Everyone in the University is busy, and nobody stays here very long, even the five year students, so why waste time and the opportunity to make friends just because no third person happens to be near enough to tell two other people that they have his permission to recognize each other on the campus.[33]

The author could have been Liddell because her attitude was to dispense with outdated formalities.

In 1918, when Liddell earned her AB degree, she became a member of the small group of people in the country with a college degree. Nationally, only two of every one hundred twenty-three-year-olds in 1918 had a bachelor's degree, and women comprised only 32 percent of them.[34]

* * *

Since the failed North Carolina suffrage amendment in 1915, the state suffragists had not been active. The North Carolina Equal Suffrage League (ESL) did not even meet in 1916. The National American Woman Suffrage Association (NAWSA) dropped its lobbying to support aid for the troops. Thus, little happened in North Carolina until the end of the war to advance woman suffrage. The NAWSA suffragists aided the war effort though Red Cross efforts and through Woman's Committees set up in each state. Laura Reilley was the Chair of the North Carolina Woman's Committee. She was an excellent choice for the job, since she had a statewide network of women with whom she had worked on social issues. She had served as President of the North Carolina Federation of Women's Club from 1909 to 1911, was the Vice-President of the national General Federation of Women's Clubs, in addition to being a charter member and Vice-President of the North Carolina Equal Suffrage League.[35]

While the NAWSA discontinued its suffrage work during the war, the National Woman's Party (NWP), led by Alice Paul, did not. In January 1917, the NWP *Silent Sentinels* began protests in front of the White House. Seven days a week, they silently walked their route, wearing purple, yellow, and white sashes, and carrying signs such as "Mr. President, How long must women wait for Liberty?" and "Mr. President, What will you do for woman suffrage?" They continued the protests, even after the country entered the war.[36]

At first, the protests amused federal officials. As the protests continued, the officials became angry. They arrested the Sentinels for blocking the sidewalk or the street. The first few times, the court only warned the Sentinels or sentenced them to at most three days in jail. However, on June 14, 1917, sixteen protesters received sixty-day sentences in the Occoquan Workhouse in rural Virginia where conditions were deplorable. Inmates slept on filthy bedding or the filthy floor, and they ate food infested with worms. This time, President Wilson issued pardons for the protesters, but he did not pardon later sentences to the Workhouse. On November 14, 1917, the court sentenced thirty-one protesters to Occoquan. The women asked to be treated as political prisoners. This request angered Occoquan Superintendent Whittaker, who ordered the forty guards to treat the women brutally. Women who received especially brutal attacks were Lucy Burns, Dora Lewis, and Dorothy Day (later co-founder of the Catholic Worker Movement). When the news media reported what happened that night, the public was outraged that White women of such high economic and social status were so mistreated. To further protest, the suffragist prisoners began a hunger strike, after the example of Alice Paul and others, who were simultaneously staging a hunger strike in the District of Columbia jail. On November 26, 2017, pressured by media coverage and fear of future media coverage if one of the women died, the government released all the imprisoned suffragists in the Occoquan Workhouse and the District of Columbia jail.[37]

Meanwhile, other women joined the military. Before WWI, women served in the military only if they enlisted disguised as men. During the Civil War, at least 400 women enlisted in the Union and Confederate Armies as men. They wore short hair and male clothing and adopted habits considered masculine, such as swearing, chewing tobacco, and fist fighting. Many continued to live as men after the war.[38]

However, the United States needed women in the military for WWI to allow men to fight overseas. Because the US Army required all soldiers to be men, the women enlisted in auxiliary units that were not part of the regular army. Thus, women did not receive the same benefits as men. They even had to buy their own uniforms. Most served stateside in clerical jobs; however, hundreds of female switchboard operators served hazardous duty in France. In contrast, the US Navy had no gender restrictions and enlisted 11,000 women as yeoman during WWI. These women received the same pay and benefits as their male counterparts. After the war, however, women served in the military only as nurses.

With the help of the United States, the Allies were winning the war, but there was now a new enemy. In March 1918, about 100 soldiers at Fort Riley in Kansas contracted the *three day fever.* Similar outbreaks occurred in Europe. Most historians consider this outbreak as the first wave of the 1918 influenza pandemic. By August 1918, a second wave of the disease emerged. Countries at war suppressed the information about the outbreak because they did not want to harm the morale of their populations already suffering from war privations and because they did not want their enemies to know their troops were weakened. Only Spain, which was neutral in the war, reported the cases and deaths accurately. Thus, the 1918 flu became also known as the Spanish Flu. The actual place of origin of the flu remains unknown, although it did not originate in Spain. A rumor surfaced that the disease was biological warfare by the Germans spread through Bayer aspirin. When US research disproved that hypothesis, the rumor eventually died down.

This second wave of the infection, more deadly than the first, appeared in both the United States and Europe. It is likely that the movement of troops within Europe and the movement of troops between the United States and Europe spread this more virulent form of the disease. The United States government suppressed news about the growing epidemic until September 1918, when cases emerged in Boston, New York City, and Philadelphia. After appearing in the Eastern United States, the 1918 flu spread westward to St. Louis and San Francisco. By the end of the second wave in December 1918, the infection had spread to the entire United States, except for a few rural or mountainous areas.[39]

Earlier flu viruses (and most afterwards) primarily killed the elderly and the very young. This 1918 flu, however, had a W-shaped curve by age for mortality, instead of the typical U-shaped curve. Many seemingly healthy adults from age twenty to forty became ill and died within a few hours or days. There were stories of people getting sick as they traveled to work and then dying during the day. Four women played a game of bridge late into the evening. Three of the women died during the night. Many who survived the initial virus became sick with a secondary pneumonia infection and died later.[40]

There were neither flu vaccines nor antibiotics for bacterial infections available. Little was known about how to treat the disease except for isolation. Some communities mandated the wearing of masks. However, the masks were ineffective in slowing the transmission of the virus, because the recommended masks were made of gauze. People treated the flu with home remedies. The *Charlotte Observer* printed a recipe for a flu hot toddy composed of whisky, sugar, and ginger with instructions to go to bed for twelve hours after drinking the toddy. Despite the earlier suspicion concerning aspirin, some people thought it might help treat the flu. Doctors prescribed up to 30 grams of aspirin daily as a treatment. Today, we know that any dose above four grams per day may be toxic. Thus, aspirin poisoning caused or contributed to many deaths attributed to the Spanish Flu. Up to 650,000 Americans died either from the initial virus, secondary infections after the virus weakened the lungs, or unsafe treatments. This was ten times the number of Americans who died in World War I.[41]

The Public Health Service (PHS) managed the US federal response to the pandemic. At first, the PHS minimized reporting of the danger from the pandemic. Yet, when it was clear that the disease was more than just the ordinary flu, the agency quickly implemented a four-part strategy. The first part was a compilation of the reports of cases and deaths by local areas. The second was the distribution of pamphlets to local areas. The third was the appointment of state health directors, who could disburse federal funds and redistribute medical staff to areas most affected. The fourth was the formation of a national Volunteer Medical Service Corps. By October 5, 1918, these four parts were in place. Then the agency ordered the states to close all public gatherings and established emergency hospitals and soup kitchens.[42]

Although the federal government assisted mitigation and treatment, local governments controlled the response to the flu. The communities that started mitigation efforts early had lower mortality rates than the communities than did not. When the first case appeared in Philadelphia on September 17, 1918, city leaders told the public not to spit on the sidewalk or cough and sneeze in public, but the city went ahead with the Liberty Loan parade on September 28, 1918. The parade attracted 200,000 spectators, after which the disease spread rapidly throughout the city. It was not until October 3, 1918, that Philadelphia city leaders shut down public gatherings, including schools, churches, and theaters. By contrast, the St. Louis city leaders closed public gatherings as soon as the first case appeared, and the city had half the peak death rate as Philadelphia. Although New York City did not require closure of businesses and schools, it started migration efforts early with a strict mandatory quarantine of infected persons. The city staggered business hours to reduce the number of passengers on the transportation system and only closed poorly ventilated theaters and movie houses. Since many schoolchildren could not go home because of quarantined family members, the city set up centers to care for them. New York City had the lowest peak death rate on the East coast. The peak death rate is important because overwhelming the public health system can increase the total number of deaths.[43]

The epidemic affected the economy in all areas of the country. At its height, businesses closed because many workers were infected. Essential services, such as mail delivery and garbage collection, were halted. Some families had to dig the graves of their loved ones who died.[44]

The peak of the Spanish flu in North Carolina occurred in October–November 1918. Almost 14,000 North Carolinians died from the disease. One of those people was Edward Kidder Graham, the President of UNC, who died on October 26, 1918 at age forty-two, after an illness of five days. There is no evidence that any of the Liddells contracted the disease during this time.[45]

On November 11, 1918, World War I fighting ended when Germany signed an armistice treaty with the Allies. The second wave of the 1918 flu ended in December 1918. With the fighting over and the flu seemingly ended, Liddell was ready to begin her career. Although she had majored in philosophy at UNC, she had not given up her childhood dream of being a famous author. New York City would be the place to start.

Writing and Voting (1919-1920)

In January 1919, Anna Forbes Liddell excitedly moved to New York City to be a writer. On weekdays, she worked at McGraw Hill Publishing Company for money to pay her bills while doing freelance writing in the evenings and weekends. Each day at McGraw Hill, she had a stack of about 100 letters that needed responses. Every letter had a note attached by her research assistant with the facts. She personalized each response, but, with so many letters each day, she had to use some stock phrases. In her spare time, Liddell worked steadily on her freelance writing. About mid-March, she sent two stories and a series of fairy stories to the Wildman Agency.[1]

During that time, Liddell dated four men: Victor Stephenson, two medical doctors, and Rawley Myers, when he came up to New York to visit. She carefully balanced her dinner and theater dates between the doctors so that neither got the message that she wanted a more intimate relationship. She went to the theater several times with Stephenson, but when he pressed for a more romantic relationship, she told him "small room for eroticism was left."[2] She was not ready to marry anyone, which she believed would force her to give up her career.

In April 1919, Liddell caught a flu that may have been part of the third wave of the 1918 Flu that swept New York City in the winter and spring of that year. No test was available to make a definitive diagnosis, but Liddell said that it was the flu that was going around New York. After attending a theater performance with her aunt, Louella Franklin, who was visiting, Liddell suddenly felt ill with a scratchy throat. Although she felt awful, she went into work the next day. Her co-workers begged her to go home. She left work early to see Dr. Kraetzer, one of the medical doctors she was dating. She told him that he had fifteen minutes to cure her because she had plans for dinner and theater that night. He took her temperature and sprayed her throat with antiseptic. He told her that there would be no dinner or theater for her that night, because her temperature was 103 degrees. It took four days for her temperature to break. She felt so sick that she thought she might have to be hospitalized. Several days later, Louella Franklin also became ill and had to be hospitalized. Fortunately, both women recovered, although it took Liddell several weeks to regain her stamina.[3]

In late April 1919, amid her illness, Liddell received a letter that she had been hoping for each day. Mr. Browne, a literary agent at the Wildwood Agency, wrote that he likely could sell two of her submissions and that her writing was good. She had been discouraged before she got the letter. His words were what she needed to hear from a professional. Friends and family could say that her writing was good, but to hear it from someone who did not care about her feelings meant everything. Although the stories were not yet sold, she now had an agent, and that was half the battle she thought.[4]

One story that the Wildman Agency wanted was her fairy story, "Arabelle and Wiggellywumps: The Wonderful Adventures of Arabelle and Wiggellywumps in the Enchanted Garden," which portrayed four adventures of a little girl named Arabelle and a cat named Wiggellywumps. The semi-autobiographical stories show her imagination. The enchanted garden was reminiscent of her grandmother's garden, where the young Liddell talked to the fairies she imagined. Wiggellywumps was based on her grandmother's cat.[5] Aunt Evelyn was likely reminiscent of her aunt Eva Liddell. Parks-The-Gardener was likely patterned after her grandmother's gardener. Modern readers may be offended by the presence in the story of Arabelle's Mammy Ellen. Yet we should consider the story in the context of the times, when it was common for affluent White families to hire a Black woman to care for the children. The young Anna Forbes did not have a mammy, but her cousin Vinton did.[6] The fairy tale shows Liddell remained young at heart into her adulthood. She had vowed as a child always to keep her child's love of imagination and play. She kept that promise to herself.

The Wildman Agency sold "Arabelle and Wiggellywumps" to *Holland's Magazine.* The magazine published the adventures as a serial in eight issues (Feb., Mar., May, Jun., Jul., Aug., Sept., and Oct. 1920). Hugh Rankin illustrated the stories with pen and ink drawings. He illustrated many fantasy stories, the most notable were the short stories published in *Weird Tales*, a fantasy and horror magazine.[7]

Serialization in magazines was popular. When the magazine arrived each month, the family eagerly read the next adventure and, perhaps, discussed the moral lessons of the story. The adventures in "Arabelle and Wiggellywumps" instruct children to keep promises, tell the truth, and call no one a liar. They, however, also point out that liars occasionally tell the truth and that everyone lies when they say things they do not mean just to be polite. They also illustrate the relativity of experience. A distance that is not far for a jaybird is far for a snail, yet the actual distance is the same in both cases. Similarly, a trip to a place feels longer and more exciting than the return trip. There are also cautions to use resources wisely. A grasshopper gives an environmental lesson when he says that humans have no purpose and are a menace—they kill insects, steal the fruits of the earth, and destroy the land. The last adventure stresses that marriage should be based on love, not obligation. In each adventure, Arabelle and Wiggellywumps get into trouble. In one, they ignore warnings to turn back. When they come upon a pit of slithering snakes, they cannot go forward. Suddenly, the forest closes behind them and they cannot now turn back.

They learn to take heed of warnings. Arabelle is a resourceful heroine who conjures up solutions to their predicaments. In a time when the culture taught that women could not manage their lives without a man, the adventures illustrated that women and girls can solve problems and make decisions on their own.

Liddell left New York City at the end of summer of 1919. Her job at McGraw Hill was not the kind of writing she wanted to do. Since her connection with the Wildwood Agency was established, she could do her creative writing from anywhere. She quickly found a job teaching high school English in Salisbury, North Carolina, which is only forty miles from Charlotte.[8] She was there in November when Victor Stephenson wrote her, "Have you forgiven me yet for trying to treat you as a woman instead of a disembodied spirit? I believe that was the sum of my offending—and the sum of yours was that you were grossly unsympathetic."[9] In December, after he reread "Confessions," an essay she wrote in 1916 about the men whom she had loved, he wrote a formal letter, addressed to "A F L" (not the usual "Forbsey Dear"). In the letter, he admitted that it had always hurt him that she mentioned him only on the last page of the essay as "a mysterious person who did not belong in the category of lovers." He also wondered about the line, in which she says that his move to Philadelphia affected her psychologically. He suggested she add chapters to bring it up-to-date. He said, "I have myself had at various time[s] widely different ideas as to the part I played in your life and have suffered some rude shocks."[10] Liddell and Stephenson continued to write an occasional letter to each other for another three years, but the relationship was now only a friendship, not a romance. Whatever she felt for Stephenson, she kept his letters all her life.

* * *

The proposed Nineteenth Amendment to the US Constitution, which would give women to right to vote in all elections, gained public support after World War I. Historians debate whether the shift in sentiment was because of the Silent Sentinel protests or the goodwill earned by women's support for the war. Likely, it was a combination of the two forces. After Congress passed the amendment in June 1919, thirty-six states needed to ratify it for it to become part of the Constitution. By March 22, 1920, only one more state was needed. Most people thought the crucial vote would come from either North Carolina or Tennessee. The entire nation watched to see what those two states would do.

Carrie Chapman Catt, President of the National American Woman Suffrage Association (NAWSA), suggested that people go to North Carolina to help get the amendment ratified. Gertrude Weil, who followed Barbara Henderson as President of the North Carolina Equal Suffrage League (ESL), insisted that only Southern women would be welcome. Previously, the North Carolina anti-suffragists had invited out-of-state campaigners, and that strategy had antagonized the men in power. Weil's strategy was to limit the campaign to only North Carolinian women and to appeal to the gallantry of North Carolinian men. Weil and the ESL hoped that their polite campaign would win the votes for ratification by the state.[11]

Some North Carolina Democratic Party precinct leaders thought women would soon be voting regardless of what North Carolina did. On March 27, 1920, they invited some women to the local meetings to elect delegates to the State Democratic Convention. Imagine the shock of the men when other women showed up uninvited and many were their wives! In the confusion, the men elected some women as delegates. When the Convention met in April, the delegates debated whether to put ratification on the party platform. The women delegates were quiet, fearing that if they spoke up, there might be a backlash. Max Gardner spoke passionately for woman suffrage and gained enough supporters to defeat the opposition led by Cameron Morrison, who spoke just as passionately.[12]

The victory was short-lived, however, as Cameron Morrison defeated Max Gardner in the Democratic Primary for governor in July. Morrison's campaign opposed woman suffrage. He used the rallying cry of "Remember the Revolution of 1898," which was a coded phrase to scare White voters with the thought that if women voted Black citizens would take over control of the state.[13]

Four days after the Democratic Primary, Governor Bickett called for a special session of the General Assembly to consider ratification of the Nineteenth Amendment. The session began on August 10, 1920. On August 11, sixty-three House representatives sent a telegram to Tennessee legislators stating that North Carolina would not ratify. They asked Tennessee not to ratify. On August 17, the North Carolina General Assembly voted to postpone the vote on ratification until 1921. The next day, August 18, Tennessee ratified the Nineteenth Amendment, and, eight days later, the Amendment was formally declared a part of the US Constitution.[14]

Since women now had the right to vote in all elections, there was no need for the suffrage associations. The League of Women Voters, previously an arm of the National American Woman Suffrage Association, emerged as an independent organization to provide education on government and political procedures without affiliation with any political party.[15]

The North Carolina suffragists did not directly influence the passage of the Nineteenth Amendment. Yet, as they lobbied for their rights, they clarified their values and strengthened their commitment to equality for all. Gertrude Weil served as the first president of the North Carolina League of Women Voters. A lifelong advocate for civil rights, she founded the Goldsboro Bi-Racial Council in her hometown. When the local public swimming pool refused to admit black citizens, Weil built a swimming pool for the Black community and jumped into the pool at its dedication ceremony. In the 1930s and 1940s, she worked to rescue Jewish refugees who fled from the Nazi regime. Gladys Avery, who led the marchers in front of the suffragist float in the 1914 Charlotte parade, became a well-respected political activist. After graduation from UNC in 1917, she married Charles Tillett and continued to work for suffrage. She was the founder of the Mecklenburg Chapter of the League of Women Voters, and in later years worked for passage of the Equal Rights Amendment. She was active in the Democratic Political Party and spoke at its 1944 national convention. She was appointed by Presidents Truman, Kennedy, and Johnson to committees representing the United States in United Nations activities. After suffrage was won, Laura Reilley served on the advisory board of the North Carolina League of Women Voters and was a delegate to the 1924 Democratic national convention. She continued as a leader in many women's, cultural, and historical clubs.[16]

Anna Forbes Liddell came from a family of women who wanted equality for women. She was twenty-eight when she got the right to vote. Her grandmother in her nineties was one of the first women to register to vote in Charlotte, North Carolina.[17] Liddell's advocacy was not just for the right for women to enter a voting booth, but for women to enter all areas of society as equals with men. For the rest of her life, Liddell would work for equality for women. Yet, at the end of 1920, she was not sure that she had found the right path in life to do so.

Cornell University (1921-1923)

The eight years between 1913 and 1921 brought changes to the Liddell family. In 1921, Anna Forbes Liddell's sister Helen and her husband Dexter McBride now had two children, Walter and Helen-Aline. Two other children, Mary Anna and Eva, would be born later.[1] Anna Forbes Liddell's grandmother, Anna Amelia Liddell, now 95 years old, was confined to a wheelchair, after breaking a hip from a fall. The lovely gardens that Anna Forbes loved as a child were no longer maintained. Her uncle, Vinton Liddell, died in 1915. His widow Jane Hall Liddell married Dr. Westry Battle, in 1918. The Battles were seldom in Charlotte. In fall 1921, Jane's daughter, Vinton Liddell, was in her senior year at Bryn Mawr College. Anna Forbes's uncle, Forbes Liddell, died in 1917. His widow Myra Ravenscroft Liddell moved in with her daughter Katherine Liddell, who was teaching English at Byrn Mawr College.[2]

Also in 1921, Liddell's writing career was at a standstill. Although she was still writing, Mr. Browne, her literary agent had left the Wildman Agency. Since then, the agency had answered none of her letters about the work she had left with them. She needed to go to New York City to meet directly with them. If it did not work out with the Wildman Agency, she would try to discover where Browne was working and sell her work there.[3]

As a woman traveling alone, Liddell had few options for her hotel. People thought that women who stayed alone in regular hotels were there for immoral reasons. On this trip, she stayed at the Martha Washington Hotel. The hotel had opened in 1903 only for professional women. Its twelve stories housed thirty-six women per floor, each in a tiny room with a sink. The women shared the floor's one bathroom that had four toilets and four bathtubs. At first, it had male bellhops, because the hotel considered women too frail to carry their own luggage. Two years later, the hotel switched to female bellhops, because they were more reliable. Except for the elevator operators, no men were allowed past the first floor.[4]

Liddell found Browne in New York City and gave him all her work to sell. When she was a child, she had dreamed about writing stories, not selling them. Actually, she felt humiliated trying to sell her stories.[5] Writing as a career was losing its glamor. Selling her work was too hard and, it seemed, she could not support herself with only her writing income. She decided to become a university professor like her uncle Robert Ogden. Philosophy would be her field.

In the fall of 1921, Liddell enrolled in Cornell University for a master's program in philosophy. She was torn—her head (and her mother) told her that Cornell was the better choice, but her heart longed to study again with Williams at UNC. A degree from Cornell would be more prestigious than one from UNC. Cornell had a long history of graduate education, and the Sage School of Philosophy there was one of the best graduate schools in the nation. UNC was just developing its graduate programs. No one had yet been awarded a PhD in philosophy at UNC. Another consideration was that her uncle Robert Ogden was a professor at Cornell and could watch over her.

While Liddell was at Cornell, her mother wrote that a Charlotte girl was flirting with Rawley Myers, admonishing Anna Forbes that she might lose him. She replied, "if Margaret Berry can get Rawley she is welcome to him. I'm just that conceited. I didn't know you wanted me to get married. I think

I can if I bend all my energies in that direction. And I might be able to acquire a perfectly new man."[6] Later, she wrote to her mother, "Please be good to Rawley—I haven't been lately I'm afraid, but I couldn't help it."[7]

Who could think about Rawley Myers when there was Ben Holtzclaw, a fellow philosophy student?[8] Liddell said about him, "I have discovered that we share a love for Jane Austin—Really that is too much!"[9] She could not find any fault with him and decided she liked her men younger, like Holtzclaw, rather than older, like Myers.[10]

When Liddell was not thinking about boyfriends or her studies, she obsessed about the bleak Ithaca winters. They were the coldest and longest she had ever experienced. Her dreaded February mood lingered into April. She complained:

> March 17, 1922. . . .Snow again.
>
> March 22, 1922. . . .Snow again! It isn't the severity, it's the *length* of the winter which wears me out.
>
> April 29, 1922. . . .The winter has lingered on until I am worn out with it.[11]

At the start of her study, she worried, "I have so much reading to do that I sometimes wish that I didn't have to eat and sleep and put on clothes. Sometimes when I consider how much lies before me I am overcome with a kind of terror—but I reckon if I can make myself do a day's work each day I'll come through."[12]

James Edwin Creighton and Lane Cooper directed Liddell's master thesis.[13] Creighton was Dean of the Graduate school and the Sage Professor of Logic and Metaphysics. He was instrumental in the founding of the American Philosophical Association and served as its first president during 1901–1902. Liddell was indeed fortunate to study under him. G. Watts Cunningham wrote of Creighton's skill as a teacher:

> Of his students, he was one of the keenest of critics—and one of the kindliest. He would tolerate neither the hasty incubation of ideas nor their slipshod expression; and yet his criticisms were so genially presented that the student felt, not hurt, but ashamed that he had fallen so far short of his real abilities as to have been content to bring such a sorry offering![14]

Liddell's thesis was "The Theory of External Relations in Neo-Realism." She explained:

> Is it true that there is a true *universe*, an organic whole of life and experience, into which all the differences and variety of life are integrated, through internal and necessary relations, or is there no true universe, but merely a plurality of distinct objects, which may or may not be or become connected. In the latter case relations would be external and accidental. . . .Sometimes I feel quite hopeless—it is such an important problem, it involves so much! Even in practical affairs—if each act is distinct and independent, we don't have to be nearly as careful as if every act connects with every other.[15]

Liddell gave Creighton three drafts of her thesis He suggested revisions to each one. Now she was calling her thesis "the damned thesis."[16] To edit or correct a line using a typewriter could require all pages after the change to be retyped. In April she wrote, "I have so much to do that I don't know when I can stop to write a real letter. I'm working on my thesis, which is hard typing as well as hard thinking."[17]

Creighton accepted the fourth version of Liddell's thesis, and she was awarded the AM degree in June 1922. She joined an even more elite group than she had four years earlier when she earned her bachelor's degree. Nationally, only 15 percent of the master's degrees conferred were to women that year.[18]

Liddell wanted to go to the University of North Carolina for her doctorate, but her mother pushed her to continue at Cornell. Anna Forbes replied to her mother, "I think you are right about it being a greater advantage to have a PhD from here than from Carolina. I shall not find another teacher who seems so great to me as Prof. Williams, but I realize that he is only one man, and not widely known. The Sage School of Philosophy has a reputation."[19]

Remarkably, the Cornell scholarship committee renewed her scholarship for study beyond the master's and that decided the matter.[20] Women rarely received financial aid for higher education. When a working woman married, she typically left the workforce. Since most college-educated women married, many people thought financial aid was wasted on a woman.[21] Her relationship to Robert Ogden likely influenced the decision of Cornell to give her the initial scholarship and renewal.

Amid her studies, Holtzclaw asked Liddell to marry him, and he wanted to marry soon. Yet she was losing interest in marriage with anyone, not only with Rawley Myers. In her mind and the opinion of society, she would have to give up her dream for a career if she married. She told him "No." In the fall of 1922 when Liddell returned to Cornell, she learned that Ben Holtzclaw had married during the summer break. She replaced him as her boyfriend with Tom Harrison, another graduate student, who had graduated from UNC in the same class as she did. Surely, they reminisced about the challenging discussions Williams had sparked.[22]

Again, the hated winter came:

> January 11, 1923. . . .The snow it snoweth [*sic*] every day. I feel pretty good—but I do hate to work in cold weather.
>
> February 13, 1923. . . .More snow last night—I suppose we are in for another month
>
> February 28, 1923. . . .The winter gets on my nerves more and more. I

can't bear to think about another year, but I don't see how it can be avoided. Perhaps the weather will be better next year. We are having a fresh snowfall now.

March 7, 1923. . . .it seems to me that I just work and work all the time and still don't get anything done. When the weather gets warmer, I shall accomplish more. Now I waste so much time taking off and putting on my boots.

March 28, 1923. . . .I hate the climate more and more, all the time. It is so irrational.

April 19, 1923. . . .I think I suffer so much from the weather because I hate it so.[23]

In April 1923, Liddell was shocked when she read a letter from Dean Creighton informing her that the committee had decided to not award her a scholarship for the next year. The committee based its decision on three criteria:

(1) Would the student work publicly in the field after graduation?
(2) Could the family afford to support the student?
(3) Would the student finish the doctorate in the minimum time?

The first criterion was often used to deny women opportunities since it was assumed that women would marry and not have a career. She failed the second criterion since her family could support her studies. On the third criterion, Creighton doubted that she would finish the doctorate in the minimum time. He wrote in the letter:

In the first place, I realize that you are not very strong and that you are not yet accustomed to the rigors of our climate. It seems to me therefore that you can scarcely expect to complete the work for the doctorate in the minimum time.

> About the quality of your mind, I have not the least doubt. You seem to have not only philosophical interest and intelligence, but real insight and understanding. If one were to criticize, it would be in the way of asking whether your insights do not remain too much in the realm of the general, and are not worked out sufficiently in detailed and concrete form. That defect, if it really exists, may be due to the fact that your health does not permit you to work hard, or it may be due to a natural tendency to rest in a general insight, and not 'labor at the dull mechanic car when the fair breeze is blowing.'
>
> You remember the difficulty you had in getting your thesis for the AM in shape. I am not sure you could or can manage to organize the more complex and extended data that would be necessary in a thesis for the doctorate. I do not want to discourage you, but merely to express frankly my doubt. There are plenty of better kinds of writing than that required for a thesis and I recognize fully your literary ability. I recognize too that I may be mistaken in my judgement.[24]

Liddell wrote her mother about the scholarship's non-renewal:

> I am not disappointed really, for I honestly don't think I could have stood the third consecutive winter. I really hesitated about making the application for that reason. Every criticism which the Dean makes is justified—I only hope that the compliments which he adds are as justified.
>
> I shall not give up working for my PhD, but I may go back to Chapel Hill, or I may teach for a while and then go back to Cornell. In answer to the Dean's letter, I asked his advice, and will talk everything over with him when I return to Ithaca. Of course, I know Daddy *could* send me right along, but I really think a third hard winter would be a little too

much. I know I have been writing and thinking I would return Scholarship or no Scholarship, but without that obligation to encourage me, the thought of the cold eats into my very spirit.

Nobody knows how I have really suffered this winter. . . .I hope you are not disappointed that I didn't get the scholarship again. Of course, I wish I had just for the sake of feeling that I did, but I don't feel well in Ithaca most of the time, and I know I never have done enough work to justify the scholarships I have already had.[25]

After meeting with Creighton, Liddell explained to her mother:

[Creighton] told me I could go to Chapel Hill next year and complete my residence *there* instead of here, and then after my thesis is written, come back here to take my examination, and receive my degree from Cornell . . . .I don't want to break into the continuity of my work—and this seems to me a most satisfactory arrangement. I don't believe I could hold out through another winter. . . .To live in Chapel Hill and yet get my degree from Cornell is just what I'd rather do than any other thing, so I hope it meets your approval.[26]

Liddell's work had been good, at least at times, since she received the 1923 Essay Prize in Sage School of Philosophy for her essay "Hegel's Theory of Absolute Knowledge."[27] She also had two book reviews published in *The Philosophical Review*.[28] She agreed with Creighton's critique that she had difficulty with her thesis and that she could have worked harder.[29] Yet one wonders if the committee would have judged a man the same. Were they influenced by the belief common then that women could not do rigorous intellectual work without harming their health? Liddell's frequent colds during the two years of study could have confirmed the gender stereotype for them. Without knowing the outcomes for men who also revised their thesis three times, there is not enough information to confirm or deny whether gender bias was a factor in the scholarship denial.

Regardless, Liddell was relieved she would not be continuing at Cornell. She had signed her Sage Essay "*filia Horati*" (daughter of Horace), signifying that she considered Williams to be her mentor.[30] The climate in North Carolina would also be more agreeable. She could also room with her cousin, Vinton Liddell, who had graduated from Bryn Mawr and who would be at UNC pursuing a master's degree in theater.[31]

* * *

In the early 1920s, women's rights reformers disagreed on a woman's role in society. Some, such as Alice Paul, viewed women as citizens who deserved equal rights in every aspect of public life. She worked to get an equal rights amendment introduced into Congress. Other reformers who viewed women's primary role in society as mothers feared the passage of an equal rights amendment might eliminate laws that protected women and children. Opponents of an equal rights amendment included the Women's Trade Union League, the National Consumers' League, the American Federation of Workers, and the American Association of University Women. The League of Women Voters remained neutral, wanting to remain nonpolitical.

Chapel Hill Again (1923-1925)

At the University of North Carolina, Anna Forbes Liddell and her cousin Vinton Liddell roomed together in a house built especially for them. Many people helped them settle into the house. Rawley Myers drew up the house plans and oversaw its construction; Ruffin Smith, a Charlotte friend, helped them move their things from Charlotte to Chapel Hill; Steve, a medical student who lived next door, hung pictures, moved furniture, and unpacked their trunks. Steve came over every night to ensure that they had enough firewood. Vinton explained, "Steve makes himself as thoroughly indispensable . . . that we feel that we have all the advantages of matrimony. As a matter of fact, Steve speaks of us openly as his two wives and gives unasked for advice just as freely as any husband."[1]

When an instructor from Maine came by and saw how tiny the house was, he asked, "Where are you going to put your collars?" At least, that is what it sounded like he said as he spoke with his Maine accent. He actually said, "Where are you going to put your callers?" From then on, the tiny house was called the Collar Box.[2]

Each night, friends dropped by to discuss theater, philosophy, or medicine or just to talk. One friend reminisced in 1967:

> I may be wrong, but I think the Collar Box still stands. Probably its interior still smells of tomato soup and innocence and full of faint echoes of intellectual beauty. Was the conversation so starrily [*sic*] brilliant as I remember it, or does time give it that luster and dimension? I always think of the meteors in the summer sky of my youth as having been much larger and brighter than the little popcorn shooting stars that I see now. Maybe I exaggerate Collar Box talk. But I can't believe I do. . . .So it's just as well that it wasn't recorded on tape.[3]

The Collar Box philosophy discussions continued the seminars Williams had in his home every Tuesday evening where students presented drafts of their papers. Judge Robert Winston, who returned to college at age sixty, remembered Liddell as a young Portia, the intelligent, quick-witted woman in Shakespeare's *Merchant of Venice*, who provided the argument that won the case. He reminisced that a paper she gave "touched the very heart of Williams' [*sic*] philosophy."[4]

Liddell planned to return to Cornell to finish her PhD, but she changed her mind and remained at UNC—a decision likely due to her fondness for Williams and to Creighton's illness. Shortly after she left Cornell, Creighton had to step down as Dean because he was seriously ill. He died on October 8, 1924.[5] Had she returned to Cornell, she would have had to start over with a new dissertation advisor.

By June 1924, Liddell finished her dissertation, "The Logical Relationship of the Philosophy of Hegel to the Philosophies of Spinoza and Kant."[6] Her hypothesis was that G. W. F. Hegel's Absolute Spirit, which many religions call God, was the synthesis of the philosophies of Baruch Spinoza and Immanuel Kant, which appeared to contradict each other. In her dissertation, Liddell explained Hegel's synthesis process. Later, as a professor at Florida State College for Women, she wrote a poem to help her students learn the many philosophers. It was an alphabet of philosophers with A is for Aristotle, B is for Bacon, and so forth. For each philosopher, she wrote a stanza of the poem. Here is what she wrote for H:

> H is for Hegel
> A contradiction does not prove
> That either term is false, because
> The way of logic is to move
> To unity through higher laws,
> So *thesis* and *antithesis*
> Are both absorbed in *synthesis*.[7]

To understand Hegel's concept of synthesis, consider the parable in John Saxe's poem "The Blind Men and the Elephant." Liddell did not use this parable in her paper, but it is a useful device to understand Hegel's concept of synthesis. The elephant in the parable represents Reality and the blind men represent philosophers trying to understand Reality. The first blind man touches the side of the elephant and declares, "God Bless Me! But the Elephant is very like a wall." The second man touches the tusk and says, "Ho! What have we here, so very round and smooth and sharp? To me 'tis mighty clear this wonder of an Elephant is very like a spear!" The statements of the two blind men appear to contradict each other, but both statements are true—partial truths. Compromise cannot resolve the apparent contradiction, because the Elephant is not somewhere between the "like a wall" and "like a spear," but it is both at the same time. A compromise would lose the truth in each statement. When a third blind man grabs the trunk and exclaims, "I see, the Elephant is very like a snake," there is another partial truth. More partial truths emerge when the fourth blind man touches the elephant's knee, the fifth blind man touches the elephant's ear, and the sixth blind man touches the elephant's tail. These blind men never share their experiences. Thus, no synthesis of their individual points of view can take place. But what if they had shared their experiences with each other and collectively sought to understand the Elephant? Understanding the Elephant (Reality) comes about through synthesis of the partial truths of all the blind men's experiences.[8]

Liddell explained the partial truths in Spinoza's and Kant's philosophies that Hegel synthesized. Spinoza and Kant had different presuppositions concerning the Absolute (God or a similar concept). A presupposition is a type of assumption. The statement "Mary no longer goes to the gym" presupposes that Mary had previously gone to the gym. Liddell asserted that Spinoza presupposed an Absolute that is Substance that remains unchanged. To understand Substance, consider water. The substance of water remains unchanged as water goes among the states of solid, liquid and gas. However, Spinoza would not have used water to explain Substance, since he thought only God had Substance. For him, trees, rocks and all nature are expressions of the Substance of God. God permeates everything in the universe. Spinoza was a pantheist who considered God is Nature and Nature is God. Since experiences of the senses are finite and God is infinite, knowledge of God cannot come through the senses, but only through reasoning about ideas. Kant presupposed the reality of knowledge gained through the senses, which is how the blind men gained knowledge of the elephant. Kant's problem was how sense experiences can lead to knowledge of the Absolute. Another sense experience might develop that would contradict the previous experiences. How can there ever be certainty? Kant concluded that we can only know our perceptions of the Absolute.[9]

Conscious thought consists of cognition and reasoning. Kant emphasized cognition of objects, and Spinoza reasoning about ideas. According to Liddell, Hegel synthesized Kant's and Spinoza's theories of the Absolute by developing the part of conscious thought that was undeveloped in each philosopher's theory. She asserted that Hegel's Absolute Spirit got its form from Kant and its content from Spinoza. As for the content in Hegel's Absolute Spirit, she wrote, "shall we not say that the substance of Spinoza is the lifeless statue and that Hegel, Pygmalion-like, breathed spirit into the static form?"[10]

In her dissertation, Liddell also compared philosophy and science. To illustrate, she described a philosopher and a botanist observing a tree. The botanist focuses only on the tree, while the philosopher focuses on the tree and on the act of observing the tree. Both the botanist and philosopher state that they have discovered the reality of the tree. Since the assertion of the philosopher contains what the botanist asserts and more, Liddell concluded that philosophy "is the fulfillment of science."[11]

In the second half of her dissertation, Liddell discussed Hegel's concept of becoming, which is a continual process. Within Hegel's model, whenever a change occurs, it does not appear from nowhere, but builds upon what currently exists. Experience is continuous, since what exists came from what existed before. She reconciled two Biblical passages she learned from her family's fundamentalist Baptist faith with Hegel's theories. For the first passage, she wrote, "the Hebrew Bible defines God as 'I am that I am.' Is not this the true definition of the absolute—existing in its own quality?" For the second passage, she wrote, "'Heaven and earth shall pass away, but my words shall not pass away.' We can think the annihilation of every existent finite thing, but we can not [*sic*] think the annihilation of process. Development must go on. Something must be and be connected with what went before, with whatever may follow."[12] In this statement, Liddell showed she was breaking away from her childhood's fundamentalist faith that asserted creation was static and not a process.

Liddell was awarded a PhD in 1924 from the University of North Carolina. Irene Dillard received a PhD at the same time. They were the first women to be awarded PhDs from UNC. In telling about this accomplishment, Liddell was quick to point out that she passed her doctoral exam before Dillard did hers. Liddell was also the first person to receive a PhD in Philosophy from UNC.[13]

The next year, Liddell received the Graham-Kenan Fellowship in

Philosophy for post-doctoral work for which she wrote a seventy-page monograph entitled "Alexander's Space, Time, and Deity: A Critical Consideration." Her monograph reviewed Samuel Alexander's two-volume *Space, Time, and Deity*, published in 1920 when the philosophy of science was a new field. Liddell noted that Alexander was as an important contributor in this new field. He asserted that philosophy, not being distinct from science, was actually the most comprehensive of all sciences. Her critique of Alexander's work, however, continued the theme expressed in her dissertation that philosophy takes the knowledge gained by science and completes it. She concluded that the purposes and methods of science were inadequate to advance philosophy.[14] Richard Hull, who surveyed the body of Liddell's works, remarked, "Forbes's courage in undertaking a critical exposition of Alexander's work is symptomatic of her desire to be on the cutting edge of speculative philosophy of her day."[15]

* * *

While Liddell was thinking about reality, Vinton was falling in love with Bob Pickens. He proposed marriage two months after they met. Vinton would not give him a definitive answer. Bob insisted on an answer and said he would not be a 'Rawley.' After a few stormy, miserable weeks, Vinton said yes. They married on April 26, 1924.[16]

Another change in the Liddell family was the death of Anna Forbes's grandmother Anna Amelia Liddell in December 1923. She was 97 years old at the time of her death and was still mentally sharp. Her death set into motion the sale of the city block where the three Liddell homes stood.[17] On this property, the city built a City Hall, which became designated as the Old City Hall, when the city built a newer City Hall in 1984.

* * *

After the Nineteenth Amendment to the US Constitution became law, politicians at all levels of government were afraid of the potentially powerful female bloc of voters. They passed reform legislation from 1921 through 1924 on issues such as maternal and infant health, consumer protection, and the legal status of married women. The powerful female voter bloc, however, did not materialize. Women voted at lower rates than men did, and they often voted the same as men. By 1925, politicians noticed the absence of the voting bloc they had feared and lost interest in advancing reform legislation.[18]

When her fellowship was over, Liddell needed a job. She had overcome discrimination against women college students to become *one of the boys* and a *good fellow*. Yet resistance to women as professors in colleges and universities remained a barrier she still had to face. Liddell was more likely to be hired to teach at a women's college. Only recently had men's colleges even admitted women as students, much less hired them as professors. Many female PhDs could not continue in their field of specialization because of this discrimination.[19] In seeking to be a college professor of philosophy, a non-traditional field for a woman, Liddell was part of the small group of women who set out to work as equals with men in the workplace. Horace Williams and Robert Ogden would serve as her mentors for this new phase, as they had for her when she was a student.

The Perfect Job (1925-1927)

Few people find their perfect job on the first try. That was certainly true for Anna Forbes Liddell. She taught history and social science at Chowan College in Murfreesboro, North Carolina, for the 1925–26 school year. Chowan College was an undergraduate Baptist women's college with only fifty-two students in 1925. The school became coeducational in 1931 and became Chowan University in 2006. In 1925, five men and ten women comprised the faculty, including Liddell. Only two other faculty members, both men, had PhDs. Fifteen faculty members seems like a high number for only fifty-two students. Only nine of the faculty, however, taught regular academic subjects while the other six faculty taught performance courses, such as piano, stringed instruments, voice, expression, china painting, and athletics. In letters to her mother, Liddell wrote that she found most of her fellow faculty members disagreeable.[1] She did not say why she felt that way.

In October 1925, Charles Weaver, the college president, appointed Liddell to represent the college for University Day at the University of North Carolina. When Liddell returned, she found the Chowan campus in turmoil. Charles Weaver had left after having a nervous breakdown. A week later Liddell wrote her mother, "Things have straightened themselves around about as well as could be expected. Dr. Burwell—the local Baptist minister is acting as President temporarily. Nobody knows whether there is to be a new President—or what. Meantime the work goes on."[2] The uncertainty about the leadership of the college provided an air of instability and chaos for the entire school year.

Liddell settled into her responsibilities as a professor, one of which was giving a talk to the student body at chapel time. Chowan College required students to attend chapel devotionals and talks, designed to inspire the young women or instruct them as to proper conduct. In November 1925, Liddell gave a radical chapel talk on the new conditions women faced. She proclaimed, "The greatest thing to be thankful for today is to be born a woman. There is no question that now men must take a second place." She proclaimed that men had no more frontiers to conquer. Women, she continued, were just beginning to achieve significant accomplishments. Liddell asked her audience to consider whether a woman could keep her womanly charm and graces as she went into jobs previously held by men. Then, she dismissed this question as excessively moralizing and pompous. She said that whenever a woman gives up something, she gains a new interest. This result, she continued, follows from the universal principle of compensation, which states that every loss has a compensation.[3]

The campus newspaper printed a summary of Liddell's talk. Next to that article was a summary of a radio talk program, "Standards of Conduct for the Modern Girl," by Herman H. Horne, a New York University professor. He exhorted young women not to follow the modern trends of drinking, smoking, dancing, swearing, wearing cosmetics, and showing overt interest in sex. Instead, he instructed them to develop their womanliness, grace, charms, and personality so that they could achieve what every woman wants most, which is "to be beautiful, to be attractive, and to win the fullest respect of a worthy man."[4] Horne's talk was the kind that Liddell would have considered moralizing and pompous.

Liddell wanted a better job for the next academic year and applied to several schools.[5] Florida State College for Women in Tallahassee, Florida, offered her a position as the sole philosophy professor. Before moving to Tallahassee, Liddell and Rawley Myers toured Europe in a party which included one of Rawley's sisters, his mother ('Miss Mamie' Myers), and two of her aunts.[6] Miss Mamie and Anna Forbes were strong-willed women whose personalities often clashed, but they got along well on this trip. Anna Forbes wrote to her mother, "I can't tell if Miss Mamie likes me *very* much or is just on good behavior. Rawley and I like each other as well as ever."[7] When the touring group was in London, Anna Forbes and Rawley slipped away from the group to go to Paris alone for a few days.[8]

When Liddell arrived at Florida State College for Women in the fall of 1926, she discovered that Walter McNutt, the professor who had preceded her, remained at the center of a controversy. It all started six years earlier, when President Edward Conradi began to upgrade the faculty. Forty of the fifty-eight faculty members had only a bachelor's degree; eleven others had a master's degree as their highest degree; only seven had doctorates. Conradi filled vacancies with professors who had at least a master's degree. He also wanted to separate the teaching of philosophy and psychology. Professor E. A. Hayden, the only professor who taught philosophy, also taught psychology courses. When Hayden committed suicide in October 1921, Conradi replaced him with two professors, both of whom had PhDs: Basil Bassell to teach philosophy and Paul Finner to teach psychology.[9]

The next year, Conradi replaced Bassell with Walter McNutt, because Bassell had been unsatisfactory. McNutt turned out to be unsatisfactory as well. He taught ten philosophy courses: Ethics, History of Philosophy, Logic, Introduction to Contemporary Civilizations, American Philosophy, English Ethics, Aesthetics, Present Philosophy, History of Science, and Problems of Philosophy. His curriculum stressed the scientific method and the 18th and 19th century philosophers. Students reported that he boasted these philosophers had gotten their ideas from him, even though those scholars had done their work before him. During class time, students wrote letters home instead of listening to McNutt's disorganized lectures. At the end of McNutt's second year, Conradi warned him that he would be fired if he did not improve. Nothing changed, and, thus, McNutt was told in April 1926 that he would not be rehired for the next school year. McNutt was angry. He developed a plan to use the anti-evolution movement to get Conradi fired.[10]

The anti-evolution movement grew out of the global debate between modernist and fundamentalist theologies in Protestant denominations. Modernism reinterpreted biblical scripture to be compatible with scientific knowledge; fundamentalism rejected scientific knowledge if it conflicted with a literal interpretation of biblical scripture. This conflict began in the late nineteenth century and escalated in the early twentieth century.[11]

In 1925, Tennessee passed a law that made the teaching of evolution a misdemeanor. That same year, the state of Tennessee charged John Scopes, a high school teacher in Dayton, Tennessee, with violating the law. In the famous *The State of Tennessee v. John Thomas Scopes* trial, Clarence Darrow defended Scopes and William Jennings Bryan was the prosecutor. Darrow was famous for being the defense attorney in the Leopold and Loeb murder trial, and Bryan ran for US President three times. The participation of Darrow and Bryan in the trial brought the case and the evolution controversy to national attention. The court ruled in 1925 in favor of Tennessee, but the Tennessee Supreme Court later overturned the verdict on a legal technicality.[12]

Liddell had witnessed the evolution debate arise in North Carolina. In 1924, Governor Cameron Morrison banned a biology book from public schools, because it included the theory of evolution. In 1925, Representative Scott Poole introduced a bill, known as the Poole Monkey Bill, in the North Carolina Legislature. The bill banned the teaching of the theory of evolution in publicly funded schools. The measure failed.[13] On May 4, 1926, the Committee of 100, composed of North Carolina religious fundamentalists, held a public meeting in Charlotte to organize a statewide anti-evolution campaign. Charles Tillett Jr., organized a group of Horace

Williams's former students across the state to argue against the Committee of 100's campaign. Williams had taught that a Christian could accept the theory of evolution. E.D. Broadbent, Robert Lassiter, Bill Shaw, and Paul Ransom were key members of Tillett's group, who called themselves the *Horatians*. When the Committee of 100 introduced a resolution to ban anyone who was not an orthodox Christian from teaching in public schools, Shaw and Ransom spoke against it. Then Broadbent spoke, "You are just a bunch of scared creatures. You had better go home and save the world by preaching the gospel instead of being here trying to pass foolish laws." At those words, a Fundamentalist rushed down the aisle, threw off his coat, and raised his fist to attack Broadbent. Audience members grabbed the Fundamentalist and restrained him. After that, the meeting broke up.[14]

Representative Poole reintroduced his bill in 1927, and it failed again. Many North Carolinian legislators opposed the teaching of the theory of evolution. They, however, voted against the bill, because they valued freedom of speech more. They also thought that state law should not endorse a specific religious belief.[15]

Horace Williams had worried that the fundamentalist movement would get a bill passed that restricted teaching. If the bill passed, he thought he should resign, because he would interpret that as a sign that he had failed to do his job of educating the future leaders of North Carolina. He said of the Committee of 100 meeting in Charlotte, "Three of my boys went into the gathering and stopped the thing in its tracks. I was deeply pleased and encouraged. I had done my duty. My boys were prepared to serve the State and would guide it wisely."[16] Actually, more than three of Williams's boys were at the meeting, since another account names five men.[17]

The evolution debate in Florida focused on textbooks. Fired Philosophy Professor McNutt gave his friend L.A. Tatum a list of textbooks and reading assignments used at FSCW that referred to evolution. In May 1926, McNutt remained in the background while Tatum ranted self-righteously to the Florida Board of Control about the textbooks and readings used at

FSCW. He demanded the removal of Conradi as college president. Conradi adequately defended himself before the Board. He kept his job, but it would be three more years before the matter died down.[18]

Meanwhile, FSCW needed a philosophy professor. Dean of Arts and Sciences William Dodd asked a contact at the University of North Carolina, presumably Horace Williams, for a recommendation and received the resume of Forbes Liddell. Liddell dropped Anna from her name, likely hoping that the masculine-sounding name of Forbes would gain her an interview. However, the resume honestly listed the candidate's height as 4' 11" (stretching the truth about half an inch). Dodd presumed that must be a typographical error, with Liddell intending to type 5, not 4, feet. Still, the candidate's weight was written as 95 pounds, and Dodd worried about hiring such a string bean. Imagine his surprise when a petite woman walked through the door. Liddell recounted, "Little did he expect to have a woman's credentials sent to him, because the enrollment at UNC was approximately ten women to 1,000 men. However, he couldn't find anything wrong with my credentials, so he hired me."[19]

From time to time, Anna Forbes Liddell had tested dropping Anna in her name and using only Forbes. After she come the Florida State College for Women, she used just Forbes with her Tallahassee friends and colleagues, although she used her full name in professional writings. Her students called her Dr. Liddell, and her family continued to call her Anna Forbes.[20]

During this time in her life, Liddell had self-doubts. For every inroad into previously male-only areas, there was a backlash. When women began attending colleges, doctors suggested that learning would harm a woman's health. As women entered the workplace, opponents conceded that a woman could do a man's job and she could be good, but argued that she could never be great, because such work was against her nature.[21] Liddell had heard these opinions her entire life.

Once Liddell learned about the state of the philosophy curriculum at

FSCW, she wrote to her mother:

> I'm PETRIFIED with fear. The gentleman who preceded me was (after three years' trial) fired for incompetence—and I was selected out of 40 male and female applicants. The department has suffered from three years of dry rot—and it's up to me to build it up. When I learned what I was up against I was tempted to beat it home—but my trunk was unpacked and I hadn't courage to repack it.[22]

With little time to develop a complete philosophy curriculum, FSCW offered only five philosophy courses in Liddell's first year. President Conradi taught at least one of the philosophy classes. Liddell's curriculum kept the introductory course *History of Philosophy*. She changed the focus of the course named *Ethics*. In the ethics course, McNutt had taught the "ethical development of the human race," while Liddell taught the "origin and development of moral customs, standards, and ideals." Liddell replaced McNutt's *Logic* course with her *Evolution of Logic* course. McNutt's logics course had stressed the scientific method, while Liddell's course focused on the "relation of thought to life."[23]

As for her fellow faculty, Liddell explained to her mother, "I am in a neighborhood of congenial people—most of them lady doctors like myself."[24] In another letter to her mother, she wrote, "Compared with last year I am in heaven, but I have not found. . .any man to play around with."[25] Liddell was still dating Rawley Myers, but she had never limited herself to one boyfriend at a time. About FSCW, Liddell further noted, "The environment is a little too feministic—rather out of balance, but at least they are normal women who surround me. If there are any faculty freaks, I have not yet encountered them."[26] Liddell was still a feminist who wanted women to have social and financial independence, but she was not of the type she had met during her time in Greenwich Village, who had thought that the entire social structure would have to change for women to be independent.

In the 1920s, young women across the country insisted on more freedom than earlier generations had. The FSCW administration resisted loosening behavior standards for students. As a result, FSCW students were subject to some of the most stringent restrictions in the country. They could not smoke cigarettes either on or off campus. They could not dance with men anywhere in Tallahassee and could go to a dance at the University of Florida in Gainesville, Florida, only if the dance was properly authorized and chaperoned. It would not be until 1928 that the college allowed students to have one dance event on campus, the Junior-Senior Prom. There were also rules about when and with whom students could ride in cars. The college regulated the dating behavior of students and considered any conversation longer than ten minutes with a man as a date. Only seniors had unlimited dating privileges. All other students were limited as to the number of dates allowed and had to introduce their dates to the residence hall director or chaperone. The college actually maintained a list of men the students could not date. Moreover, all students had to state their destinations on the sign-out form in their residence hall before leaving campus. If a student went anywhere else, she could be disciplined. The college administration also despised short skirts and short hairstyles, but was unsuccessful in establishing rules about either. Hemlines creeped up to knee-length and sixty-nine percent of the students in 1924 had bobbed hair.[27] Of course, the college prohibited alcohol on campus, since the Eighteenth Amendment to the US Constitution prohibited the sale and transportation of alcohol beverages. Meanwhile, other young women were flappers, who did everything forbidden to the FSCW students, such as smoking and drinking alcohol in illegal speakeasies.

Women faculty also had rigid behavior rules. Liddell limited her smoking, since women were not allowed to smoke on campus. Men faculty, however, smoked on campus in designated smoking areas.

Daisy Parker Flory, a student of Liddell and later her colleague as Dean of Students, credited Liddell with influencing both students and colleagues. She said, "One can hardly deny that many FSCW customs—lights out at 10:30 p.m., signing out and in for any kind of trip off campus, rigid dress and personal conduct codes, etc.—might have had disastrous and narrowing effects but for the free and fiery spirit of Forbes Liddell and other strong and liberated women who came to the faculty and stayed because Forbes was here."[28]

Living in Tallahassee had benefits. The climate was warmer than the extreme cold ones in New York City and Ithaca, New York, which she had detested. The hot weather made her feel lazy.[29] Air conditioning was not yet invented. People opened the windows in homes and depended on attic fans to create a breeze by drawing in the outside air through open windows, circulating it through the house, and drawing the air into the attic. Homes had high ceilings to allow the hotter air to move up and the cooler air to stay low. Liddell wrote her mother:

> The climate and way of living here must agree with me here, for I have been remarkably well. . . .My time is all taken up, one way or another, and I work pretty hard—but I do not feel any strain of working. While I was striving toward my advanced degrees and even when I was working on my monograph, I was conscious of a definite objective and that made a sort of pressure. Last year I was not doing the sort of work, which I most enjoyed, and that was in itself an obstacle. But this year I am studying what I like to study, without any straining to get through.[30]

Yet the town of Tallahassee was smaller than most places Liddell had lived. She missed the bustle of a big city. She said, "I yearn now and then for Broadway and the Avenue, for stores and theatres and crowded streets."[31] As she thought about New York City, she nostalgically remembered attending theater performances in Greenwich Village and the people she met during her time there in 1916. Her experiences in the Village were influential to the sequence of decisions that landed her at FSCW as a philosophy professor. The Greenwich Village that Liddell knew in 1916 no longer existed. She wondered what Bobby Edwards, the Troubadour of Greenwich Village with whom she defiantly smoked cigarettes in the Washington Square, was doing now.[32]

When the Village bohemians opposed the United States entering World War I, public opinion turned against them. The federal government brought charges against several for their anti-war activities. Emma Goldman was arrested in 1917 for distributing pamphlets that encouraged men not to register for the military draft. She was imprisoned, and, upon her release from prison, was deported to Russia. Once a supporter of communism, she became disillusioned with the system when she saw that free speech was more limited in Russia than in the United States. She left Russia for London in 1926, where she used her free speech to warn about the communism system in Stalinist Russia. John Reed, the communist whose lectures Liddell attended, traveled to Russia to cover the Bolshevik Revolution in 1917. A supporter of the Revolution, he wrote *Ten Days That Shook the World* about his Russian experiences. In 1918, he returned to the United States, but was arrested and tried for sedition for articles he had written for *The Masses*. His first trial and second trial ended in hung juries. Indicted again for sedition, Reed fled to Russia in 1919. By 1920, he questioned the results of the Bolshevik Revolution, but continued to defend the revolution to Emma Goldman when she arrived in Moscow. He became ill with spotted typhus and died in Moscow in 1920. Given a hero's funeral in Moscow, he was buried at the Kremlin Wall Necropolis.[33]

Susan Glaspell lived in Milligan Place when Liddell lived there in 1916. Now, she lived in Provincetown, Massachusetts, writing novels. The Provincetown Players, founded by Glaspell and Cook, had produced Eugene O'Neill's first play, *Bound East for Cardiff*, in 1917 and several of his other plays. The Provincetown Players dissolved about 1922 as O'Neill began producing his plays on Broadway. Glaspell and Cook moved to Greece. She returned to Provincetown after Cook's death in 1924.

Romany Marie and Bobby Edwards remained in Greenwich Village long after Goldman, Reed, Glaspell, Cook, and other Villagers had left. Marie was still running Marie's Tavern in 1926, nurturing young talent such as Stuart Davis (artist) in 1920 and Paul Robeson Sr. (musician) in 1924. Bobby Edwards was still singing ballads and playing his homemade ukuleles in Greenwich Village. However, in 1926, he took a regular job in an art department of a department store.[34]

As Liddell thought about the past and her journey to FSCW, she noticed that her life as a college professor was not what she had thought it would be. She said:

> I had always supposed that a college community was quiet and peaceful, but I find that on the contrary something is going on all the time. And as for the old saying that Woodrow Wilson would not know anything about practical politics because he had spent his life in college communities—well the folks who said it didn't know colleges. Politics is just what you don't have nothing else but. The present excitement is between students and administration—student government against higher authorities, but there is faculty backing for each side[35]

One such conflict started in 1925, the year before Liddell arrived, when President Conradi hired Mina Kerr to fill the vacancy of Dean of the College Home when Sarah Cawthon retired. Cawthon had been beloved by students and administration. During her fifteen years at FSCW, she was the arbitrator of Southern values for the young women while also being their confidant—any girl's personal problem became her personal problem. Her replacement, Kerr, did not understand that her role was to be a substitute mother to the students, many of whom were away from home for the first time. Because she was not from the South, she did not understand what the Southern culture expected of young women. She steamrolled through campus traditions, gutting those she considered adolescent or outdated, rousing up animosity toward herself. Consequently, she was gone at the end of the 1926–1927 school year. Kerr, however, did accomplish something good. Before she came to FSCW, she had been the Executive Secretary of the American Association of University Women (AAUW). While at FSCW, she convinced two AAUW members to join the faculty: Kathryn T. Abbey (history) and Bessie Randolph (political science and history). Abbey became Liddell's close friend. Liddell joined the Tallahassee AAUW branch, a group in which she was active for over fifty years.[36]

Students quickly learned that Liddell was a good, yet unorthodox teacher. She strode across her classroom, lecturing and questioning her students. She was shorter when she stood than some students were when sitting. Sometimes she hoisted herself up to sit on the teacher's desk in the front of the room so that she could see all the students. Students arrived early at her classes to get the best seats, which were on the second row. As Liddell spoke, projecting her deep, raspy voice to the back row, she released a flow of spittle upon the first row.

Liddell combined the teaching methods of James Creighton and Horace Williams. From Creighton, she required students to read extensively. Imitating Williams's practice of debating ideas with the students, she challenged them to question everything, to choose their own path in life regardless of what others may think, and to take responsibility for their choices. She told them wisdom was not an abstract, but was the practical ability to determine what is true and to make the best choices for one's life. She also wanted her students, using logic and reason, to develop their own philosophy and not simply repeat what they had read in textbooks or heard in lectures. Dorothy Bullock recounted years after she had Liddell as a teacher:

> She gave us a topic to write on and gave us a reading list on the subject; books to check in the library. So we went to the library and read and read and read, then wrote our papers. Well, of course, we were repeating what we had read. We all got "D-." That was not what she wanted. So we would take the topic and write it out, then do our reading. After that, we got "As."[37]

From the moment Liddell started teaching at FSCW, she influenced young women from all parts of Florida and even from other states. In 1926, higher education in Florida was segregated by race, and for White students, also segregated by gender. White women from all areas of Florida attended FSCW, since it was the only public higher education school available to them in the state. Florida State College for Women was unique in its focus. Most Southern women's colleges were specialized schools that trained women as teachers or nurses. FSCW's primary purpose was to provide a high quality liberal arts education. The Southern Association of Colleges and Secondary Schools accredited FSCW in 1915, making it the first state women's college to be accredited. This gave FSCW national prominence.[38]

Many FSCW professors hired in the 1920s stayed throughout their professional career. They guided the college through an economic depression, a world war, and the transition to the coeducational Florida State University. Robin Sellers, FSU Historian, cited Liddell as one of those influential early professors.[39]

At FSCW, Liddell had indeed found the dream job she wanted. She quickly settled into a routine of teaching and preparing for classes, attending campus activities and church, reading books for a book club, playing bridge and golf, enjoying visits from Rawley Myers, and spending time with her new friends Ephraim and Bess Brevard. Bess had grown up in Charlotte and her heart never left North Carolina. She must have been delighted to have Liddell to talk with about the people they both knew in Charlotte.

On Sundays, Liddell attended St. John's Episcopal Church with the Brevards. Afterward, she went home with them for a formal noontime meal, which they called dinner. Joining them for Sunday dinners were Ephraim's sister, Jane Brevard Darby, and her fifteen-year-old daughter Mary Call Darby.[40]

Jane Darby and her husband Thomas had lived in New York City, where he had a business. Their daughter, Mary Call, had been born in New York City, but Jane moved to Tallahassee when Mary Call was young, because the Darbys considered Tallahassee a better place to raise their daughter. Jane and Mary Call moved into the home of Jane's mother, Mary Call Brevard, who was the daughter of Richard Keith Call, a territorial governor of Florida. Jane's sister Caroline Brevard also lived in the home. Thomas Darby split his time between New York City and Tallahassee, with plans to build eventually a permanent home in Tallahassee. Sadly, Jane's mother and sister died in 1920 from the flu. Three years later, Thomas Darby died suddenly in his hotel room in New York City. His business partner took the money from the business, including the Darby share, and sailed to Europe. His ship sank somewhere in the Atlantic Ocean. The business partner drowned, and the Darby money was never recovered.[41] After Thomas's death, Jane's brother Ephraim Brevard stepped up to provide the family's male guidance for the young Mary Call.

Before Sunday dinner, Ephraim Brevard poured exactly one glass of Scuppernong wine for everyone, presumably even the teenager Mary Call, and made a grand display of carving the meat when everyone sat down at the formally set table. When Mary Call was in her nineties, she reminisced how smart Liddell was, yet how easy she was to talk with. She recalled that Liddell never talked down to her because she was a child.[42]

Now that Liddell planned to stay at FSCW, it was time to build a house. In spring 1927, she built a duplex at 647 West Pensacola Street, where she would live until she was in her eighties. The duplex provided rental income. Liddell lived on one side with Kathryn Abbey. Eleanor Scott, Professor of

English, and Rebecca Hubbell, Professor of Foods and Nutrition, lived in the other side. The boxy one-story wood building was yellow with white trim. Front and back porches ran the full width of the house. The front porch had four white posts supporting a simple gable roof. Bricks faced the concrete foundation on the sides and the front of the porch. The front of the house was simple and elegant with what looked, at first glance, like four full-length windows with a fan-shaped transom above each window. Upon a second look, the inner two window-looking openings were actually the doors to the duplexes. The gable above had an identical transom window. Lush St. Augustine grass filled the lawn, and flowers planted in side gardens grew so high that they covered up the concrete foundation. Depending on the season, there were pansies, calendula, bamboo, lantana, zinnias, and white periwinkle-like flowers. Working in the garden relaxed Liddell.[43] Her house and garden provided a sanctuary where she sat on the back porch smoking without censure.

* * *

In May 1927, Liddell wrote to her mother that she could no longer be a Baptist and had joined the Episcopal denomination. She wrote:

> I decided after last year's experience that whatever I might be I could not be a Baptist. The theory of the Baptist church is altogether satisfying, but the practices of the brethren, especially now that Modernism and Fundamentalism are raging abroad are such that I can not subscribe to. At first I thought I'd stay out of any Church, but that did not seem quite right, and finally I compromised and decided to be confirmed in the Episcopal. . . .Use your own judgement about telling the rest of the family. I don't want to hurt the feelings of my Baptist Aunts, but if they are real Baptists, they will have to admit that a woman thirty-five ought to join the church of her choice. I don't think any one

> denomination is altogether satisfying, but I have closely examined three and the Episcopal comes nearest suiting me.[44]

In her letter, Liddell did not name the experience that prompted her change because her mother would have known what it was. It was likely the anti-evolution campaign of the fundamentalist Baptists in North Carolina and Florida. Liddell thought that Christianity and the theory of evolution were compatible.

In the spring of 1927, the Florida textbook controversy returned. A bill passed that required the removal in tax-supported schools of books that were "detrimental to good morals and clean thinking."[45] Delighted, L. A. Tatum created a Purity League whose goal was to rid "all state libraries of objectionable publications and all state schools of 'objectionable teachers.'"[46] Under pressure from the Purity League, Conradi restricted access to books deemed objectionable to faculty and certain students.[47] There is no evidence that Liddell took part in the 1927 textbook debate. She, however, spoke up in the 1960s when academic freedom was again threatened.

Establishing Herself (1927-1929)

For 1927–1928, Anna Forbes Liddell's second year, she changed the name of the logic course to *Modern Logic* and added four courses: *The Relation of Thought to Life, Greek Life and Thought, Nineteenth Century Idealism*, and *Philosophical Ideas in Nineteenth Century Literature.* In the fall semester, she taught six philosophy classes with forty students per class. Presumably, Conradi taught at least one philosophy class, but it is unknown which course or courses he taught.[1] However, concerning *Nineteenth Century Idealism*, Liddell wrote to her mother in the previous spring, "I made a great hit with the dean [William Dodd] by offering to give it, and he is putting people into the class right along. . . .I am rather terrified, because I have never given it before and I shall have to work it up this summer. I really ought to go somewhere to study—Ithaca perhaps."[2] Although she only taught for nine months of the year, she knew she needed to study during the other three months to excel as a teacher. Her uncle, Robert Ogden, often reminded her that she needed a lifetime professional focus that would leave her mark on the philosophy field. She decided her legacy would be an authoritative textbook on ethics.[3]

It is unknown if Liddell studied in Ithaca in the summer of 1927. However, we do know that she toured Europe with her parents on a three-week trip the following summer. They saw the Follies-Bergere, the Louvre, Westminster Abbey, Hampton Court, Eton, Anne Hathaway's cottage, Oxford, castles, such as Winsor, Edinburgh, and Linlithgow, and many other sites and traveled far enough north to see the Northern Lights and icebergs.[4] Travel was a life-long passion for Liddell.

For the 1928–1929 school year, Liddell added the course *Form and the Simple Principle of Beauty* to the curriculum and dropped *Greek Life and Thought*. The new course covered the *Poetics* of Aristotle, selections from the *Dialogues of Plato*, Wordsworth's *Preface to the Lyrical Ballads*, Arnold's *Culture and Anarchy*, and other related readings. As in previous years, Conradi taught at least one philosophy class.[5] Liddell felt the strain of refining the curriculum each year. She noted in the spring of 1929:

> My difficulty here is that the number of activities is so great that continuity of study is almost impossible. After I have had more teaching experience, I shall probably be able to let my course work run along on momentum much more than I can as yet, and can do my study in advance of my classes, work up some articles, etc.—whereas now I have to spend hours just getting my lessons. Now next summer I want either to get one or two courses systematized, and thus leave myself more leisure for general "scholarly pursuits."[6]

In March 1929, Liddell went to her first meeting of the Southern Society of Philosophy and Psychology (SSPP) in Lexington, Kentucky. Philosophy and psychology once had similar methods, as the field of psychology emerged from the field of philosophy. At the meeting, Liddell noted that the presentations of philosophers and psychologists were very similar. One presentation, "Subjective of the Objective" by Professor C.A.S. Dwight of the University of Oklahoma, had the premise that pure objectivity was not possible, since the researcher's experiences prevented knowledge of the pure object itself. Another presentation by Professor H.H. Johnson of

Melton Institute discussed how a researcher's presuppositions influence the structure of research. On the first day of the SSPP meeting, Liddell felt ill at ease. She asked the other attendees if they knew her uncle, Robert Ogden. Of course they did. They then warmed up to her, and she had fun. On the last day of the meeting, Liddell was elected to a three-year term as a council member of the Society. No one had asked her beforehand whether she would welcome such a nomination. She credited her election to her coming so far to attend and to the Society's desire for more women and more philosophers on the council.[7]

As for romance, Liddell had a mystery relationship in 1928, with a man identified in her papers only as C.R. No details of the romance are known. She wrote this poem to him:

I could see your destined high road
Like a satin ribbon stretch,
White lengths through crimson clover fields,
And purple blooming vetch.

When I lured you to a byroad
Around a hidden turn.
It led through jasmine scented woods,
Deep carpeted in fern.

And was it very wicked,
When I heard the wood thrush call,
To wander with you down a lane
That led nowhere at all.[8]

After her short fling with C.R., only Rawley Myers remained. He was now forty-eight-years old and had become portly. With his vested suit and pocket watch, he looked quite the distinguished businessman that he was.

He was associated with the Stephens Company, which developed the Myers Park area in Charlotte. He was also a director of the Mutual Building and Loan Association. With his real estate and financial connections, he helped many people with limited incomes to buy homes.[9]

Myers had courted Liddell since 1914. Each year, she relied on him more and more, until he became her partner in life in reality, although not legally. Yet she often took his steadfast love for granted. It was about 1928 when Anna Forbes and Rawley finally became engaged to be married. She wrote this poem to him,

I can not tell my love for you in song,
There is no measure for its joy and tears.
Since my whole heart will now to you belong.
Take from me, these my follies through the years.[10]

Rawley gave Anna Forbes a diamond engagement ring, but they set no wedding date, an arrangement satisfactory to them both. Neither wanted her to give up her career, and both thought that marriage would destroy their love if she made that sacrifice.[11] Yet the engagement formalized the commitment each felt for the relationship.

With Liddell now settled in her job, home, and romance, she was amazed with all that she was doing—teaching, writing, and going to college activities—that she still had time to "enjoy each day with simple childish glee."[12] When she was a twelve-year-old, she wanted to never grow up and become an adult who would not sit on the grass for fear of ants. Somehow, she kept her youthful joy of life well into adulthood. Working in her garden or walking through the campus, she remembered the flower fairies she first met as a child. She wrote:

In my grandmother's garden
I would play for hours

With the fairies and the elves
Who lived among the flowers.

Once you've made their friendship
They will not forget.
Walking through the campus,
I often meet them yet.[13]

When Liddell was a child, she had introduced her cousin Vinton to her fairyland in her grandmother's garden. Now, she had Vinton's daughters with whom to share her fairyland. Vinton and Bob Pickens's first child, Jane, was born in February 1925 and their second child, Cornelia, was born in February 1927. Vinton and Bob asked Anna Forbes to be Cornelia's godmother.[14] The Pickens moved often to follow Bob's career as a journalist. Since Jane and Cornelia did not live in Tallahassee, Liddell wrote, even when the girls were babies, letters to them, full of images of fairies they might encounter.

* * *

Before Liddell was in her mid-thirties, she had traveled to Europe three times. She had, however, experienced few interactions with American sub-cultures other than her own. Most everywhere Liddell went in the South was for *whites only*. If an event was racially integrated, the Black people occupied a separate inferior section, and there were separate restrooms and water fountains labeled *white* and *colored.* Liddell's experience with Southern Black culture was with the cooks, gardeners, housekeepers, and handymen who entered her world. An invisible veil concealed from her the life of the Black help when no White people were present.

Like many White Southerners, the Liddell family had loving relationships with the Black help. Anna Forbes's uncle, Vinton Liddell, and his wife Jane financed the education of W.S. Daniels, who was likely the son of one of the Black help. Daniels later had a distinguished career as a traveling instructor for all the chefs for the B&O railroad.[15] George Harris, a Black handyman, lived in the home of Walter and Nellie Liddell for decades. Anna Forbes wrote her mother when she learned of Harris's death, "Of course you miss him most of all of us. . .but I shall miss him too. I had a real love for George, and I can scarcely remember when he was not there."[16]

Progressive for their time, the Liddells had advocated for the end of slavery. When W.J.F. Liddell started the Liddell Company, he paid the workers, who were Black men, more than they were previously paid. This pay raise likely was needed to entice skilled workers to a start-up factory. W.J.F., however, may have also felt a social justice satisfaction, especially when the other factories in response had to increase what they paid skilled Black men.[17] Yet, although the Liddells considered the Black household help as family, they did not consider them as equals. Neither did they consider the Whites who worked in the factories and mills as their equals. The Liddells belonged to the White protestant upper class, which was the dominant class in North Carolina. The dominant class often believes that its dominance is due solely to merit and that those without power are such because they have less merit. White women's clubs worked for better sanitation for poorer neighborhoods, because they thought of themselves as good and benevolent people and not because the poor had a *right* to clean water and proper sanitation. A belief that merit is the sole factor in determining one's place in society can be challenged when experiences are seen from the perspective of a sub-culture different from one's own. It was in 1929, when Liddell was thirty-seven years old, that she had two such experiences—one that pulled back the veil on the Black culture and one that showed her common humanity with a poor, less educated, White Appalachian guide.

The new experience of the Black culture involved a concert of the African-American tenor Roland Hayes at Florida Mechanical and

Agriculture College (FAMC) in Tallahassee. Born in Georgia, Hayes struggled to get his education and musical training because of his race. Moving to Boston to train and perform, he still could not get the recognition he felt he deserved. Thinking he might fare better in Europe, he toured several European countries. In England, he gave a concert at Buckingham Palace for King George V. When he returned to the United States, his European fame opened doors for him in America. He gave concerts mainly in the North, venturing only a few times to the South.[18]

Hayes insisted that his concert at FAMC be integrated, but the integration had a twist—the Black concert-goers sat in the best seats (the center section and balcony seats), while the White concert-goers sat in the inferior seats on the sides of the main floor. Liddell attended the concert and, for the first time, she was in a place where Black people were treated as superior to the White people. Before the concert started, Liddell was acutely conscious of race. She curiously watched the crowd, gazing at the fancy dresses and shawls that the Black women wore. She was seeing Black culture as she had never seen it before.[19] Concerning Hayes's performance, Liddell recounted, "Caruso is the only other tenor I have ever heard with as golden a voice, and although Hayes has less power, he has more art. . . .It was a perfect performance. And as an experience, it was most interesting. . . .After the man began to sing, I thought no more of race, color or previous condition of servitude."[20]

The second new cultural experience occurred on a four-day Appalachian Mountains hiking trip Liddell took with Vinton and Bob Pickens, Ted Livingston, and Francisca Rowland.[21] An Appalachian guide named Frank accompanied them. The hike was in the area now known as the Great Smoky Mountain Park. The group planned to hike to the summits of Bull Mountain and Mount Guyot during the day and to camp at night with bedrolls spread under the stars.

Vinton Pickens wrote a twelve-page story about this trip. In the following account of the hike, the dialogue is as Pickens wrote it in her story. At that time, Appalachian speech was viewed as an illiterate variant of standard American English. Although today's scholars debate the language's origin and influences, they agree that it is a unique and rich language, distinct from standard American English.[22] The city hikers also held stereotypes of the Appalachian people based on their poverty and lack of education. When they met their guide Frank at his cousin Bill's house, their first impression confirmed their stereotype.

Bill provided two packhorses named Tom and Dan. Frank and Bill disapproved of what the city hikers brought—the blankets and cans of vegetables—but they loaded the gear on the horses without saying a word. The city hikers, except Liddell, wore heavy boots. She wore brand-new shoes that sat low on her ankles, because high boots were uncomfortable on her short legs. Frank agreed with Liddell that boots were too hot for hiking, but he insisted hiking shoes should be high-topped to prevent blisters on the heels. He wore high-topped shoes, faded denim overalls, a shirt, a hat, and a thin coat. The coat had two layers zipped together. Everything for hiking for a month could be stashed between the layers of the coat or packed on a horse.

As the hikers started up the mountainside, they enjoyed the beauty of the abundant wildflowers: jewel weed, yellow touch-me-nots, Turk's cap lilies, pinky-violet phlox, yellow daisies, golden anemone, pink and red dianthus and deep red horse-mint. Hummingbirds darted among the wildflowers. After a brief break, Frank ordered the horses to start up by shouting "Gee" and "Haw" at them. Tom obeyed, but Dan did not want to leave his sweet patch of grass. When Frank hit Dan on the rump with his axe-handle, Liddell indignantly ordered him to stop hitting Dan, because horses were intelligent creatures who would respond to reason. Frank replied that horses were like men—some you could reason with, but others you could not. Then he turned to Dan and said sweetly, "Come, honey, let's go." Dan ignored him. Liddell said nothing else about the intelligence of horses, but every time Frank hit Dan on the rump, she screamed. When Frank finally had all the screaming he could handle, he pulled Bob Pickens aside and said, "Bob, if you don't make that little sawed-off gal quit hollerin' at me every time I spank my horse up the trail, I'm goin' to throw the axe at her." Bob Pickens told Frank to ignore Liddell and her ignorance. The hiking party made it to the campsite without the axe being thrown. Their progress was slower than planned, and after the first day, they were a day behind schedule. They camped at a lean-to, where two Appalachian men, Ben and Ed, were also camping.

The atmosphere on the hike up to the campsite had been awkward between the city hikers and Frank, each feeling superior to the other. They had no common ground for discussion. Around the campfire, the Appalachian men traded tall tales. Bob Pickens joined in with a tall tale of his own about the time he took a trip out West. Frank peered at Bob with respect and moved to sit closer to him. Frank continued his storytelling, "You may not believe it, but the mist up here's so thick sometimes you can't see the match you light your fire with." Bob Pickens came back with, "Reminds me of a sandstorm I saw out West, the dust was so thick the prairie dogs were digging holes eight feet off the ground." The Appalachian men burst out laughing. From then on, Pickens was accepted as a fellow Appalachian. But when the talk around the campfire turned to politics, the two groups disagreed. Next, the city hikers sang college songs. No one else knew these songs. The singing ended and there was silence. Then Frank, while putting a new log on the campfire, started whistling a song that Liddell recognized. She began singing it and everyone else joined in singing:

> When the trumpet of the Lord should sound, and time shall be no more,
> And the Day shall break eternal, bright and fair,
> And the saints of God shall gather, upon the distant shore
> And the roll is called up yonder, I'll be there!

Everyone sang the song several times, each time more in unison than the time before, until the fire burned low.

All settled in to sleep by the campfire. The mountain men lay on the bare ground. Ed and Ben had no covers, and Frank had only a saddlecloth. The city hikers put on sweaters and tucked themselves in between heavy blankets. Time passed, and the only sound was the low popping of the campfire and the whirring of crickets in the distance. Suddenly, Bob Pickens exclaimed, "There's a stone under my head and I always did think the fellow in the Bible who used a rock for a pillow was an ass." He dug out the small rock. Frank retorted, "You couldn't say that if my mother was here. I remember when I was a kid an' used to argue with her about things in the Bible that didn't seem to me to make sense, when she couldn't make me agree any other way she jest took a stick of stove wood an' beat the tar out o' me." Frank paused and then continued, "My mother ain't much hand to read. If you was to walk in an' give her a newspaper, she'd just say 'I cain't read thet, but I'll read you from my paper,' an' get out her old Bible. It's a big'un an' she's read it from lid to lid. She'll tell you too thet whoever shall take away from or add to this book is worse an infidel."

Frank had told them that he did not read or write much, but he continued to talk about the Bible. The educated city folk were dumbfounded. They disagreed with his interpretations at times, but recognized he knew more about the Bible than any of them, except Bob, who was a minister's son. Liddell leaned over and whispered to Vinton, "We never think of the Greeks who knew only Homer as illiterate, but these people are considered a disgrace to us because the only literature they know is so good we don't appreciate it."

In the morning, the hikers said goodbye to Ed and Ben, who were going in a different direction, and set off with Frank. This day was easier, because their trail was mostly downhill, but, by the end of the day, Liddell had ugly red blisters on her heels.

The next morning, the group had a decision to make. They could continue on to Guyot Mount and return to the campsite that evening. Then they would have to hike in one day the distance they had done in the first two days. Or they could turn back now. There was silence. Everyone wanted to turn back, but no one wanted to admit it. Finally, Bob Pickens said that since vacations were for resting, not for getting tired, Bull Mountain satisfied his need for climbing. Liddell's blisters settled the matter. The men would have to carry her up and down Mount Guyot if they continued, since the horses could not make that leg of the journey. The hikers turned around, since, if they turned back now, she could ride on a horse.

Returning was uneventful, except for the problem of getting Tom, the horse Liddell was riding, to stay on the trial. She kept the reins so slack the horse decided himself where and when to go. Whenever anyone took the reins to lead Tom, Liddell gave so many orders that they gave the reins back to her. It became a game with the group to slip behind Tom, where Liddell could not see them, and give the horse a light slap on the rump, slyly exchanging grins among themselves. Liddell was oblivious to the drama happening behind her. By the time the group reached cousin Bill's house, the city hikers and their Appalachian guide had developed a respect for each other and came to see their own prejudices.

* * *

In September 1929, prices on the New York Stock Exchange began falling. In late October, the share prices collapsed, creating the Wall Street Crash. The crash affected economies around the world. In the United States, it led to the Great Depression, which would cause the loss of fortunes and jobs. Families and institutions worried about how they would survive financially. In that uncertain time, people again questioned the role of women in society.

A Turning Point (1930)

For the 1929–1930 school year, Anna Forbes Liddell was appointed as Full Professor and taught all of the philosophy courses.[1] She also wanted to advance her career beyond the college. In April 1930, she attended the annual meeting of the Southern Society of Philosophy and Psychology and presented her first professional paper entitled "Challenging the Major Premise." In this paper, she asserted that philosophy completes science. She likely knew that the scientists in the audience might take offense, but her nature was to speak her truth regardless of whether people agreed. Joseph Peterson of Peabody College, a psychologist and scientist, critiqued each presentation of the annual meeting in *The American Journal of Psychology*. His critique of her talk was a blistering rebuttal bordering on a personal attack:

> [Liddell] apparently regards philosophy as having a rather large supervisory function over science. . .She showed signs of lack of acquaintance with the spirit of advanced scientific work today. . . .How this view among certain philosophers. . .arose and received its justification among these individuals is an interesting question. . . .It may well be questioned whether those unverified assertions by certain philosophers are not made to justify their own existence in a day when

> science has turned to its own method with the excellent results known to everyone.[2]

Was Peterson's review negative because Liddell was a woman? Probably not, because he analyzed another woman's talk in a neutral way. That woman was a fellow psychologist. He appeared to have a disdain for philosophers who criticized the work of scientists. He was outspoken in the belief that the methods of philosophy and psychology had diverged so much that the Society should now have separate sessions for the two fields.[3] We do not know how Liddell received Peterson's criticism, but she likely was not as bothered as other people might have been. She had always liked a good argument and did not care whether other people agreed with her. She remained in the Society and continued to make presentations at the annual meetings.

In July 1930, Liddell had a six-page article "In Defense of Absolute Ethics" published in *The Journal of Philosophy*. She began the article with a concern that the current emphasis on the scientific method as the best way to discover truth was causing humanity to lose its values. This concern showed the influence of Horace Williams on her thinking, since he had also expressed that concern.[4] Science, she continued, seeks to explain, but it does not evaluate. It does not declare whether anything is good or bad. For centuries, scholars viewed humanity on Earth as the center of the universe. Then science showed that humankind is but a speck of life on one planet in one solar system in the Milky Way. If human beings are so insignificant, what does anything they do make any difference and how can anyone find meaning in life? Why should anyone strive to be good? In the article, Liddell explained that although humankind is not the center of the universe, each person assimilates knowledge, even scientific knowledge, according to what it means for that person and asks how this information affects life choices. Ethics is centered on human thought. If human beings did not exist, neither would ethics.

The dependence of ethics on human thought might lead one to wonder whether values such as goodness also depend on human thought. To answer this question, Liddell used the following example: Suppose she killed her neighbor, and immediately after that act, a cataclysmic event destroyed all human life. Since her act of murder had no consequences to herself, her neighbor, or the future of humankind, was her act a sin? She noted that human acts, institutions, customs, and laws exist in a certain place and time. Is the value of goodness also dependent on place and time? She asserted that although acts of goodness are located in particular place and time, the abstract notion of goodness is an absolute that does not depend on place and time? Thus, the goodness of human acts does not depend on where or when the acts occur. She concluded that her hypothetical act of murder was a sin.

In the same article, Liddell discussed the effect of scientific discoveries on the Christian concept of Heaven. She pointed out two of Jesus's statements: "The Kingdom of Heaven is within you" and "In my Father's House are many mansions." The first statement, she argued, reveals Jesus's belief in Absolute Goodness, while the second has led the average person to expect to walk in Heaven on physical streets of gold. She asserted that religion must accept scientific truths and quoted medieval Catholic theologian Thomas Aquinas, "For the truth of our faith becomes a matter of ridicule among the infidels, if any Catholic not gifted with the necessary scientific learning, presents as dogma what scientific scrutiny shows to be false."[5] Although science had debunked the idea of Heaven existing as a physical place, it had not affected the belief that the Kingdom of Heaven resides within each person or the belief that the Father's house is spiritual. Liddell concluded with an assertion that ethics must seek value, but science must be disinterested.

While her article emerged from her study for an ethics textbook, she had abandoned writing such a textbook. She now sought as her professional legacy the translation of the major work of Nicholas of Cusa (1401–1464) from Latin into English. Today's scholars also call Nicholas of Cusa by the name Cusanus. He was truly a Renaissance man in the scope and depth of his studies, which included mathematics, science, philosophy, and theology. He saw no conflict between science and religion. For him, learning more about the physical universe leads to a greater knowledge of God.[6] As a theologian, Cusanus was a Christian mystic. The fundamental question throughout his writings was how human beings, whose existence is finite, can understand an infinite God. His major work, *De Docta Ignorantia,* was his first published philosophical treatise. *Docta ignorantia* means human beings must use faith and inspiration to understand God.[7] Cusanus rose to become a Cardinal in the Catholic Church, yet he studied non-Christian religions, including Islam. He taught that Christians should resolve conflicts with Muslims, Jews, and all other non-Christians using persuasion, not force. He considered all religions to be "one religion in a variety of rites."[8] Liddell said of Cusanus's philosophy, "I find it the most satisfying philosophy I have ever studied."[9]

Liddell first learned about Nicholas of Cusa in her undergraduate study at the University of North Carolina. At Cornell, she searched all the libraries for everything he had written. She could not, however, find, even in the Library of Congress, any of his works. She would have to travel to Germany to access a copy of *De Docta Ignorantia.*[10]

The foremost Cusanus scholar in 1930 was Ernst Hoffmann, Professor of Philosophy at the University of Heidelberg in Heidelberg, Germany.[11] Liddell knew that she would have to go to Heidelberg to study Cusanus. Studying at the University of Heidelberg was satisfying in another way because all three of her mentors, Robert Ogden, James Creighton, and Horace Williams, had studied there during their careers.

Liddell asked Horace Williams about her idea of producing an English translation of *De Docta Ignorantia.* He replied, "Your plan for the Cusa study is fine. By all means go to Germany and produce it there."[12]

Encouraged, Liddell set off to Germany to study with Hoffmann in summer 1930. Here is her first impression of him: "He is about forty, rather fat, very German and most pleasant. He can't speak English at all, so, although my German isn't the best, we speak German. I can understand at least 90% of what he says, and I believe he understands me."[13] She was relieved that he spoke slowly at his Cusanus seminars so that she could keep up.[14]

Nicholas of Cusa wrote in Latin. Hoffmann's seminars were in German. Liddell was translating from Latin into English. She found thinking in three languages hard. She knew she could translate better at home with better Latin-English dictionaries, but Heidelberg was the place to be to study and discuss Cusanus.[15]

Liddell's goal of translating *De Docta Ignorantia* required her to translate a five-hundred-year-old manuscript written in an archaic, degraded form of Latin into modern English. A modern Latin/English dictionary could not give the nuances of meaning to the writings of a German fifteenth-century cleric. She would have to rely on Hoffmann's Cusanus seminars for the nuances. Yet Liddell's German was not fluent enough for her to feel confident that she adequately understood the seminar discussions. Nicholas of Cusa said that he wrote his ideas simply. However, no one else thinks that his writing is simple. His writings require study and reflection. In addition, the task for any translator becomes more difficult with the passage of time. How can someone of the twentieth century set aside the cultural milieu in which they live to get into the mind of a fifteenth-century scholar to determine what that writer meant in his time?

Liddell was disappointed that she had so little opportunity to contact Hoffmann outside the seminars, since she had hoped to develop an ongoing professional relationship with him.[16] She wished for the seminar discussions to spill over into conversation afterwards over tea or supper, in the way she had enjoyed the home seminars Horace Williams had with his students. But that did not happen. She talked with Hoffmann and other scholars in the seminar and then went back to her rooming house to study.

The language barrier likely contributed to that. Hoffmann may not have understood her German as well as she imagined. She gave Hoffmann the first few pages of her translation, but she wrote, "Prof. Hoffmann knows so little English, I don't know how he can tell whether my translation is any good or not. It is very difficult, because if the translation is literal, it is awkward—if it is free there is danger of losing the meaning."[17]

Most of the time, Liddell was lonely in Germany. She ate many of her meals alone, walked alone, and attended concerts alone. It was only at the end of the summer that she began to have more contact with Hoffmann and his wife Thea, going to their home for tea and discussions. She wrote her mother, "The next time I come—whenever that is—I think I shall probably make more friends and have a more social time. It takes the Germans a little while to take you in. Also the outsider is supposed to make the first advances, and that is awkward for a person who isn't used to it."[18]

While on this trip, Liddell met Marie Baum, Professor of Sociology at the University of Heidelberg, who had worked for factory reform and for welfare of women and children during the German Weimar Republic period after World War I. Liddell had learned about Baum though the American Association of University Women, and she had corresponded with her before her trip.[19] Their first meeting was formal over tea in Baum's home. Liddell's first impression was, "She is a rather dumpy little old lady. . . .We sat side by side on a little sofa and drank tea and ate little cakes like nabiscos [*sic*] and talked about family life in Germany and America and whether married women should earn money or not, etc. We talked English, which was a great relief to me."[20]

In her free time, Liddell walked around Heidelberg and visited other areas such as Baden-Baden, Oberammergau, and Munich. The tranquility of the beautiful German scenes was at odds with the undercurrent of unrest due to the economy. Liddell wrote "if the Americans think they are hard up, they ought to see the Germans."[21] The German people had been suffering from an unstable economy since the end of World War I in 1919.

Liddell, however, could not foresee how the economy and governmental ineffectiveness would create the environment for the National Socialist German Workers' Party (Nazi) to emerge from obscurity. She, instead, focused on Cusanus and her professional relationships. Neither Baum nor Hoffmann were yet alarmed by the growing hatred of Jews, liberals, intellectuals, Catholics, and any others who were not conservative or of pure Aryan heritage.

Several weeks before Liddell returned to the United States, she received a letter from Rawley Myers that stunned her. He would be going to Paris for business and suggested they travel back on the same ship. Although they were engaged, she worried that the scandalous behavior of traveling alone with Myers would cause her to be fired.[22]

The modern reader may not understand Liddell's predicament. In that time, proper American women did not travel alone with a man unless he was a relative. Doing so might start rumors of immorality. It did not matter whether the couple had a torrid affair or simply sat side-by-side as friends. The appearance of immorality was nearly as scandalous as the immoral deed itself. Consequences for the woman could include social shunning and loss of her job. If she lost her job for immorality, then it would be hard to get another one. However, there was a double standard in society. A man involved in such a scandal would rarely face consequences. Although Liddell and Myers had gone from London to Paris unchaperoned in 1926, that trip was before she was employed at a publicly funded college. She had no job to lose then.

As Liddell thought more about the situation, she rationalized she would not be fired if she traveled unchaperoned with Myers. She wrote her mother:

> Naturally, I cannot forbid Rawley to buy a ticket on whatever ship he prefers, and I can't ask the Deutcher-Lloyd Co. not to sell him one Second Class on the *Columbia*. However, if I can prevent it, I shall. I

> don't think, however, that I should lose my job or even be scandalized among my Tallahassee friends if he did follow me over and back. I have lived there four years. My reputation's established. Rawley has been down several times and people like him. He looks awfully safe. . . .He might not be complimented to hear me say that because of his age and his grandfatherly manner nobody would mistrust his motives or his behavior. . . .I never had a real friendship that I didn't have to purchase at a great price, and Rawley's no exception. I seem to have the fatal faculty of picking as my best friends people who are in one way or another sharply different from ordinary conventional folk—Horace Williams says they are always the most interesting, but they are also the most trouble.[23]

While Liddell was worrying about her response to Myers, he wrote that he would have to stay in Paris a little longer. Thus, it turned out that he could not travel back with her after all. She was relieved.[24]

Before returning home in late September, Liddell attended the World Congress of Philosophy in Oxford, England. There were only a few women attendees. She saw her friend Katherine Gilbert, who was the Professor of Philosophy at Duke University.[25] Liddell was excited to attend the prestigious Congress, which met at that time only every four years. She noted that the three daily sessions were intellectually strenuous and that "it was most thrilling just to be in Oxford, that great seat of learning whose history dates back over almost 700 years."[26]

On October 10, 1930, the unthinkable happened. Rawley Myers died suddenly from a heart attack at age fifty.[27] Presumably, Liddell received the terrible news in a phone call in Tallahassee from her mother in Charlotte. It devastated Liddell. She was deeply grieving when she wrote to her mother about her first week back in Tallahassee after Myers's funeral in Charlotte:

The week that I have been back has gone by rather quickly; there are always so many people around and so many things to do that the days are gone before one can realize it. Until yesterday I felt so utterly exhausted that I didn't have the strength for anything more than my class attendance and the ordinary business of dressing and eating and walking about. I slept and slept and slept. Sometimes I just lay down without thinking or feeling or anything, (daytime), but I didn't try to exert myself at all and now I'm quite a lot better. Tonight I haven't any headache. Bodies are curious things, aren't they? It seems so strange, so irrational that an emotional grief should have a physical reaction.

It still doesn't seem quite as if I were myself. Part of me is gone, and I suppose that part of me won't ever come back.[28]

Liddell had loved Rawley Myers deeply, but had taken his presence for granted. She did not realize how much she depended on his strength, energy, support, and advice until he was gone. She wrote the following poem to him after his death:

The constant sun has never left the sky.
And so
How could I know
That you would die?[29]

In a letter to her mother, Liddell struggled to put her mother's mind (and her own) at peace. She wrote, replying to her mother's concerns for her:

I don't sit around and grieve. I had a wonderful friendship. It was a dominant factor in my life for sixteen years. I shall enjoy it as long as I live. Nothing can replace it. But I had lived to be twenty-three before it

> began and life was interesting and joyous. I know it will be interesting and joyous again. But I have to find a new focus. Everybody tells me I have my work. I don't suppose many people even suspect how much Rawley was the driving force which kept me at work, how much I depended on his energy. Now I've got to go on alone, but I'm naturally indolent. He pushed me all the time. Now I've got to keep myself from slumping without him.[30]

Beyond losing a love, Anna Forbes's life was going to change immensely, since she had relied on Rawley in so many ways. She would now have to rely on herself more than she had thought she would ever have to.[31]

Photographs

Walter Scott Liddell, Liddell family photo.
Courtesy of Anne Bentley

Nellie, Anna Forbes (age 3), and Helen Liddell,
Liddell family photo. *Courtesy of Anne Bentley*

1914 Charlotte Suffrage Float.
Courtesy of the Robinson-Spangler Carolina Room, Charlotte Mecklenburg Library

Liddell at Florida State College for Women.
Courtesy of Special Collections & Archives, Florida State University Libraries

Liddell's Tallahassee house, *drawing by Kelli Swan*

Liddell about 1939, Liddell family photo.
Courtesy of Anne Bentley

Liddell with Ernst and Thea Hoffmann, Liddell family photo.
Courtesy of Mary Anna Dunn

Liddell and Robert Miller,
Courtesy of Special Collections & Archives, Florida State University Libraries

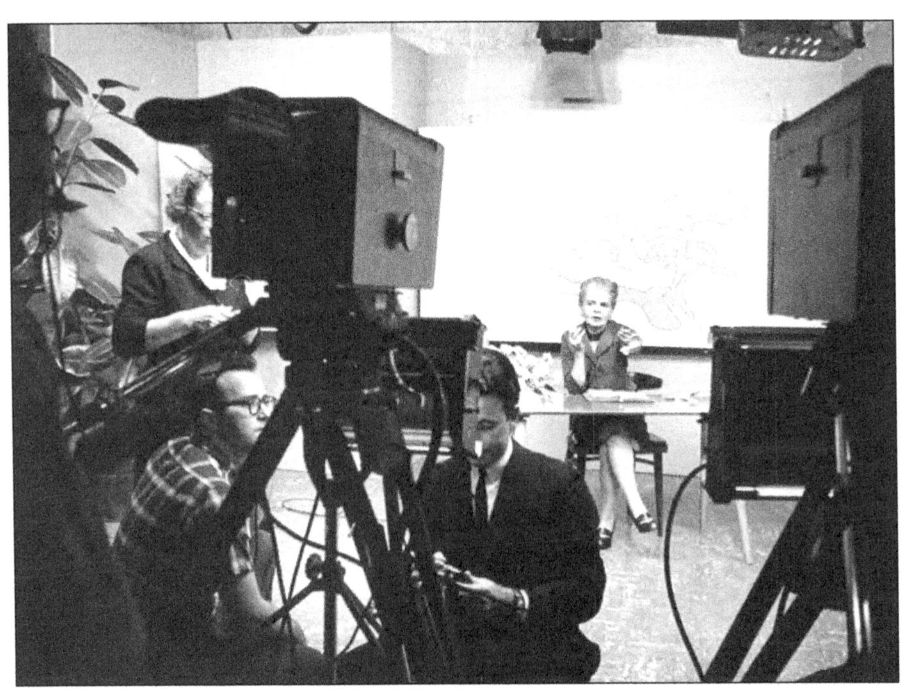

Liddell on WFSU-TV.
Courtesy of Special Collections & Archives, Florida State University Libraries

Liddell talking with Florida Governor Farris Bryant, (L-R Marian Irish, William W. Rogers, Dorothy L. Hoffman, Wiley Housewright, Anna Forbes Liddell, Michael Kasha, Gov. Bryant). *Courtesy of Special Collections & Archives, Florida State University Libraries*

Anna Forbes Liddell, *FSU Lawton Distinguished Professor, courtesy of Richard Parks, State Archives of Florida, Florida Memory*

Liddell Speaking to 1973 Florida Legislative Committee.
Courtesy of State Archives of Florida, Florida Memory

Rebuilding (1931-1932)

After Rawley Myers's death, Horace Williams wrote to Anna Forbes Liddell to express his belief that she would be compensated for her loss. He said, "There is a fineness, a stability of purpose, a beauty of the spirit that come [*sic*] out of such experience. So one must carry on. I expect a new note will come into your teaching, the quality of individuality."[1]

Yet in 1931, Liddell was not seeing any compensation. She was exhausted, with little energy for teaching, much less for working on her Cusanus translation. Even so, she presented a calm demeanor as she went about her day. She prepared for classes, taught, and went to concerts and bridge parties. She made light conversation with her colleagues and friends, not wanting to burden them with her personal problems.[2]

Distracted by her grief, Liddell forgot to send her godchild Cornelia Pickens a letter for her fourth birthday. Liddell's belated birthday letter had the following fairy story that shows her state of mind:

> Once upon a time there was an old maid who lived in a little yellow house with white columns in front. It looked a little like a slice of lemon custard pie with meringue on it. She didn't have any children. Old maids never have any children. They aren't even supposed to.

This old maid knew a great many things—really she could tell you quite a lot. (Old maids usually can, and generally do—ask Budhie [Cornelia's name for her mother] and Bob if that isn't true.) She knew that Columbus landed at San Salvador on October 12, 1492, and The Mecklenburg Declaration of Independence was signed May 20, 1775, but she couldn't remember when really important events occurred like the birthdays of Jane and Cornelia Pickens. She knew that they came very close together in the shortest month of the year, but on which days, she didn't know any more than a puppy knows how to read. And then she knew some things which she thought were important like the difference between Nominalism and Realism, but she didn't know what little girls liked for their birthdays. She had *been* a little girl, but she had never *had* a little girl, which is very different.

And so you see she was a very stupid and useless person.

The fairies had been very fond of her when she was a child herself, because she never disturbed them when they were sleeping in the roses or inside the tulips or riding on the backs of June bugs and fireflies. But that was long before she became an old maid. Fairies never forget. Because she had been a nice child, they decided that they would give her a chance to escape the spell of black magic which had converted her into an old maid. So they let her be a godmother. That is a great opportunity if a person only realizes it. It keeps you right in touch with the fairies. All of the fairies are godmothers. I mean, all of the women fairies. Perhaps there are godfather fairies too, but I never heard of any. If you are a godmother, you can keep right on going to fairyland on the Moonbeam Express, or the Southwind Special. But of course you have to buy your own ticket. The ticket isn't difficult to buy, if you have plenty of wishes and dreams in your pocket, and wise people never are without wishes and dreams. But grownups, especially old maids, get so careless. They forget their glasses, and their fountain pens and their school books—that's bad enough, but they forget their wishes and their dreams and that is a million times worse. And so this little old maid, with all of the privileges of going to fairyland, was so careless that time after time when she got to the big station where the Moonbeam Express had stopped and the Star Conductor was already calling "Aaalll a BooARD" she had to turn back because she couldn't buy a ticket. That was very sad, much sadder than she realized herself. She had grownup and was getting grownupper and grownupper all of the time. She not only forgot the dreams and the wishes she forgot to go to the station where the fairy trains come in. The fairies felt badly. They had given her a great privilege (done up in gold paper and tied with blue ribbon) the privilege of riding on the fairy trains, (Of course she had to buy the ticket, but most grown ups aren't allowed to ride, ever) and she had forgotten all about it. They were sorry she was a godmother. She wasn't a good one.

And then one day when the fairy godmothers were talking together at a fairy reception the Queen said, "Isn't there a little girl with blue eyes and blond hair who hasn't an [*sic*] godmother? Isn't she being allowed to grow up without being taught when to come to the fairy court and how to entertain fairies in her own garden?" And a fairy waiting maid said, "do you mean the fair child Cornelia, verily she has a godmother, but a most unworthy one. In her youth she was the companion of fairies, but now she is nothing but an old maid. Verily I think we should pick a new godmother for the fair child Cornelia."

But that very day the little old maid saw the sun shining on blud [*sic*] water. "Oh, I wish I had the power to go to the depth of this Silver Spring," she said, "I know it is a fairy spring." And sure enough it was. And she put a beautiful wish in her pocket. "I wish I could see the fairy

> castle at the bottom of the spring." And now there were two wishes in her pocket. "Oh, I wish I could take my god child by one hand and her little big sister by the other, and go to the fairy castle down under the water, and play with the Duc de Turtle and ride on the backs of cat fishes." And then there was such a big wish in her pocket, that the next time the Moonbeam Express leaves for Fairyland she can go all the way. And if you want her to I think she will, and tell you all about it when she comes back.[3]

The fairy spring in the story was likely inspired by Wakulla Springs, just fifteen miles south of Tallahassee. Liddell went there when she first came to Tallahassee and described the experience, "Yesterday afternoon I went with the Brevards to Walkulla Springs—it is a very interesting place. A whole river rises right out of a big spring, and you can go out in a glass bottomed boat and look down at the rocks and seaweed and fishes under the water."[4]

Liddell resolved to be the kind of aunt that Jane Liddell Battle had been to her. She was already providing clothes and lessons for her nephew and three nieces. Now she wanted to show them the world through travel. At family gatherings, she played with them, but being in charge of them for days frightened her more than going to Germany alone had the year before.[5]

Thus, in June 1931, Liddell, excited and nervous, boarded a train with her fourteen-year-old nephew, Walter, and twelve-year-old niece, Helen-Aline. They were the two oldest children of her sister Helen McBride. The trio rode the train to Washington, DC, to visit the Pickens family—Vinton, Bob, Jane, and Cornelia.

Bob Pickens reported on the daily activities of President Herbert Hoover as a White House Correspondent for the Associated Press. With his White House connections, Pickens arranged for Walter and Helen-Aline to have a private meeting with President Hoover.[6] Presumably, Liddell escorted the children for the meeting with the President.

The next stop on their trip was New York City to see the usual tourist sights. Liddell likely took Walter and Helen-Aline to see Greenwich Village, although its grand bohemian time had ended. She must have shown them where the Provincetown Players had performed, the apartments where she had lived, and the New York Post and McGraw Hill Buildings where she had worked. Surely, when they saw Fifth Avenue and the Washington Square Arch, Liddell told them about marching in the suffrage parades and what a grand time it was! They did go to the top of the Empire State building to see the entire city in miniature. If it had been a clear day, they could have seen a distance of some eighty miles into parts of Connecticut, Pennsylvania, New Jersey, and Massachusetts. The building was completed in April 1931 and was opened to the public in May, a month before the children visited. All the marble, steel, and terrazzo would have been sparkling. At its opening, it was the tallest building in the world. Nonetheless, Helen-Aline mentioned none of those sights when she recounted the trip. The highlights of the trip for her were going to Coney Island, meeting President Hoover, and playing with her cousins Jane and Cornelia Pickens.[7]

* * *

The year 1931 had been a time for grieving and for more responsibility for the family's children in her role as the *old maid aunt.* Liddell felt she had muddled through her professional life. Yet it was likely that was not how others perceived her, because, for the 1931–1932 year, she was promoted to Chair of the Department of Philosophy. Prior to this time, the department did not have a chair. She also remained the only professor in the department. Promotion to Full Professor two years earlier and now promotion to Department Chair were significant. Gaining respect in the professions was harder than women had thought it would be. At that time, women often stayed in the lower tier of academia—as instructors or associate professors. Few women achieved the rank of full professor, much less department chair. Some lack of advancement for women in academia stemmed from their preference for teaching over publishing. However, some was likely due to gender discrimination.[8] In addition, many women did not know how to advance in their profession. It was not enough to have the professional credentials. One also had to know the rules of the game. Many did not even know that there were rules of the game of being promoted. Women in this generation generally did not have women role models to follow, and few had male mentors willing to guide them professionally.

Liddell wanted to return to Heidelberg to study with Hoffmann. Yet the political unrest continued to grow in Germany. In April 1931, she received a letter from Hoffmann, which contained this excerpt:

> Our winter semester has been very restless and has given cause for serious concern. The entire student body of Germany has now been swept up in an extremely nationalistic current, which we faculty members painfully regret and painstakingly fight against. But even we cannot remain closed to the realization, that most likely, no student body in the world, in the same situation, if at all still in possession of any sense of national honor, would behave differently. It really is an unreasonable burden placed on our youth. On the right, to see a weapon-staring and with gold overflowing France, to the left, the continuously progressing Polonization [imposition of Polish culture] of the East under the protection of the League of Nations and in-between both, to live in a Germany that in the midst of daily increasing poverty, hears the accusations from the world over, that it cannot satisfy its creditors and is maliciously preparing for wars. I'm only telling you of this, so that you may properly understand why we've had street clashes between police and students.

In spite of the political unrest, Liddell applied in the fall of 1931 for sabbatical leave for the spring 1932 semester with plans to extend her German trip through the summer break. In November 1931, she received a letter from Hoffmann with this excerpt:

> Germany has been in such a dire situation since June, that all laws are suspended and the governing of the state merely relies on the issuance of emergency decrees. It is such a considerable crisis, that in some months, a civil servant is required to pay more in taxes than the state can afford to pay him in salary. Crazy but true. Thirdly, add to this that since September, I am Dean of Faculty and you yourself may grasp what this means under the current circumstances. But now I can share with you the pleasant fact that the Cusanus enterprise will continue nevertheless, even if our means have been reduced to a minimum. *The Apologia doctae ignorantiae* is in finished print and will be available in all bookstores in the coming days. The *Docta ignorantia* is itself also almost finished and should appear around Christmas. When Miss Liddell comes to Heidelberg in 1932, she will see first, the university built with American money; second, she will reunite with Dr. Klibansky, now lecturer/associate professor, and third, find in me an old friend. One who will with greatest pleasure, join her in the continued quest to discover the mysteries of the Cusanic philosophy.[9]

Hoffmann's letter did not change Liddell's plans. In January 1932, she told her mother why she felt compelled to go to Germany:

> Rob [Ogden] told me last summer that if I wanted to accomplish anything professional, I must write. In Tallahassee, I simply can't. I have too many classes, too much general college, *too many* friends. I haven't arrived professionally, but I have made a good beginning, and I have

> had some rather lucky breaks. I feel that it is now up to me to show what I can accomplish, and the only way to do it is to go to it. It will be easy for me to settle down in Heidelberg this time; it won't seem strange at all, and I know the Hoffmanns well enough now to regard them as real friends. I shall be homesick, but I am in Tallahassee.[10]

Liddell left for Germany on March 9, 1932. Before settling in Heidelberg for study, she went to Berlin to visit friends. When she arrived in the German capital, she found that most of her friends had gone to Rome for Easter. Liddell had assumed the economic conditions would have prevented such travel. Her German friends however, were from the middle and upper classes. Many were intellectuals still working in the universities. Some, such as the Krasmanns, whom she was able to see when in Berlin were wealthy. The Krasmanns paid 65 percent income tax, yet still had money for a car, expensive clothes, a maid, and a nanny for the children. Frau Krasmann would neither wear her furs nor drive her car for fear of being mobbed by the many Germans who were starving. There were frequent deadly riots in the street. In letters home, Liddell downplayed the conflicts, likely so her family would not worry.[11]

After World War I, the democratic German Weimar Republic replaced the German monarchy. The Republic had an elected President, an appointed Chancellor, and an elected legislative body, called the Reichstag. The President as the head of state negotiated with foreign governments and was Commander-in-Chief of the army. He appointed the Chancellor who appointed a cabinet. The Chancellor and the cabinet implemented the policies of the government. The President could dissolve the Reichstag and call for an election of new members. The Reichstag could remove cabinet members.

The Reichstag was ineffective. There were so many political parties that none could win a majority of the seats. A political party won a seat for each 60,000 votes in an electoral district. Thus, the number of Reichstag seats changed with each election. After the 1930 election, the Social Democratic Party, the largest party, had 25 percent of the 577 seats, the National Socialist German Workers' (Nazi) Party had 18 percent, the Communist Party of Germany had 13 percent, and the Centre Party had 12 percent. The remaining seats were divided among nine other political parties., Because the Reichstag could not get legislation passed, President Paul von Hindenburg in 1930 invoked Article 38 of the German Constitution, which allowed him to use emergency powers to pass decrees without legislative consent.

Hindenburg, a former field marshal in the Imperial German army, had been elected as President of the Weimar Republic in 1925. In spring 1932, when he was eighty-five years old, he reluctantly ran for reelection. The Nazi Party wanted to run Adolf Hitler against the incumbent Hindenburg. However, the Austrian-born Hitler was not qualified because he was not a German citizen. He became a naturalized German citizen on February 25, 1932, to be eligible to run for office. There were several candidates. Hindenburg got 49 percent of the votes and Hitler got 30 percent. Because no one had a majority of the votes, a runoff election between Hindenburg and Hitler was scheduled for April 10.[12]

Liddell traveled to Stuttgart to sightsee around the time of the runoff election. The night before the election, she strolled by a 10,000-seat auditorium there, where people were lining up for a Hitler rally. She thought about stopping to hear Hitler speak, but decided against it. The crowd was so large she might wait in line a long time and still not be able to get in. The next day, Hindenburg won with 53 percent of the vote. Liddell's friends were pleased with the results.[13]

Because Hindenburg won the election, Heinrich Brüning continued as Chancellor. After the April 10 election, Brüning, with a decree, banned political parties from having military organizations. This ban was directed toward the Nazi's SA paramilitary unit, known as the *Brown Shirts* or *Storm Troopers.* The Storm Troopers had about 440,000 rowdy members who started street fights.[14] Liddell wrote to her mother about the ban saying, "You probably have read in the paper that the military organizations here in Germany—(not the national troops)—I mean those political parties with military drill as part of their activity, especially Hitler's group—have been disorganized by government ordinance. . . .The parties of course can continue to exist as parties, but the *military* aspect must be eliminated. German papers are funny. The news stories are much like editorials, and very few mere news items—unelaborated. Yet their papers give much information in a few pages."[15]

Political tension escalated because of the back room scheming of Hitler, and Kurt von Schleicher, an ambitious army general. Hitler agreed to support Schleicher's plan to have Franz von Papen appointed as Chancellor. Papen would be Schleicher's puppet. In return, Schleicher promised to get Papen to lift the ban on the Storm Troopers. Hitler and Schleicher then undermined President Hindenburg's support of Brüning. Schleicher suggested to Hindenburg that the aristocrat Franz von Papen be appointed as Chancellor. Hitler agreed that Papen was acceptable to him. Thus, Hindenburg ordered Brüning to resign, which he did on May 30, 1932. Hindenburg appointed Papen as Chancellor that same day. Papen's cabinet was composed of aristocrats and industrialists. Liddell wrote to her mother, "We are all distressed over Brüning's resignation, but of course it has happened too recently for anybody to know what effect it will have. . . .I do not suppose it will affect me personally, but I do hope that Germany isn't in for more trouble."[16]

On June 15, 1932, the government lifted its ban on the Nazi Storm Troopers, who quickly returned to the streets. As they marched, they blasted out a Nazi song, which is translated into English as, "Blood must flow, blood must flow! Blood must flow as cudgel thick as hail! Let's smash it up, let's smash it up! That goddamned Jewish republic!" [17]

Communist supporters, looking for a fight, were also marching. Hundreds of shootings erupted between the Nazis and the communists.

On July 19, the Storm Troopers, with a police escort, entered a communist enclave near Hamburg. Shooting broke out between the communists and the Nazis. Nineteen people were killed and almost three hundred wounded in this battle, known as Bloody Sunday. The Nazi Party rallies where Hitler spoke now drew crowds of over 100,000 people.[18]

On July 31, there were new elections for the Reichstag. The Nazi Party won 230 seats, an increase of 123 seats from the previous election. The Nazi Party, with 37 percent of 608 seats, now had the most seats in the Reichstag. Hitler demanded to be appointed Chancellor. Hindenburg offered him the Vice-Chancellor job instead. Hitler not only turned the job down—he did so angrily. He threatened to let the Storm Troopers ravage the country. In addition, he refused to work in a coalition with leaders of the other political parties. Hindenburg, the former German field marshal, gave Hitler, the former corporal, a proper military-style dressing down. Hitler backed off his demand, but the government was at a stalemate.[19]

After Liddell left Germany in August, the back room scheming continued. On September 12, the Nazi Party led the Reichstag in a no-confidence vote for Papen. That same day, Hindenburg dissolved the Reichstag, and ordered new elections for November 6. In this election, the Nazi Party lost seats. With 33 percent of the seats, however, it still had the most of any political party. The Nazi Party had lost popularity because of the violent street fights of its storm troopers, and because a faction of the party had joined with the communists in a labor strike. Many Germans feared a communist takeover more than a fascist one. Hitler himself was distracted before the elections because his girlfriend Eva Baum had attempted suicide by shooting herself in the neck.[20]

The political scheming continued. On November 17, Papen resigned as Chancellor because he could not form a workable government coalition. With the backing of business leaders, Hitler again demanded to be Chancellor. Hindenburg refused. Papen asked for his job back with conditions. He wanted to rule by decree with the Reichstag permanently disbanded. Schleicher, who had the support of the army generals, asserted that the army would not accept the reappointment of Papen. Underestimating Hitler, Schleicher further promised that he could create so much discord within the Nazi Party that it would break into factions. Reluctantly, Hindenburg appointed Schleicher as Chancellor of a shaky government on December 2, 1932.[21]

* * *

On her 1932 German trip, Anna Forbes Liddell focused on her profession and tried to ignore German politics. She hoped to have her discussion of Cusanus's work finished by the end of the year. Professor Hoffmann encouraged her. She reflected:

> It seemed to me so stupendous as to be frightening, but he [Hoffmann] thinks I can do it, so I shall try not to show him I can't. He has an almost magnetic effect on me. He has so much enthusiasm for his work himself that I seem to imbibe it. He really is a marvelous teacher too. I can learn more about teaching from attending one of his seminars one time, than from a whole summer school course in education.[22]

Liddell rented a room in the picturesque old-town section of Heidelberg in a house that was directly on a streetcar route. Yet Liddell walked many places as the Hoffmanns lived only a ten-minute walk away, and her friend Marie Baum lived around the corner. Liddell's daily routine was writing in the morning, attending lectures in the afternoon, and socializing in the evening. After supper, she often went with Marie Baum or the Hoffmanns on a walk or to a musical concert.[23]

Marie Baum introduced Liddell to Marianne Weber, who had been one of the female leaders in the Weimar Government and who was the widow of the renowned sociologist Max Weber. A sociologist herself, Marianne

Weber wrote and spoke about the place of women in society. After her husband's death in 1920, she fell into a deep depression for about four years. Afterwards, she resumed her public speaking about the status of women and began organizing and promoting her husband's work.

Liddell described a meeting that she and Baum attended in Marianne Weber's apartment. There were small tables set up for the social time before the lecture. Weber served tea, cakes, and cigarettes. After an hour, she had the small tables removed, one large table for the speaker added, and the windows closed to keep out the street noise. Thus, cigarette smoke filled the room. On that day, the speaker was a German professor who had just returned from the University of Wisconsin. He critiqued American universities. Liddell responded that she thought his critique was reasonable. Next, everyone commented. The whole affair lasted three and a half hours. Liddell attended the weekly Weber meetings several times. Ernst Hoffmann occasionally attended these meetings.[24]

One evening in early July, Liddell attended a concert by a famous organist, who was an authority on Bach. In addition, he had a PhD in theology and a MD and was a visiting lecturer at the University of Oxford. Yet, he spent most of his life in Africa at a mission hospital, which he founded. The organist was Dr. Albert Schweitzer. His concerts were fundraising events for his hospital or other mission work. Although Schweitzer achieved significant accomplishments in the fields of music, theology, and medicine, his African mission work became his best-remembered legacy. Liddell was so impressed with Schweitzer's character and work that she felt her accomplishments had amounted to little.[25]

In the same week that Liddell attended the Schweitzer concert, she finished the first draft of her discussion of Cusanus. She remarked, "The whole thing will have to be worked over and then edited and polished off and copied, but at least I have a working summary. Next I shall write the biographical sketch—not much, just enough to serve as an introduction to the public, and then I shall put the two together."[26]

During this time in Heidelberg, Anna Forbes Liddell wrote a three-page letter that would be published in the *Journal of Philosophy*. The letter, entitled, "Communication with Regard to the Cusanus Commission of the Heidelberg Academie der Wissenschaften," was her first published work on Cusanus. In the letter, Liddell discussed the failure of historians to recognize the contributions of Nicholas of Cusa. She stated that he was a prominent Catholic theologian in his time. While many of his beliefs were questioned during his lifetime, they would be considered heretical a century later by the Catholic orthodoxy. In theology, Cusanus stated that there is only one God and that all religions contain some truth even if they are inadequate. He even tried to reconcile the Koran with Christianity. In astronomy, Cusanus wrote that the earth is not the center of the universe and that all heavenly bodies move in an orbit that is not a perfect circle. The earth appears to us to be the center of the universe because the earth is our focal point. His writing was before the that of Johann Kepler and Galileo Galilei. Liddell suggested that perhaps the Catholic Church ignored his works rather than attack a Church leader who had been a staunch supporter of Pope Eugene IV. Or perhaps, his works were no longer popular in the next century. In either case, his works slipped into obscurity. Liddell pointed out that Cusanus had been cited by Giordano Bruno, Johann Kepler, and Leonardi da Vinci. The last section of her letter discussed the work of the Heidelberg Academie der Wissenschaften to revive interest in Cusanus.[27]

Liddell left Heidelberg on August 7, 1932, for three days of sightseeing in Frankfurt before meeting her uncle Robert Ogden in Hamburg. After sightseeing in Hamburg, they both went to Copenhagen to attend the Tenth International Congress of Psychology where they met many distinguished academics from Europe and the United States. The opening of the Congress was a ceremonious event since the King of Denmark was present. Congress attendees enjoyed exclusive sightseeing trips to the opera house, the city hall, a seaside resort, and private homes, in addition to free admission to Trivoli Gardens. Interviewed three years later, Liddell said of

Copenhagen, "It is very beautiful with its handsome red brick buildings, wonderful flowers, well kept lawns and streets. The display of goods of all kinds in the stores was the perfection of artisty [*sic*] and the window arrangements were indescribably lovely—in fact, it is the only city I ever visited where I wanted everything I saw in the shop windows."[28]

Liddell returned to the United States in early September. In November, Ernst Hoffmann wrote to Liddell:

> As often as my wife and I walk along Hauserstrasse [street name], the Haus Drach [Drach house] always appears lonely to us, because we can no longer expect the front door to open and for you to join us, so the three of us might take a stroll together. It was wonderful with you and we've come to hold you dear in our hearts.
>
> The month of August brought along a surprise for Cusanus: A long rumored and missing script of the *Docta ignorantia* appeared in an Austrian monastery. I sent Klibansky there; luckily the variations were few, but they still had to be inserted/integrated into the already printed *Docta ignor.*, which delayed publication a bit. But now, the printing is finally completed.[29]

While in Germany, Liddell had fretted about conditions back home because of the economic depression. She had worried that her brother-in-law, Dexter McBride, might lose his bookkeeping job at the textile mill, which was laying off workers and cutting the salaries of those still employed. She even had a nightmare that she had lost her job, although she had already received her reappointment for the 1932–1933 school year at the same salary. Besides her FSCW salary, Liddell had income from Rawley Myer's estate and from her duplex rentals. However, she was going to have to lower what she charged as rent since rent prices had dropped sharply in Tallahassee.[30]

Liddell also missed the summer 1932 wedding of Mary Call Darby and Thomas LeRoy Collins. The couple met when they were both students at Leon High School in Tallahassee. Four months before the wedding, Mary Call Darby moved into the home of Ephraim and Bess Brevard after the death of her mother, Jane Darby. Although Mary Call had dropped out of Florida State College for Women when her mother became ill with cancer, she returned to college to complete her bachelor's degree after the wedding. Finishing a degree after marrying was not typical at that time, but Mary Call had promised her mother she would do so.[31] Mary Call Darby Collins never took a course from Liddell. She had planned to do so, but after hearing her family and friends talk about how difficult Liddell's courses were, she changed her mind. Years later, she regretted not having taken the course, because she knew everyone who took a course from Liddell vividly remembered the course and the professor.[32]

Advancing (1933-1939)

In the 1932 US presidential election, Franklin Delano Roosevelt (FDR) had a landslide victory (472 of the 531 electoral votes) over the incumbent President Herbert Hoover. Hoover's rugged individualist philosophy led to his belief that the federal government should not regulate the economy or provide economic relief to citizens. Two years into the Great Depression, he thought the country was experiencing only a temporary mild recession that would soon end. Thus, he only enacted temporary economic relief programs.[1]

Roosevelt campaigned on two issues: jobs and liquor. People wanted something done about the economy, and they were tired of the prohibition of alcohol. FDR offered his New Deal policies as a fix to stabilize the economy and promised to repeal prohibition.

Anna Forbes Liddell had voted for Hoover, because she had not thought the country needed to change leadership amid the Great Depression. Once Roosevelt won, she fully supported his leadership and hoped that his policies would improve the economy.[2]

In 1933, the US economy was in its lowest point during the Great Depression that ran from 1929 through 1939. Fifteen million people were unemployed compared to 1930 when only four million people were unemployed. Runs on banks began in 1931; by 1933, almost half of the banks had closed, and banks that were still open were in danger of closing. A severe drought in 1930 created the Dust Bowl from Texas to Nebraska. Dust storms killed people, animals, and crops. Because farmers could not afford to harvest their crops, crops rotted in the fields, while hungry people formed long lines at soup kitchens and bread lines. Families fled their farms.[3]

Anna Forbes Liddell wrote to her cousin Vinton Pickens in February 1933:

> Conditions in America don't seem to be picking up. I have about two or three men a week coming by looking for work. Usually they seem in earnest. I rarely can do anything more than give them a sandwich, a cup of coffee, and a 25¢ job, not always even a little job like that. I always feed them. Most of them have been decent white workmen. The one today was an electrician, from Wilson NC. We had a long talk. His sister-in-law is a student at N.C.C.W. [North Carolina College for Women], but if he can't get work soon, he'll have to have her come home.[4]

In February 1933, between the November 1932 election and the March 4, 1933, presidential inauguration, Congress passed a proposed amendment to the US Constitution, which repealed the prohibition of alcohol. The states quickly ratified the proposed amendment, and it became the Twenty-first Amendment to the US Constitution later that year.

In the 1932 elections, the Democrat Party increased its majority in the House and gained control of the Senate. With a Congress favorable to his ideas, FDR could get his policies passed quickly into law, which allowed him to accomplish much in his first one hundred days in office, which spanned from March 4 to June 11, 1933. On March 12, Roosevelt had the first of his cozy radio fireside chats, in which he calmed the nation's fears and delivered one of his most famous quotes, "the only thing we have to fear is fear itself." By the end of March 1933 (first 28 days), 75 percent of the banks that had closed had reopened after a four-day bank holiday and the passage of the Emergency Banking Act. During the administration's first 100 days, legislation created the Tennessee Valley Authority and the Public Works Administration. Congress also passed bills that boosted the price of agricultural products, reduced surpluses of those same products, gave workers the right to unionize, and suspended antitrust laws. On Roosevelt's 105th day in office (June 16), he signed into law the Banking Act of 1933, which created the Federal Deposit Insurance Corporation (FDIC) and introduced other banking reforms. By the end of July 1933, Liddell was already seeing fewer men coming to her back door asking for work, although there were still many people unemployed.[5]

Despite the New Deal reforms, the unemployment rate hovered at 20 percent even as late as 1935 (down from 25 percent in 1933). People were worried and angry. Thus, Roosevelt launched his Second New Deal in 1935, which created the Works Progress Administration (WPA) and the National Labor Relations Board. The WPA provided jobs. In August 1935, FDR signed the Social Security Act into law. In 1936, FDR won reelection for a second term in office with an even greater margin of victory that he had four years earlier. He garnered 523 of the 531 electoral votes against his challenger, Alfred Landon.

The economy remained unstable. Factory workers organized into unions. In December 1936, a United Auto Workers strike lasted forty-four days and affected 150,000 workers in thirty-five cities. By 1937, there were 8 million union members among the various industries. In 1937, the economy worsened when Roosevelt reduced federal subsidies to balance the federal budget. The Great Depression lasted until 1940, when the country increased defense spending as war raged in Europe and Asia.

The Great Depression did not affect everyone the same because of systemic gender and racial segregation of jobs. Jobs were still categorized as men's jobs or women's jobs. Ninety percent of jobs for White women were in nursing, teaching, or civil service. Black and Hispanic women were limited mainly to domestic work. The number of women employed actually increased by 2.5 million during the Great Depression. Fewer women than men lost their jobs because women's jobs were less likely to be eliminated. The government expansion under the New Deal created thousands of clerical jobs filled mainly by White women. Because the marriage rate declined by 22 percent during the 1930s, there were more single women who needed to support themselves.[6]

Women faced competition with men for teaching jobs. Schools counseled women to study feminine fields such as home economics or home design to avoid competition with men. The percentage of working women who were in professional positions fell from 14.2 to 12.3 percent during the Depression. Discrimination continued against women in the medical and legal professions. Medical schools limited female students to 5 percent of the enrollment. Women could not join the New York Bar Association until 1937.[7]

Women were also paid less than men for their work. Black women fared worse than White women. Domestic workers, mainly Black women, often had their already low wages further reduced during the Depression. In industrial jobs, women were paid 50 to 65 percent of what a man earned. Some of this disparity was rationalized by the fact that women and men generally did different work. However, even when men and women did the same work, the men usually earned more. For example, in 1937, in a New York box factory, a male finisher earned $35.50 a week, whereas a female finisher earned $17.83 a week. In 1939, male social workers earned $1,718 annually, compared with $1,442 for female social workers.[8]

The economic protections of the New Deal programs differed among employment groups. The Social Security Act excluded farm and domestic workers. The National Recovery Administration adopted lower pay for women's jobs for its wage codes. The Works Progress Administration created jobs that were segregated by gender and that provided lower pay for women's jobs.

Yet women did progress in public policy making under the Roosevelt administration, primarily due to the influence that Eleanor Roosevelt, the first lady, had on her husband. FDR appointed Frances Perkins as US Secretary of Labor, making her the first woman to hold a Cabinet position. In addition, FDR appointed Ruth Bryan Owen (known as Ruth Bryan Owen Rohde after marriage) as ambassador to Denmark. She was the first female US ambassador. FDR also appointed Florence Allen as a US Circuit Court judge. She was only the second woman appointed to a federal judgeship. Later, she became the first woman to serve on a state supreme court (Ohio). Several other women held executive positions in New Deal Agencies.

When the Great Depression began, many people thought married women should not work outside the home. Many still believed that married women worked only to provide luxuries for their families and that their employment would take a job away from a man who was supporting his family. That belief persisted even though a wife's salary was often essential income and even though most women worked in different jobs than men.

Even women who had achieved positions of political influence supported the idea that it was wrong for married women to work. California Congresswoman Florence Kahn, who won her husband's congressional seat after his death, said that a married woman's place was in the home and not in the workplace. Frances Perkins said married women who worked were selfish and should be ashamed.

There was even a law that restricted the employment of married women in the federal government. The Federal Economy Act of 1932 required that if a married couple both had federal government jobs, one had to quit or be fired. Usually, it was the wife who left her job since her pay was typically lower. Beginning in 1933, married women with federal jobs were required to use their husband's last name as their last name, thus preventing them from circumventing the Federal Economy Act.[9]

State and other local governments and private businesses followed the lead of the federal government in restricting the employment of married women. Seventy-five percent of school boards would not hire a married woman as a teacher. By 1939, half of the state legislatures had bills introduced to prohibit any married woman from working regardless of whether her husband was employed.[10]

Black Americans made some progress in federal employment during the depression. FDR appointed Mary McLeod Bethune as Director of the Division of Negro Affairs of the National Youth Administration, making her the first Black woman to lead a federal agency. The daughter of former slaves, she was a renowned civil rights advocate and educator (founder and first President of Bethune-Cookman University). FDR eventually appointed over 100 Black advisors on race in federal agencies. These advisors formed an informal *Black Cabinet* that Bethune led. The influence of the advisors varied among the agencies. Although the issue of race was often recognized, New Deal programs had no civil rights initiatives.[11]

State governments experienced revenue shortfalls throughout the Great Depression years. Florida State College for Women (FSCW) professors worried about layoffs and salary cuts. In 1933, Liddell noted:

> My job is safe for another year, but I think I am in for a little cut. We all are, and some people are being let out entirely. It is hard, but unavoidable. I feel somehow that if everybody put to and worked together as we did during the war we could straighten things out, but unfortunately this sort of situation doesn't seem to arouse patriotism in the same way. I think it is the time for Christian brotherhood, and I think that few of us, myself included, are doing all we can. We are all so afraid that we won't be ready for the morrow.[12]

Eleanor Scott, who lived in Liddell's duplex, was one of the FSCW faculty fired in 1933.[13] The professors who kept their jobs had their salaries reduced. Worries about job security continued throughout the decade. Liddell said in 1938, "We have reason to be afraid that there may be delayed salary payments next year. . . .The State *has* the money. It is earmarked for something else. The Governor and the Comptroller are at outs as to whether or not the money can be transferred. Many State accounts are unpaid. Thus far, salaries have come through on time and with no hitches—but we get jittery every now and then."[14] Liddell fretted whether she was investing her money wisely. She used to rely on Rawley Myer's advice for her investments and she missed that.[15]

Besides money, Liddell worried about the political division in the country. She wondered what would happen after Roosevelt's New Deal. The Communist Party of the United States of America (CPUSA) had drawn more people to it as the economy remained weak. Its membership grew from below 20,000 in 1933 to some 66,000 in 1939. Several writers, artists, and other intellectuals promoted Marxist ideas. Fifty-three American writers, including Sherwood Anderson, John Dos Passos, Langston Hughes, and Lincoln Steffens supported the CPUSA's 1932 presidential candidate William Foster. Some, like Dos Passos, later opposed communism, especially the Stalinist regime of the Soviet Union. A major focus of the CPUSA was strengthening the labor union movement. Liddell was one of the many people who wondered whether its labor activism would lead to a communist proletarian revolution. Fear that a communist revolution would overthrow democracy led some Americans to consider communism as un-American. Liddell also wondered if fascist-leaning groups would restrict labor unions and reduce workers' pay to an even lower level of economic subsistence if they gained power.[16] Fear of communism was one factor that led to mainstream acceptance of fascist ideas in the United States in the 1930s. Also important was not only the acceptance but also the promotion in the United States of racial segregation, white supremacy, and anti-Semitism.

There was no American Fascist organization identical to the German

Nazi Party. Yet several groups and prominent individuals promoted fascist values. Catholic priest, Father Charles Coughlin, ranted anti-Semitic views on his radio show, which had ratings second only to those of FDR's fireside chats. Automobile manufacturer Henry Ford was strongly anti-Semitic and anti-union. The white supremacist Ku Klux Klan (KKK) experienced a resurgence in the 1920s with between three to six million members at its peak membership. In the 1930s, the KKK still existed, but its membership declined. The KKK did not seek to overthrow the government. Instead, KKK members sought to influence policy by election to political office. In addition, the Klan terrorized and killed the targets of its hatred, which included Blacks, Jews, Roman Catholics, and foreigners. The Black Legion, which got its name because its members wore black robes instead of white ones, broke off from the KKK in 1925. In 1935, the Black Legion had between 60,000 and 100,000 members. Its most radical members sought to overthrow of the government and exterminate American Jews. Another fascist group was the American Bund, a small organization that used the swastika as its symbol and had 15,000 members of mainly German heritage.[17]

Many prominent Americans praised European fascism. Charles Lindbergh stated that Adolf Hitler was a great man. Lindbergh even attended the 1936 Olympic Games in Berlin as a guest of the Nazi Hermann Goering; he also received the Service Cross of the German Eagle in 1938. Lindbergh seriously thought about moving permanently to Germany. William Randolph Hearst portrayed a favorable opinion of Hitler through his publications. In 1937, *Fortune* (a Hearst magazine) listed the virtues of fascism as "Discipline, Duty, Courage, Glory, Sacrifice." *Reader's Digest* (a Hearst magazine) characterized Hitler as "an exceedingly able man." In 1938, *Better Homes and Gardens* (a Hearst magazine) described Hitler as a "nice, humble, personable man of taste."[18]

Even FDR's administration was soft on European fascism at times. FDR supported neither communism nor fascism in the United States. Yet, as late as 1937, the US State Department praised German and Italian fascist governments, for their anti-communist position. The department thought German and Italian fascism kept those countries open for American business expansion. Over time, FDR, however, began to see fascism as a greater threat to American capitalism than communism and worked for an improved relationship with the Soviet Union to restrain the expansion of fascism.[19]

Adding to the political divide were the anti-Roosevelt Share-Our-Wealth clubs of Huey P. Long and the pro-Roosevelt National Union for Social Justice that Father Charles Coughlin founded.[20] Liddell said of the political division in the country:

> I confess I don't know what to think, so I have sunk back into my private professional life, try to spend my own little income as wisely as I can, and to spend my days honestly and to some good purpose by sticking to my own last [staying with what one knows]. Sometimes I think our whole order is going to blow up and bust, again I think it is merely perishing by the slow process of decay. Perhaps my own life will end in a period of turmoil, perhaps I shall go quietly on scarcely realizing, excepting in a little pinch here and there how tremendous are the changes which are slowly taking place, but certainly the very major premis [*sic*] upon which our social and economic life is founded in undergoing a tremendous change. It is thrilling to be alive and watch it, even though one feels often the desire to have done with thrills.[21]

* * *

As soon as Kurt von Schleicher became German Chancellor in December 1932, Franz von Papen and Adolf Hitler joined forces to undermine his administration. On January 29, 1933, a false rumor circulated that Schleicher was going to let the military take over the government and arrest

President Hindenburg. The next day, Hindenburg appointed Adolf Hitler as Chancellor of Germany. Hitler exclaimed to his supporters, "We've done it!"[22] Hitler, however, was not yet a dictator; he was the Chancellor of a democratic republic, which consisted of twenty-three states and three city-states. Neither did the Nazi Party have a majority in the Reichstag. Hitler would use the democratic processes of the republic to undermine democracy. On his first day as Chancellor, he persuaded Hindenburg to call for new Reichstag elections on March 5, 1933.

On February 27, 1933, the Reichstag building in Berlin burned. A twenty-four-year-old anarchist, Marinus van der Lubbe, started the fire. Once Lubbe's fire started, the Nazi Storm Troopers set additional fires in the building. Nonetheless, Nazi newspapers blamed the communists for the fire. Hitler exclaimed, "The German people have been soft too long. Every Communist official must be shot. All Communist deputies must be hanged this very night. All friends of the Communists must be locked up. And that goes for the Social Democrats and the Reichsbanner [WWI veterans' organization] as well."[23]

The following day, Hitler persuaded the now extremely tired eighty-five-year-old Hindenburg to sign an emergency decree called "Presidential Decree for the Protection of People and the State." It restricted free speech, freedom of the press, and the right to assemble. Mail, telegraph, and telephone communications were no longer private. It also relaxed restrictions on search warrants and confiscation of private property and prohibited any meeting or publication against the Nazi party. It further became illegal to campaign against the Nazi Party. Even with the restriction under the emergency decree, the Nazi party won only 44 percent of the Reichstag seats in the March 5th election. Hitler sought to weaken the Reichstag, yet that would have to come later.

Under the emergency decree, with the help of the Storm Troopers, Nazi party members replaced elected local officials in Prussia, the largest German state. Next, Hitler imprisoned thousands of his political enemies in detention centers. Additional decrees further restricted personal liberty. One decree set up special courts to try political prisoners. These special courts did not have a jury or allow 'defendents' defense counsel. Judges rendered verdicts after hearing evidence only from the prosecution.

The newly elected Reichstag met on March 23, 1933, in an air of intimidation—armed Storm Troopers surrounded the legislators ready to act. The legislators voted on an Enabling Act, entitled "Law for Removing the Distress of the People and the Reich." The Act would transfer much of the powers of the Reichstag to Hitler. Before the vote, Hitler promised that, if the Act passed, he would use the new powers with restraint—only to the extent needed to end unemployment and improve relations with France, Great Britain, and the Soviet Union. He needed thirty-one non-Nazi votes for the Act to pass. Those came from the Catholic Centre Party, which Hitler had promised that he would restore some liberties that had been taken away. Of course, Hitler did not keep his promise. When the Enabling Act became law, democracy ended in Germany. President Hindenburg remained as titular head of state. This meant he kept his title as Commander-in-Chief of the army and the right to negotiate with foreign governments. Hitler controlled the rest of the government.

Hitler began ruling the German people with terror. On March 22, 1933, the day before the Enabling Act passed, the government opened Dachau, the first permanent concentration camp. The next month, Hitler set up the Gestapo, a secret police force that was above the law. It had authority to arrest, interrogate, and send a person to a concentration camp or for execution with no other judicial procedure. Telling an anti-Nazi joke, for example, was one crime that could get a person arrested. The Gestapo relied on citizen informants. People could no longer trust their co-workers, their neighbors, or their milkman. Children informed on their schoolteachers and their parents. The Gestapo sometimes used torture. People walking on the sidewalk in front of a Gestapo building could hear screams coming from inside.

Soon after the Enabling Act became law, the government began restricting sources of intellectual knowledge. On May 10, 1933, Berlin university students assisted the Storm Troopers to throw 20,000 books deemed improper into a huge bonfire. The flames devoured the works of John Dos Passos, Albert Einstein, Sigmund Freud, Ernest Hemingway, Helen Keller, Jack London, Karl Marx, Marcel Proust, Margaret Sanger, Upton Sinclair, H. G. Wells, Emile Zola, and many others. That same night, there were book burnings in eighteen other university towns. On May 17, University of Heidelberg students held a book burning. Students, Storm Troopers, and other Nazi paramilitary members marched to the bonfire site carrying torches and singing the German national anthem and the *Horst Wessel Song* (a Nazi anthem). At the site, the students gave speeches about the anti-German spirit in literature and then threw books into the fire.[24]

From 1933 through the 1935, the government 'cleansed' German universities by removing professors based on racial or political criteria. The University of Heidelberg dismissed 47 of its 189 professors who were teaching in 1932 by the end of 1935. It fired sixteen of the fifty-two philosophy professors.[25] In July 1933, Raymond Klibansky and Marie Baum were among the first purged. Klibansky had proudly affirmed that he was Jewish. He left Germany in July 1933 with only what he could carry and settled in London. During World War II, he worked with the British Political Warfare Executive (PWE), a clandestine body which distributed war-related propaganda. He gathered intelligence for the Allied invasion of Italy and persuaded the Allies not to bomb St Nikolaus Hospital in Kues, Germany (now Bernkastel-Kues, birthplace of Cusanus), which had a collection of Cusanus's manuscripts. Although a Lutheran, Marie Baum was likely fired for racial *and* political reasons. The Nazi government considered her Jewish as a descendent of the German-Jewish philosopher Moses Mendelson. Since Baum had worked in the Democratic Weimar Republic, she was also politically unacceptable to the Nazis. After her dismissal, she remained in Germany.

Before and during World War II, Baum helped German Jews slip out of the country. Because the Nazi government suspected her pro-Jewish activities, she was under daily surveillance. In 1941, a police raid confiscated many of her professional research and personal papers. None of the confiscated papers were incriminating—she carried the incriminating papers on her body. The Gestapo interrogated her several times. At an interrogation in 1941, an officer demanded to know why Baum had not left the country since she disliked the government. She replied, "Because I'm 67 years old and have always faithfully served my country." The officer let her go.[26]

Caught up in passionate nationalism, most of the University of Heidelberg faculty and students supported the faculty dismissals. Some professors, initially critical of Hitler, supported his regime once he became Chancellor. When Hitler came into power, Marianne Weber suspended her weekly open forum meetings, which Liddell had attended in 1932. She restarted the meetings with a small group of trusted intellectuals. After the war, Weber said about these meetings:

> During the whole time of the Nazi tyranny I managed to keep together a group of people holding opinions like my own, and every Sunday afternoon, as well as on other occasions, we had meetings for discussion of matters vitally important to us. We did not, however, directly deal with political matters; we restricted ourselves to philosophical, religious, and esthetic topics, making our criticism of the Nazi system between the lines, as it were. None of us were of the stuff of which martyrs are made. Perhaps this is unfair, for there is no sense of being a martyr when there is nobody to witness the martyrdom and be affected thereby. We were in no such situation as the early Christians, who were devoured by lions in public. We would have been quietly exterminated in the dark, so to speak, and with no one to witness our agony.[27]

In August 1933, Liddell received a letter from Ernst Hoffmann, which had this passage:

> It appears to me from your letter, that you have generally gained an accurate impression about Germany from the newspapers. It is an enormous, to the depths shaking, and metamorphosing revolution. With much courage toward work and with strong will toward improving our circumstance. A few, small misconceptions of yours I wish to correct: Of course, it is not forbidden to import English or American books into Germany, and it is also false, that only German books are allowed for reading, and that the foreign language ones are being burned. The book burnings were merely symbolic acts of the students against the Jewish spirit and against a type of literature, which in its dissemination to the people is being deemed as harmful. The universities are expecting a great reform this winter, but what that consists of, has not been made public. Among the Jewish colleagues that have been laid off in Heidelberg is, regretfully, Klibansky and you can imagine how infinitely difficult it is now for me to be able to discuss each individual question with him, only via correspondence to and from abroad.[28]

In November 1933, Liddell received a disturbing letter from Thea Hoffmann which said:

> About politics, you are able to read in the paper; I want to tell you only about personal matters. The conditions are splitting humanity into two camps; the fervent adherents of the new regime + those who masquerade as such (out of fear) + the Jews + those who, because of past liberalism, or because of past activities due to differing political orientation are, seen as [not legible] or not safe people. You won't be astonished to hear, that my husband was subjected to questioning in Sept. in Karlsruhe and he was accused of being hostile toward the new

state. He was able to completely invalidate these preposterous accusations, but because the time for the reappointments for the higher education institutions continues until April, it's not yet certain that he doesn't get replaced, or perhaps he will be transferred to a different place. The Cusanus room had to be dissolved.

Klibansky is now in London, where he continues to work on Cusanus. For now, the resources for him are still sufficient, that is, I believe, just until the spring. As you can see, work is being made very difficult for my husband. But he wants to continue, despite all difficulties + K. will continue to help him; only, it will progress at a slower pace. Our circle of friends is quite small, but we are together very often. The friendship with Mr. and Mrs. Rickert has unfortunately been destroyed due to the circumstances. Prof. v. Baeyer, who gave me back my health, has lost his post because his grandmother was not entirely Aryan. I do not know any other family with anywhere near as high an intellectual level. You will presumably read about it in the newspaper. To experience all of this in such proximity; calm work is hardly possible. We do not know yet if + how long we will or can stay. But hopefully one will be able to come to rest once again. Be careful, when you're writing to Germany; Not a single word about politics is best, only personal + scientific matters; that's the most important for us as well.[29]

The disturbing letters from Ernst Hoffmann continued:

January 1934. . . .We are giving this letter to our friend Gutzwiller, who will take it to the post office in Basel, as I as a Democrat, am under police surveillance and my mail is being checked. I'm faring much like you are: I too now only have a *very* small salary. And it isn't certain at all yet, whether I will keep my professorship.

Pentecost Sunday 1934. . . .It is Pentecost–but my heart is in mourning,

> in great and deep grief. I have lost my brother. He has, at fifty years old, on April 16, departed from life voluntarily. Physical illness and financial worries had made him melancholy. I have taken over the care for his wife and for his daughter. He was very close to me and my wife, our brotherly love had not dimmed for even one day during the past 50 years. . . .Your friendship makes our life more beautiful, it adds to our well-being, even in sorrow. Hopefully, in the summer, we will be fated with a reunion.[30]

In June 1934, Hitler strengthened his hold on the Nazi party and squashed any remaining political challenges in a three-day rampage of executions, called the Night of the Long Knives. Under Hitler's orders, the SS Nazi Paramilitary group (rival paramilitary group to the SA), the Gestapo, and Hermann Goring's private army executed several hundred people. The exact number executed is unknown since the relevant documents were destroyed. The SS was completely loyal to Hitler. However, the SA had always acted somewhat independent of Hitler, and its leaders now questioned his actions. Thus, the SA leaders were at the top of Hitler's list of people to be executed. Also at the top of the list was Kurt von Schleicher, who was trying to pull off a political comeback. He and his wife were executed at their home. Also executed were people who had known Hitler as he rose to power because they knew incriminating information about him.

The Night of the Long Knives shocked the foreign press corps and the German people. Hitler had acted above the law. In a two-hour speech, he admitted that he had seventy-seven people executed, but he rationalized that those executed were traitors. He said, "If anyone reproaches me and asks why I did not resort to the regular courts of justice, then all I can say is this: In this hour I was responsible for the fate of the German people, and thereby I became the supreme judge of the German people!"[31] Hitler had firmly established that he was above the law and that the SS could execute anyone upon his command.

President Hindenburg died on August 2, 1934. On the day of his death, Hitler required all soldiers to take a Hitler oath in which they swore allegiance to him instead of to their country. Next, Hitler combined the offices of President and Chancellor and appointed himself to fill that office. The German people voted overwhelming in a referendum to accept the combination of the offices. Hitler was now the dictator of Germany.[32]

In late August 1934, Liddell stopped in Heidelberg to visit briefly with the Hoffmanns before traveling to Prague for the World Congress of Philosophy held in early September. After she returned home from Prague, she received sad letters from Ernst Hoffmann:

> October 15, 1934. . . .I'm writing to you as a convalescent. When you were in Heidelberg, you may have noticed that I was at the end of my strength. I sought to hide it from you, as not to burden the short get-together with you. Then came the time in Berlin, where I was obliged to get a clear picture of the last months in the life of my unhappy brother. After everything that had preceded it and the amount of work-related exhaustion in the summer, it was too much. At the sea I experienced an utter nervous breakdown. Bloodletting, absolute rest, and diet have helped me a lot; the doctor says that if the recovery continues to progress like this, I will be healthy again by November. I will await it calmly.

> December 19, 1934. . . .Since I've had your dear and friendly letter for a long time now, and I still haven't replied back, you may have already thought that I am still sick; and that is indeed the case. But life-threatening danger no longer exists. But writing is becoming a difficulty for me, as the blood stagnation occurs rather easily while writing. But my deepest gratitude shall not remain locked in my heart forever: I was profoundly joyed by your words, every last one of them. On your birthday we made our journey to you, unfortunately only in spirit, and

we presented you with many loving wishes. . . .From me you will receive three works: No. 1.) Platonism and Mysticism, No. 2.) Show of the Gods in Eckhart and Cusanus, No. 3.) Platonism in Augustine's philosophy of history. All three are in print. From you, I hope to receive your wonderful seminar paper on philosophy and religion. Live well, very dear Liddellchen [the addition of *chen* makes the name a title of endearment.]. *Par aspera ad astra* [through hardships to the stars] are good words. Let's hope together that we may see each other again.

February 5, 1935. . . .I'm able to work again and I'm progressing.

My treatise is now finally finished, but it has become a book, and you will be reading it for a long time, you poor dear Miss Liddellchen.

In the lecture, I said that the first concept of infinity did not come about when the pre-Socrates called the largest whole of the universe infinite, but that instead the Hellenistic philosophers discovered the infinitesimally smallest of the creative minimum. With that, I thought of the dear Liddellchen: quantity so small, quality so great![33]

On December 5, 1935, the German government issued this press release, "On his own request, full professor for Philosophy and pedagogy at the University of Heidelberg, Dr. Ernst Hoffmann was released from his official duties." The press release contained this biographical sketch of Hoffmann:

Ernst Hoffmann, who was born in 1880 in Berlin and has taught in Heidelberg since 1922, is first and foremost a preeminent historian of philosophy whose exceptional accomplishments are focused on the form and interpretation of Greek philosophy, as well as on the philological creation of the compositions of Nicolas Cusanus, the publication for which he is owed thanks. Philosophically he is closely

> aligned with that form of neo-Kantianism, which is closely tied to the name of Ernst Kassirer. To each one who ever listened to Hoffmann, in particular the many who have been his students, the vigorous thoroughness of his lectures, permitted by his manner of speaking, the philological solidity and the memorable orderliness with which the material was elucidated, remain unforgettable.[34]

Researcher Stephen P. Remy has included Ernst Hoffmann in a list of professors dismissed for racial reasons.[35] It is clear from Hoffmann's letters to Liddell that he did not identify as Jewish. However, the Nazi regime may have considered him as such. In addition, his political affiliation with the social democrats and his intellectual work clearly made him unacceptable to the government.

Hoffmann now worked on his Cusanus translations at home. His stress lessened since he no longer had to teach and he was not as harassed by the Nazi government. He wrote this passage to Liddell:

> October 20, 1936. . . .In April of this year I was in Sweden with my wife. I was invited, in Goteburg, Stockholm, Uppsala, to hold lectures about Plato, Cusanus, and Kepler. The lectures found much approval and I was invited to write an article for the Swedish journal *Theoria* for which I was asked to construct my point of view of the "issue of the historic philosophical method." I have now completed it. It is supposed to be printed in January. It is the first time that I have talked in principle about the meaning of our work. If I receive any Separata [offprint], then the dear Liddellchen will receive one as well.
>
> What Cusanus knew about Plato? I believe, as an old man he may well have known everything of Plato's. Because he had a close friendship with the Florentine Platonists, therefore had access to Plato's writings, and he was called "Il grande Platonista" by the Italians. What is more,

> he knew of Plato's Theory of Forms in *Diogenes Laertios* and the rich scholastic orthographic literature about Plato's teachings, which still today are in the libraries in handwritten form and have never been printed. Aristotle, he appears to only have studied as a young man in the scholastic sense, and with the scholastic commentaries.[36]

During these unsettling times, Ernst and Thea Hoffmann took comfort in the beauty of nature and architecture and in the strength of friendship. Thea wrote poetically to Liddell in February 1935, "This winter, Heidelberg lies dressed like a vain woman, in completely snow-covered dress. . . .it was gloriously splendidly snow-covered, fine powdery snow let all the ski-hearts beat faster." Five months later, while on a retreat for Ernst's health, Thea wrote this passage about the beauty of a mountain village, "One must always and again be astonished at the magnificent architecture, every farmhouse resembles a castle with its thick walls, an innate sense of beauty is reflected in quirky alcoves, or a balcony—or window grates. It all appears so cheerful, peaceful, freeing, that we have the feeling of bringing home new strength—[plus] how much we will have in need of it!" Ernst wrote to Liddell in May 1937, "Yes, dear friend, the chestnuts are blooming, the Neckar Valley flaunts its shining beauty in full luster, and *we have a deep yearning for our Liddellchen*." Thea Hoffmann wrote on the bottom of her husband's letter, "We miss you, you should be, at this moment, be sitting with us in our dining room, where the sun-flooded green wilderness of the neglected garden looks in—it's like a fairytale, so surreally beautiful."[37] In November 1938, Ernst Hoffmann wrote, "My wife and I continue to live our quiet and reclusive life here. Quiet work, a small, intimate circle of friends, and wonderful memories make our life a happy one. For you, you dear and good friend, we always have longing. Hopefully, a reunion with you is to be granted."[38]

* * *

Liddell calmed her stress about economics and politics in both the United States and Germany by joining the national craze over jigsaw puzzles. When the Great Depression started in 1929, people, who were no longer able to afford a night of entertainment on the town, stayed at home assembling puzzles. Skilled artisans produced puzzles in their homes to sell or rent. Drugstores and libraries rented puzzles for three to ten cents per day. Mass production of cheaper puzzles began when manufacturers switched from wood to die-cut cardboard. Advertisers gave free puzzles to customers who bought their product. In 1932, newsstands began selling puzzle series with a new puzzle available each week. In 1933, ten million puzzles were sold weekly.[39]

Liddell put together four or five puzzles until she noticed she had to add just one more piece before she could leave for class or a meeting; and she had to add just one more piece before she could settle down to work on her translation of Cusanus's work. After that piece, there was just one more piece that beckoned her. The puzzle had become an addiction. It robbed her of getting things done, as her martinis and cigarettes did not. Liddell taught her students that they were responsible for their choices in life. Now she realized she had to take charge of how she used her time. She reluctantly gave up jigsaw puzzles and threw herself into sorting out Latin syntax for her translation, an activity not as addictive as assembling puzzles. Her strategy of working on her Cusanus translation to reduce stress succeeded—her worries about her family, friends, and county went away for brief periods of time, and she made excellent progress on her translation.[40]

From 1933 through 1939, Liddell not only worked on her translation, she also wrote journal articles and presented papers at professional conferences. In 1932, the members of the Southern Society of Philosophy and Psychology (SSPP) elected her as President for the 1933 year. She accordingly presided over the 1933 conference held in Washington, DC. and gave the presidential address on "Instructed Ignorance, The Philosophy of Nicholas of Cusa," her first presentation on the philosopher.[41] Liddell's address started with the phrase "to know is the being of the intellectual soul, and the desire to know is its life." The phase was her English translation of a phrase Cusanus wrote in Latin. She then expounded on the limitations of thought. She said, "We can not examine any datum without assuming its presence in experience. The intellect intuits the whole which it does not comprehend. Instructed ignorance makes proper use of the intellectual intuition, or faith. In dealing with any question we make those inferences which seem to us reasonable. Thought has faith in itself." She ended her address with the implication for Christian faith. She said, "The life of the spirit is the desire to know. In Christ the desire and the end are one. And those who follow Him, who live by faith in the love of truth, shall share in the immortal life of the spirit, eternally desiring to know, and eternally satisfied in their desire."[42]

In 1934, Liddell chaired the philosophers' program of the Southern Society of Philosophy and Psychology Conference and presented a paper, "A Basis of Modern Ethics."[43] Also in 1934, Liddell gave a presentation at the World Congress of Philosophy in Prague. She was the first woman from the Southern United States to do so. Her paper, "Philosophy and Religion," was presented in a large auditorium to hundreds of philosophers from around the world. One can imagine her walking upon the stage with accommodations made for her short stature. Was there a pause in the program as they lowered the microphone or provided a box for her to stand on? She wrote about her presentation, "Thank God my own paper is over. . . .I wasn't nervous, and rather enjoyed reading it. The discussion later was harder, for some of it was in French and German and I was not perfectly certain that I followed all of it."[44]

In 1935, Liddell attended the meeting of the Southern Society of Philosophy and Psychology and represented Florida State College for Women at the Eastern Division of the American Philosophical Society annual meeting. In 1936, Liddell published, "The Relation of Philosophy to Religion" in *The Personalist.* She presented "The Knowledge and Use of Aristotle Displayed by Nicholas of Cusa in '*De Docta Ignorantia*'" at the 1936 SSPP annual meeting and "God and the Cosmos in the Philosophy of Nicholas of Cusa" at the 1937 SSPP annual meeting.[45]

Liddell maintained her professional relationship and personal friendship with Horace Williams. When Williams learned the SSPP had elected her president for the 1933 year, he wrote to her, "If all one's friends were as you there would be no need of retiring to heaven. I did not suppose the Southern Society was so discriminating. I congratulate the body."[46] Another time Williams wrote to her, "[I] took my case to Saint Peter. Man alive said He, Don't come to me. I had no end of trouble with Philosophers. Spinoza was difficult. Hegel was worse. But I never dreamed that women would profess Philosophy. A brilliant woman, alas I am not equal to them. When they add Philosophy I throw up the case."[47] In Williams's autobiography, he noted Liddell's 1934 presentation to the World Congress was evidence that the decision by the University of North Carolina to admit women students was good. Concerning the opposition to the admission of women, he said, "but the women came and have justified the action."[48] Yet, he followed that opinion in his autobiography with this one, "Girls make good students. But they lack the fine sense of honor that mark our boys."[49]

That opinion shows the complexity of stereotypes. It is clear that Williams thought that Liddell and other women he knew were honorable. Yet the unexamined stereotype persisted through confirmation bias. People use stereotypes to respond quickly to a stranger who is not like themselves—to decide if the stranger is safe—to decide whether to stay, flee, or fight. Yet, people may not apply the stereotype to people they know who do not fit the stereotype. They respond to those people as individuals.

Liddell must have written to Williams about the difficulty of her work and her frustrations with it. He wrote back encouragingly, "I am pleased that you are dissatisfied with your work this fall. To be in a process and be content is to be an insect. . . .I should be glad to fly to Tallahassee, to embrace the dearest of women, to sit and listen to her golden words,"[50] Another time he wrote, "You must have a vacation. Loaf, swim, sleep, loaf, swim, sleep, and then loaf some more. What is the value of fame with health gone?"[51]

* * *

Enrollment at Florida State College for Women (FSCW) did not drop significantly during the Great Depression. What changed was how students paid for their education. In 1931, 409 students applied for financial aid, up from 55 students the year before. After 1934, many students had campus jobs through funds provided by the Federal Emergency Relief Administration and the National Youth Administration.[52]

Professors saw many students on campus they did not know, whereas before the 1930s, professors knew most of the students. Informal interactions outside the classroom between professors and students accordingly became less common.[53] Anna Forbes Liddell, however, still invited students to her home for dinner and conversation.

In the early part of the 1930s, the social restrictions for students at FSCS remained some of the most restrictive in the country. Societal attitudes, however, had changed. Many behaviors restricted by the college were ones the women could do freely at home. In 1932, a FSCW biology professor, Alban Stewart, visited six women's colleges and spoke with the Dean of Students at each. The colleges were Smith, Simmons, Wellesley, Mt. Holyoke, Radcliff, and Goucher. These six colleges had a combined enrollment of 7,994. They had dismissed only six students for breaking the social conduct rules in 1931–1932. None of the dismissals had been for riding in cars with men. For the same year, FSCW with an enrollment of 1,776 had dismissed 18 students with 15 of the dismissals for infractions of the rules about riding in cars with men. The six comparison colleges did not allow students to smoke openly, but provided pleasant places for the students to smoke. FSCW allowed students to smoke only outside a particular dormitory. If a student smoked anywhere else, she could be placed on restrictions for four to six weeks. Based on his survey, Stewart recommended that FSCW revise its rigid social conduct rules.[54]

In 1934, after Olivia Dorman became Dean of Students, she relaxed some of the rules. Students could now smoke in designated smoking lounges. The lights-out time changed from 10:35 to 11:30 pm. Rules about riding in cars with men were also relaxed, though they were still strict. Rules on dancing with men were also relaxed, but it was hard for the women to find men as dance partners, since there were no men enrolled However, any conversation with a man longer than ten minutes was still considered a date, and, except for seniors, the number of dates allowed was still limited. The college continued to maintain a list of men that the women could not date.[55]

In the mid-1930s, Dean of Arts and Science William Dodd revamped the curriculum by extending several two-year programs to four-year programs. In the 1935–1936 school year, he added four integrated courses that surveyed the fields of biology, physical science, humanities, and social studies. These courses were required for freshmen and sophomore students to ensure that all students had a basic liberal arts education, regardless of their major field of study.[56] Liddell taught humanities and English composition classes for the integrated courses. Another academic change for the 1935–1936 school year also affected Liddell. The Department of Philosophy was renamed as the Department of Philosophy and Religion. Robert Miller was hired as Assistant Professor; Liddell remained the Department Chair. Five religion courses were added. There remained five philosophy courses with *History of Philosophy* dropped and *Adventures in Thought* added. The new humanities integrated course was cross-referenced in the Philosophy curriculum. Dropping the history of philosophy course did not remove content because the essential material was now covered in the integrated course. Instead, all students in the college would now have an introduction to philosophy and exposure to the excellent teaching of Liddell.[57] Carolyn Gaines, a student in one of Liddell's classes in summer school in 1937, reminisced in 2006 about her experience in an integrated course:

> We [Carolyn Gaines and her sister] didn't take her [Liddell's] course, which was philosophy, but she taught one of those introductory compulsory courses in English. And it required that [*sic*] a lot of basic grammar and writing skills. But she was a *good* teacher. It didn't matter what she was teaching. I thought that if I ever came back to winter school and had a chance to elect some course that I would like to add a course in philosophy from her because she was such a scholar and such an educated person. Anything she taught was worth taking. . . .You worked hard from sitting in any class she taught. Because she was a real scholar and a wise person. And she was very smart. I think she was smarter than we knew. . . .But she packed a wallop in her soul. Everybody thought that way about her. . . .She would sometimes invite people over [to her home] and have cocktails or something with her. I never had a chance to go because I worked in the dining room.[58]

As FSCW expanded and added depth to its curriculum in the 1930s, it enhanced its reputation for intellectual excellence. It installed the first Phi Beta Kappa chapter (Alpha Chapter) in Florida in March 1936. The University of Florida, the men's college in Gainesville, would have to settle for the Beta Chapter three years later.[59]

FSCS expected faculty members to be involved in college life as faculty advisors and to be active in local civic organizations. As head of the Philosophy and Religious Studies Department, Liddell felt compelled to involve herself in everything religious, not just Christian, occurring on or off campus in Tallahassee. She was the faculty sponsor for the campus

Jewish student organization and for the campus Young Women's Christian Association. She was a college representative on the Religious Workers council, a local group that included Tallahassee ministers. Liddell was also the faculty sponsor for the annual Religious Week, in which an invited speaker gave a talk each weekday of the weeklong event. After the talk, the speaker presided over an open forum that covered topics, such as "Does God Care?," "Is the Universe Friendly?," "What of Leisure Time?," and "Why are we here?"[60]

Liddell was an Episcopalian from the time she came to Tallahassee until her death. During her lifetime, women could not hold mainstream leadership roles in the Episcopal Church. Instead, they did their church work through the Women's Auxiliary, which by its very name signified that it was a secondary organization. Liddell was as active in the Episcopal Church as allowed—she held offices in the Fifth District Women's Auxiliary.[61]

When Liddell came to Tallahassee, she attended the downtown St. John's Episcopal Church with Ephraim and Bess Brevard. After the Ruge Hall Episcopal Student Center was built on the campus in 1931 down the street from her house, she began attending services at the Chapel of the Resurrection there. Liddell gained a reputation for being quite a character at Ruge Hall. Rector George Bedell remembered that Liddell would give him a grade for his sermon as she left the service. Lex Matthews was chaplain at Ruge Hall when Liddell became older. One day, the tip of her walking cane came off. For a temporary fix, Matthews put a champagne cork on the end of her cane. He thought it was endearing that she continued to use the cane tipped with a cork. Once, Matthews put up stakes and strings to keep students from making walking paths in the grass. He found Liddell swinging her cork-tipped cane to knock over the stakes. She said, "We are trying to get people in the church, not keep them out." [62] Judy Matthews, the Chaplin's wife, remembered that during a church discussion on the budget, Liddell said, "I just want to say one thing. Whenever we have a service at this church, we ought to pass the plate. We should not have any service here without passing the plate." Matthews continued, "And so we all got a kick out of that. Now I think about that every time I go to a service and for some reason they don't ask for an offering." Judy Matthews remembered Liddell fondly saying:

> She had that brilliant mind and she could engage anyone in conversation of an intellectual level. . .as deep as anyone wanted to go. But yet, she was also an excellent conversationalist and could talk about anything with anybody. She was one of those people that could speak, be speaking with a brilliant boring educated person on one side and have a stifling run-of-the-mill person on the other side. She could speak with both kinds. . . .I just remember there always being a smile on her face and [she was] fun to be with.[63]

Liddell's fellow parishioners recognized the wisdom and intellect packed into her short frame—a frame so short that her feet dangled when she sat in a pew. Paul Picard was taller when he kneeled than Liddell was when she stood. One day when he was kneeling, he looked down at her and said, "Kneeling or standing, I'll never be as tall as you, Anna Forbes Liddell."[64] Everyone who met Liddell noticed the large personality and remarkable intellect of a person no taller than a child. One day, as she left the beauty shop, her beautician remarked, "My! But she's little outside to be so big inside."[65]

At the Tallahassee Branch of the American Association of University Women (AAUW), Liddell networked with women like herself. She served as president for the 1935–1936 program year. The membership included many notable FSCW administrators and faculty members, such as Dean of Students Olivia Dorman, History Department Chair Kathryn Abbey, and Political Science Professor Bessie Carter Randolph, who later became the third president of Hollins University in Roanoke, Virginia.

As trailblazers, most AAUW members were not living the lives of their mothers—they had few women role models to follow. Yet, like women who chose a traditional path, these women also had laundry to do, meals to cook, clothing to mend, and letters to write in addition to their professional obligations. Many were university professors, who, at the end of the day, still had student papers to grade and stacks of professional books to read. Liddell was often discouraged at the many things she left undone.[66] Meeting with other women like herself was more than just socializing over tea and cookies. On some occasions, going to another AAUW meeting may have felt like just another obligation to meet, but more often, it likely felt renewing and recharging, especially when the group worked to help younger women realize their dreams.

In 1929, the national AAUW surveyed the 500 graduate fellowships and scholarships open nationally to women. Even $1,000 a year was not enough for a woman to study without financial worry. The survey found that only 80 of the stipends provided $1,000 or more. About half were for less than $500. Tallahassee branch members raised money for the national association's Million Dollar Fellowship Fund and for their own local fund, which provided a loan for graduate education. A recipient paid back the loan after becoming established in her field.[67]

The monthly programs of the Tallahassee Branch of AAUW varied from social networking to serious studies of art, music, literature, and current issues. Located in Florida's capital city, the Branch brought in state leaders as speakers for public forums, such as Florida Superintendent of Schools Colin English, who talked about upcoming Florida legislative issues. The Branch also brought in out-of-town speakers. These speakers included Will Durant (author and historian), Jessie B. Rittenhouse (author of anthologies of modern poetry), and Richard Halliburton (travel author). FSCW provided speakers who were experts in their field—some were members of the Branch. The topics of these forums and meetings covered a wide range of topics, such as the Hitler regime in Germany, factors of the current economic situation, the Italian-Ethiopian controversy, the tax system in Florida, underlying causes of the Sino-Japanese war, and the history of chamber music. Members discussed how the status of Florida women had changed little since the nineteenth century. The rights of women still varied by state. In Florida, women could not yet serve on a jury. Nor could a married woman enter into a contract or sell property without her husband's permission. In case of divorce, the court gave the father preference for custody of the children.[68]

* * *

Toward the end of the 1930s, Anna Forbes Liddell worried about her parents and aunts who were in their seventies or eighties. After her uncle Thomas Franklin died in 1926, his widow Luella lived with her sister, Eva Liddell. In 1937, when it became harder for the two women to manage a household alone, they moved in with Walter and Nellie Liddell. In 1939, Luella Franklin died.

Before the stock market crash in October 1929, Liddell's Aunt Jane Battle had enough wealth that she never had to live on a budget. After the crash, she was still wealthy, but now had to make choices among potential expenditures. She chose to provide education and experiences for her granddaughters and for her nieces and nephew. Liddell also helped with the college expenses of the McBride children: Walter, Helen-Aline, Mary Anna, and Eva.[69]

In 1937, Helen-Aline McBride graduated from St. Mary's College with the equivalent of an AA degree. She then enrolled in Florida State College for Women for the additional two years for a bachelor's degree. Anna Forbes Liddell now had what she never had before—a house full of young people. She had invited her students to parties for years, but this was different. Helen-Aline and her Chi Omega sorority sisters dropped by several times a week, with or without an invitation. They filled Liddell's home with laughter, gossip, and the hopes of young women and with flirtations and young love when boyfriends came for dinner.[70]

Liddell remained young at heart. Yet she did not romanticize youth. She remembered her own struggles with finding her path in life. She said, "People talk about the joy of youth. I don't think it is a true description. Young people suffer so much that if they weren't strong they couldn't endure it. They have to learn to live, and it is hard."[71]

Helen-Aline McBride graduated from FSCW in 1939. She reminisced in 2006, "When I graduated from college, she [Liddell] gave me a trip to Europe as a graduation present which was one of the highlights of my life because World War II started the month after we got home and it was a long time before anyone went to Europe again just to sightsee." The trip was a six-week tour for young people of most of the countries of Europe. The group would be in Germany for two or three days and would stay one day in Heidelberg. Since it was also Mary Anna McBride's birthday and she had just graduated from high school, Liddell paid for her to go on the trip with her sister.[72]

Liddell worried about sending her nieces to Europe when everyone thought Germany would soon start a war. The family story says that Liddell consulted with a history professor at FSCW about the prospects of war breaking out when the young people would be in Europe. The professor reassured her that it would be safe because war would not break out until after the harvesting of the crops. The history professor likely was Kathryn Abbey, since Abbey had lived in the duplex with Liddell since 1927.[73] Before Helen-Aline and Mary Anna left for their trip, Liddell told them that the Germans would greet them by yelling, "Heil Hitler!" In jest, she said for them to respond by yelling, "Rah, Roosevelt!"[74]

While in Heidelberg, Helen-Aline and Mary Anna visited with Ernst and Thea Hoffmann. Most of the communication was by short phrases and pantomime, since the McBrides did not speak German and the Hoffmanns' English was not much better than when Liddell had visited them. The tour group returned to the New York on July 30, 1939.[75] In August, German farmers harvested their wheat and corn crops. On September 1, Germany invaded Poland from the west. The war years had begun.

The War and Afterwards (1940–1947)

Anna Forbes Liddell was uncertain about the appropriate United States response to the German invasion of Poland. She knew the dangers of Nazism better than most Americans did. To her, Nazism was not only a threat to democracy, but also a threat to Christianity.[1] Yet, like most Americans, Liddell had favored isolationism throughout the 1920s and 1930s. Many Americans thought it had been a mistake for the country to fight in WWI, which they thought to be essentially a European war. Could not the European countries now halt Germany's expansion without the help of the United States?

Americans also worried about Japan since the United States competed with Japan for the same Asian natural resources and markets. Southeast Asia supplied most of the oil, tin, and rubber the United States used. The Middle East was not yet a major supplier of oil. Japan, with few natural resources of its own, planned to expand its territory to gain the natural resources of Southeast Asia and the lucrative markets of China and Korea. The United States wanted to keep those resources and markets out of Japanese control. Tension between Japan and the United States was high as Japan started the second Sino-Japanese war in 1937 and invaded French Indochina in Southeast Asia in 1940.

While Americans viewed Japan as an economic threat, they viewed Germany as a political threat that might lead the United States into war. Two days after Germany invaded Poland on September 1, 1939, France and Great Britain declared war on Germany. Two weeks later, the Soviet Union invaded Poland from the east, fulfilling a pact made between Hitler and Stalin in August to divide Poland. At that time, only 29 percent of Americans supported sending US troops to fight in Europe.[2] To most Americans, Europe seemed far away. They believed that what happened in Europe did not affect their daily lives.

German aggression continued. In April and May 1940, Germany invaded Denmark, the Netherlands, France, and Belgium. On June 10, 1940, Italy joined with Germany and declared war on France and Great Britain. Twelve days later, France was defeated, leaving Great Britain as the only major power left to fight Germany. In the summer of 1940, Germany bombed British military industrial sites in daytime raids. Great Britain responded by bombing Berlin. Angry about the Berlin bombing and frustrated by the British Royal Air Force superiority in British skies, Hitler changed his strategy. He replaced the daytime attacks with nighttime bombing raids on London and other British cities. On September 7, 1940, three hundred German bombers dropped 227 tons of bombs on London. This was the first of 57 consecutive nighttime bombings of London designed to break the will of the British people. Called the Blitz, these bombings continued through mid-May 1941.

In June 1941, Germany turned its attention towards the Soviet Union. The 1939 Non-Aggression Pact between Germany and the Soviet Union had been only a temporary alliance that Hitler needed at that moment. On June 22, 1941, in a surprise attack, three million German soldiers and three thousand tanks battered Soviet troops along two thousand miles of the Soviet border. This attack started the war's Eastern front, where the bloodiest fighting and atrocities to non-combatants occurred. Germany was not only fighting the Soviet army but also exterminating the Slavic and Jewish populations.

It was not until September 1940 when Germany started bombing British cities that a majority (52 percent) of Americans supported entering the war to help Great Britain. Support for war continued high through 1941, going from 60 percent in November 1940 to 68 percent in November 1941.[3]

The United States government was preparing for war as early as September 1940, when the Selective Services Act authorized drafting 900,000 men between the ages of 25 and 45 into military service. Bob Pickens, at age 40, tried unsuccessfully to join the US Army throughout 1940. Finally, in March 1941, he was called to work at the Pentagon as an army major. He served as a liaison office between the War Department and the Senate committee that investigated defense installations to prepare for war.[4]

On the morning of December 7, 1941, Japan attacked the US naval base at Pearl Harbor by air. In the surprise two-hour attack, Japanese aircraft strafed airplanes sitting on the ground and torpedoed ships in the harbor. A bomb hit the ammunition magazine of the *USS Arizona.* The ammunition exploded, and the ship sank with 1,177 men trapped inside.[5] The attack killed some 2,400 Americans and wounded thousands others. Congress declared war on Japan the next day. Germany and Italy declared war on the United States. Americans united and overwhelming supported the war. Over sixteen million men joined the military during the war.

Women entered the workforce to fill office, factory, and technical jobs previously held by men who left for war. Women already working in women's jobs could move into higher-paying and higher status jobs. Although earning higher pay in the wartime jobs, women were still paid less than men doing comparable work. Yet, many women hesitated to apply for wartime jobs now open to them. They had been told their entire lives that a woman could not do a man's job. To encourage women to apply for defense factory jobs, the government waged a media campaign with videos and posters, including the well-known Rosie the Riveter poster. The campaign told women, "If you've used an electric mixer in your kitchen, you can learn to run a drill press."[6]

Women also joined the military in all the branches, filling a myriad of jobs. The military could not function unless women filled non-combat jobs so that men could fight overseas. To allow this level of participation by women required new legislation, since there were laws, regulations, and a military culture that previously restricted the enlistment of women and allowed discrimination against them when they enlisted. In 1941, US Representative Edith Nourse Rogers introduced a bill that created the Women's Army Auxiliary Corps (WAAC). Rogers had served as a Red Cross Nurse in WWI. She had seen the inequities when women supporting the US Army were not part of the regular military. She wanted female soldiers treated the same as male soldiers. Yet, Rogers had to compromise to get the bill passed; she removed the provision of equality from her bill. The women in WAAC would not receive life insurance, pensions, or equal pay. Nor could they serve overseas. Rogers felt that the compromise bill was the best that could be passed at that time, since many in Congress and the military establishment opposed the creation of WAAC altogether. The debate on the bill voiced fears that women would become generals and give orders to men, that there would be no one left to do the cooking and the cleaning, and that such military service by women would destroy the sanctity of the home. Regardless, the bill became law in May 1942.

In January 1943, Rogers introduced a new bill that incorporated WAAC into the regular army and renamed it as the Women's Army Corps (WAC). This time, the US House of Representatives stalled the legislation by demanding a report on pregnancy and venereal disease rates among WAACs. The bill finally became law on July 1, 1943. Since WACs were now members of the regular army, they could serve overseas and receive the same benefits as male soldiers. Over 150,000 women joined WAC during WWII.

In July 1942, two months after WAAC was created, the Navy created Women Accepted for Volunteer Emergency Service (WAVES). Over 20,000 officers and 70,000 enlisted members joined the WAVES. In November 1942, the Women's Reserve of the Coast Guard, which had the acronym of SPAR after the Coast Guard motto, Semper Paratus—Always Ready, was created. In February 1943, the Marine Corps Women's Reserve (MCWR), was created. Women in the WAC, WAVES, SPAR, and MCWR worked in many types of jobs, such as air traffic controllers, parachute testers, weather specialists, scientists, lawyers, radio operators, and clerical workers. The Army Air Force also used over 1,100 civilian women pilots in an experiential program called Women Airforce Service Pilots (WASP). At that time, the Air Force was a part of the Army and not a separate military branch equal to the Army and Navy.

Since WASPs were civilians, the military did not give them the training needed to get pilot licenses. Women had to pay for the training for their pilot licenses before joining the program. Margaret Phelan Taylor, a nineteen-year-old Iowan farm girl with two years of college, borrowed $500 from her father for her lessons. Later, when asked why she joined WASP, she reminisced that she did it out of patriotic loyalty and for fun. In addition, her brother was in training in the Army pilot program. She reminisced, "Everybody had left and it was wartime. You didn't want to get stuck in a hole in Iowa; you wanted to see what was going on."[7]

The WASPs flew military aircraft, including B-26 and B-29 bombers, on non-combat flights, such as transporting new planes from the factory to military bases and testing planes that had been repaired. This freed up male pilots for combat duty. One dangerous duty of the WASPs was towing targets while ground and aircrews shot live ammunition at the targets for practice. On one flight ferrying a plane between Arizona and California, Margaret Taylor's cockpit filled up with smoke. The pilots had been instructed to bail out in an emergency. However, the parachutes assigned to the women were designed for a man's body. Taylor's parachute was too large for her. The force of the wind in a jump might rip her small body out of the parachute. She decided to wait until she saw flames instead of only smoke before risking a jump. As it turned out, she did not have to jump after all; the smoke came from a single burned out instrument on the dashboard.[8]

Thirty-eight WASPS died in service during the short two-year program. Since they were civilians, they were entitled neither to military transport of remains home nor to a military funeral with a flag-draped coffin. The family of Mabel Rawlinson, who died when her plane crashed in a nighttime training exercise, draped an American flag over her coffin anyway.[9]

When the WASP program began, US Army Air Force commanding general Henry "Hap" Arnold doubted "whether a slip of a girl could fight the controls of a B-17 in heavy weather." When the program disbanded in 1944, he admitted his earlier doubts and added, "Now in 1944, it is on the record that women can fly as well as men."[10]

Before WWII, two pioneering women showed that women could break codes as well as men. Agnes Meyer Driscoll was the chair of the mathematics department at a high school before she enlisted as a yeoman in the Navy's Code and Signal Section in 1918, one year after the country entered WWI. In her career that continued through WWII and the Cold War, Driscoll broke Japanese, German, and Russian codes. Genieve Grotjan Feinstein had been an unemployed mathematics teacher when she joined the Army Signal Intelligence Service as a civilian in 1939. In 1940, she discovered a pattern that lead to breaking the code used by Japanese diplomats. In 1943, she worked on Soviet KGB communications. She discovered how to recognize when the Soviets were reusing a key for the coded messages. This discovery was used throughout the Cold War to decipher coded messages· With Driscoll and Feinstein showing that women could do the job, the government recruited and trained civilian and military women as cryptanalysts for the Army and the Navy during WWII.[11]

The government also needed women to make military maps, another field not typically filled by women before the war. The demand for these Military Mapping Maidens was great. Maps were hand drawn since computers did not yet exist. It took an average of 600 hours of work for one map from the original hand drawing to the printing of copies. Each military operation required many maps, such as large area maps, small area maps, topographical maps, and strategic maps. Navigators on bombers needed florescent and red light maps for nighttime raids. The D-Day invasion of Normandy required 3,000 original maps and 700 million sheets of copies. To recruit and train women as mapmakers, the government approved a 60-hour course taught in twenty-two colleges and universities. Florida State College for Women was the first school in the South to offer this course. The twenty-seven students who completed the first course at FSCW were all were hired by the federal government in Washington, DC.[12]

The demand for workers eliminated unemployment and provided better jobs across gender, age, and racial lines. Both teens and older workers readily found jobs. Black men and women entered jobs previously restricted to White workers. President Roosevelt banned racial discrimination in defense plants and created the Fair Employment Practices Commission to investigate charges of bias. Restaurants, laundries, and farms could not find enough employees for their lower-paying jobs. Farms did not have enough workers when they were asked to increase production to feed the troops. Men got military deferments to work on farms. Over 400,000 German and Italian prisoners of war worked on farms as laborers.

Everyone sacrificed during the war. The government rationed food (processed and canned) and gasoline, because the military needed those items. Even fresh foods in markets were rationed because they required transportation; coffee, sugar and other imported items were also rationed. The military needed rubber and various metals to build airplanes, ships, and other equipment. However, the war cut off rubber and tin imports from Asian countries. Scrap drives asked Americans to make do and recycle rubber, aluminum, tin, other metals, and paper. People scoured their homes for items to recycle. They took the bumpers and fenders off their cars and donated them. Some recycled items were unusable, but the scrap drives were great builders of morale, unity, and patriotism.

In their hometowns, Red Cross volunteers—mostly women—shared their wartime worries and sorrows along with rationing tips as they gathered to repair military uniforms and to pack medical supplies and care packages for the troops overseas. Other women volunteered with the Red Cross Motor Corps to drive their own cars across the country transporting supplies, other volunteers, nurses, and wounded soldiers. Forty-five thousand women drove over 61 million miles with the corps. Since cars break down, many learned how to maintain and repair their cars.

Anna Forbes Liddell volunteered with the Red Cross two evenings a week and occasionally volunteered at the local club for servicemen that the United Service Organization ran. Over fifty FSCW faculty volunteered at the club to brew coffee, make sandwiches, give dance lessons, or simply talk with the servicemen.[13]

Liddell viewed teaching as important war work. She said, "Education seems to me indescribably important. Behind the lines, we must not merely *preserve* but *push forward* the principles of democracy and Christian culture, which we are fighting to maintain. It is a terrifying responsibility to be a teacher—especially now."[14]

* * *

Liddell experienced many changes in her personal life from 1940 through 1946. She lost people who were dear to her and worried about aging relatives. In 1940, her father died from throat cancer at age eighty-seven. That same year, her teacher and mentor Horace Williams died. The next year, her Aunt Eva Liddell died from cancer of the stomach. In summer 1944, Liddell's mother Nellie sold her house, which she could not afford to maintain alone. After staying with various relatives or living in a hotel for a year, she reluctantly decided in fall of 1945 to live permanently with Liddell in Tallahassee.[15]

Liddell also fretted about family members who were fighting in the war. In 1942, Bob Pickens, now a lieutenant colonel, was stationed in London.[16] Liddell's only nephew, Walter McBride, enlisted in the army infantry as a private first class in 1942. By 1944, he was a lieutenant serving in the Pacific.[17]

Yet Liddell delighted that she had another niece enrolled in FSCW. Mary Anna McBride enrolled as a freshman in fall 1939. She joined the Chi Omega sorority and lived in the sorority house, like her sister Helen-Aline had done. Late one evening, the housemother at the Chi Omega house was annoyed by the loud music she heard. She stomped upstairs to order Mary Anna and the other girls to turn down the music. To the housemother's surprise and Mary Anna's embarrassment, the loud music was coming from a party at Liddell's home behind the sorority house.[18]

During this time, the relationship between Liddell and Kathryn Abbey changed. In 1941, Abbey, who had lived in Liddell's duplex since 1927, married Alfred Hanna after twelve years of courtship. Hanna was a fellow historian teaching at Rollins College in Winter Park, Florida. Abbey was likely reluctant to marry because she would retire from teaching as was customary for women at the time. She had been Chair of the history department at FSCW for fifteen years. She gave up teaching, but did not give up her career. After marriage, she was president of the Southern Historical Association in 1953 and collaborated on research and writing with her husband. Together, they jointly published *Lake Okeechobee: Wellsprings of the Everglades* (with Milo Quaife) in 1948 and *Florida's Golden Sands* in 1950. For a quarter of a century until her death in 1967, she assisted her husband with his scholarly research on Napoleon III. They co-authored *Napoleon III and Mexico: American Triumph over Monarchy,* published in 1971.[19]

Katheryn Abbey's marriage and move to Winter Park affected Liddell's life significantly, because the two women had a close friendship that was both professional and personal. In the evenings after supper, they likely relaxed on the back porch of the house, sipping martinis and sharing the day's college gossip.

Liddell kept up her friendship with Mary Call and LeRoy Collins. With her passion for historic preservation, Mary Call was thrilled when she and LeRoy bought The Grove in 1941. The Grove was special to her—it was the home built by her great-grandfather Florida Territorial Governor Richard Keith Collins. The Grove sits next to the Florida Governor's mansion, located one block from where she grew up in the Brevard family home. Serving as a hotel from the mid-1920s, the house and grounds had been neglected. Partitions were added to form extra bedrooms and tangled vines and briars covered the Cherokee roses. The war delayed the plans for restoration. LeRoy Collins stepped down from his Florida state senate seat to serve in the Navy.[20]

During this time, Liddell deepened her friendship with Spessard and Mary Holland. She first met them in the 1930s when Spessard Holland was a Florida state senator, who advocated better funding for public schools and higher pay for teachers.[21] In 1941, Holland became the twenty-eighth Governor of Florida, serving until 1945. During his term as governor, the state created a retirement system for public school teachers and reformed the tax system. With consistent sources of tax revenue, the funding of education became more stable.

While Holland was Governor, Liddell usually went to the Governor's mansion once a week—sometime for parties, but generally for informal lunches or Sunday night dinner with the entire Holland family. Liddell said of the Hollands, "Spessard is a scholar and a gentleman; Mary is a musician and much too original to be classified merely as a lady."[22] Mary Holland was known as Florida's First Lady at War. She led by example as she scoured the Governor's Mansion from top to bottom for scrap metal for the country's defense needs. In September 1943, her husband appointed her as the Florida Chair of the All-States Women's Army Corps (WAC) Recruiting Campaign. Her goal was to recruit 1,000 women in Florida. One of the five WAC training centers was in Daytona Beach, Florida. [23]

* * *

When the United States entered WWII, most of the students at the male-only University of Florida (UF) in Gainesville, enlisted for military service.

The government used part of its facilities for military training. For the 1943–1944 year, there were 1,000 civilian students and 1,500 servicemen on campus. The number of servicemen varied from month-to-month as air crew units moved in and out of training.[24]

There was no longer a stream of university men traveling from Gainesville to Tallahassee on the weekends. However, the UF men were not missed, because Florida State College for Women now had two military installations nearby—Dale Mabry Field, three miles from campus, and Camp Gordon Johnston, on the Gulf coast. Liddell remarked, "We are swimming in a sea of soldiers here in Tallahassee; we have an air base and an amphibian camp. The second is fifty miles away, but the boys come to town in thousands on the weekends. Really, all Florida is an armed camp."[25]

The FSCW students, delighted with so many men on campus, hung out the windows of the dormitories to see the parade of cars packed with servicemen. Aviators from Dale Mabry Field flew their planes low over the campus buildings, especially Landis Hall, where the women sunbathed, sometimes topless, on the rooftop. Some women cheered on the pilots, while others scrambled for towels to cover up.[26]

The college administration enacted strict curfews for the women to prevent contact with servicemen. However, when the college accepted that the students and the servicemen would find ways to see each other, it relaxed the school's code of conduct, but only in structured situations where there were two women for every man. The college did not allow students to attend United Service Organization events.[27]

Air raid sirens regularly blasted, announcing mandatory air raid drills. Because of its location to military installations, Tallahassee was considered a prime target if Germany bombed the United States. Students were disciplined for leaving a room with lights on, because a single light could aid German bombers.[28]

Military service and support jobs beckoned FSCW alumnae, students, faculty, and staff. Some faculty members, men and women, took leaves of absence to enlist in the military or to work in federal government jobs. Many students left before graduating to enlist in the military or take war support jobs. The college added twenty-four emergency war courses with condensed coursework. Besides the military mapmaking course, there were courses on news censorship, meteorology, x-ray technology, radio code practice, radio broadcasting, first aid, photography, wartime social services, seed analysis, and victory gardening. After only one or two semesters, a student could work in an essential war job.[29]

FSCW wartime graduates quickly found jobs. Many became teachers; some filled other traditional women's jobs, such as nurse, secretary, clerk, and airline stewardess; still others filled professional and executive positions, such as language translator, budget analyst, chemist, non-profit director, and social worker.[30]

* * *

In September 1939, Anna Forbes Liddell received a letter from John O. Riedl of Marquette University that must have thrilled her. He had recently returned from working with Ernst Hoffmann in Germany on a translation of one of Cusanus's writings. Riedl asked to see her translation of *De Docta Ignorantia* with the idea of it being published by Marquette University Press.[31] Liddell replied to Riedl, in part:

> I began this work more than ten years ago to satisfy my own interest. Even the partial and inadequate knowledge of *Nicholas of Cusa*, which I had obtained as an undergraduate, convinced me of his tremendous importance. I undertook the study because I wanted to understand his teaching. I hoped that at some time I might publish a translation of, but that was a pleasant hope rather than an actual plan. The demands of a very busy teaching schedule have interfered with my working on *Nicholas* as much as I had wanted to. I completed an English translation of the

> entire text; I revised it once—some portions twice; I used my own manuscript for study and for a small advanced class, and I have presented a number of papers on Nicholas before the Southern Society for Philosophy and Psychology, and published a few short articles about him. Thus, though my interest has never lagged, yet I fear that I have not done nearly enough work on the manuscript to make it ready for publication without a good deal more editing. I am telling you this quite frankly, so that you will know that I expect to have to do a lot of work on the text to get it ready for publication. There is no other work which I would more gladly do, I can assure you. I hope to follow this letter with a part of the manuscript within a very few days.[32]

Liddell sent the manuscript to Riedl in batches though the summer of June 1941. After receiving the entire manuscript, Marquette University Press accepted her manuscript for the translation series. Her correspondence with Riedl showed Liddell's concern about the accuracy of her translation, including the translation of the title. She had translated *De Docta Ignorantia* as *On Instructed Ignorance.* She had considered *On Cultivated Ignorance* and *On Learned Ignorance*, but she was less satisfied with those phrases than she was with *On Instructed Ignorance.*[33] *On Learned Ignorance* is the title used by modern translators. Liddell was positive that she understand what Cusanus meant and the importance of increasing awareness of his work in the field. Yet she worried that her translation might be inadequate. Her letters to Riedl have these excerpts:

> November 6, 1939. . . .My own criticism of the translation is that it lacks smoothness and ease. I have been afraid to translate freely lest I might change the emphasis or intrude my own style. I am not a Latin scholar, and I admit that I feel reluctant to submit a Latin translation to the Marquette Press. My defence [*sic*] is that I am confident that I have worked out and do understand the philosophy of Nicholas of Cusa, its basic

principle and its essential implications. I may stand in need of correction in the reading of phrases, and I should welcome such assistance.

April 26, 1940. . . .The place of Nicholas of Cusa in the history of philosophy is so important, yet to the average student he is so little known, that the presentation of his fundamental principles and most significant works is very important. I can assure you that I am not only willing but anxious to do everything within my power to make my translation adequate.

June 13, 1941. . . .Nobody knows better than I how imperfect my translation is. I often wonder at myself for having dared to make it. My justification is that nobody else could have been more genuinely interested, more anxious to get at the full meaning and set it forth for others. I am sure that I translated the whole not less than five times and many portions more than that.[34]

On September 6, 1942, Riedl wrote to Liddell that her manuscript would be the next one printed. However, he informed her that he did not know when that would be, since he was reporting for active duty in the US Navy in two days. He said he would continue to work on her manuscript in his spare time if he had any.[35]

During the war years, Liddell attended the annual meetings held by the Society for Philosophy and Psychology, but she did not present papers at those meetings. In another academic pursuit, Liddell sent stories to Howard W. Odum at the University of North Carolina at Chapel Hill for his groundbreaking work *Race and Rumors of Race: The American South in the Early Forties*, published originally in 1943. Odum asked professors teaching in White Southern colleges and universities to poll their students about stories they had heard about Black people planning racial uprisings. He received over 2,000 stories that he catalogued and researched. There were stories of Black men armed with ice picks or guns (ordered from the Sears Roebuck catalog) planning massacres of White people and stories of Black men seducing or raping White women when so many White men were overseas. These stories ended with the Black men who refused to *stay in their place* being jailed or killed. Or the men just disappeared never to be seen again. There were also stories of Eleanor Roosevelt traveling across the South encouraging Black people to revolt against racial segregation. There were stories about Black women refusing to work in White homes after joining Eleanor Clubs (named after Eleanor Roosevelt). In these stories, Black women boasted that they would soon be living in the big houses and the White women would be their servants.

Odum had noticed an upturn in the number of these stories as the country entered the war. Southern White anxiety increased as Black men and women now worked alongside White women in factories that previously employed only White men and as Black soldiers walked Southern streets looking dapper in their crisp uniforms. Odum determined that most of these stories were not based on fact. They were rumors, similar to modern day fake stories posted on social media. A few were mostly false—exaggerated tales mixed up with actual specific isolated incidents. Black men were not planning massacres; neither were they seducing and raping White women; Eleanor Roosevelt was not inciting Black people to overturn segregation; Black domestic help were not joining Eleanor Clubs. There were indeed fewer Black women working as domestic help during the war, but that was because they could get better jobs.[36]

Odum's work was groundbreaking because the wartime racial rumors would have been lost if not collected and studied. Odum also analyzed Southern racial tension at the beginning of the war. This analysis provided context for the rumors and described the roots of the civil rights movement that emerged in the 1950s.[37]

* * *

World War II ended on September 2, 1945 with Japan's surrender. Victory in Europe had been declared earlier on May 8, 1945. Liddell's German friends, Marie Baum, Marianne Weber, and Ernst and Thea Hoffmann all survived the war. Baum was one of the few Germans considered Jewish by the Nazis who had not been executed or sent to a concentration camp.

When the Allied soldiers entered the concentration camps, they saw the surviving prisoners, so emaciated that they looked like living skeletons. Dead bodies that the Germans could not hide in their hasty retreat were stacked in piles. Through the concentration camps, gas chambers, and mass shootings, six million Jews were killed, two-thirds of the European Jewish population. Marianne Weber talked about German responsibility in a 1951 interview:

> I must hang my head in shame at belonging to a people who, in the persons of some of its members, have committed crimes at which the whole world stands aghast. There is no evading a certain collective responsibility. Many of us could more or less justly say that we knew little or nothing of the diabolical perversions that made the concentration camps such scenes of horror, but we cannot therefore wash our hands of the whole filthy business. We are all in some sense guilty and must all try to make amends, however slight these may be in view of the immeasurable extent of German criminality in this war.
>
> We knew, to be sure, that the concentration camps existed, and that in all probability they were far from pleasant places. One after another of our acquaintances disappeared, never to be seen again. Nevertheless, it was impossible even to imagine the refined cruelty of these camps; no decent German—and there were and are many—could form the slightest image of the actual horror.[38]

Heidelberg had been spared the bombing that left much of Germany in shambles. That did not prevent the city from severe deprivations of food and other items after the war. Liddell sent packages to Marie Baum and the Hoffmanns. In Baum's thank you letter, she told Liddell about the conditions in Heidelberg:

> Unchanged by the outward appearance may be, the town has immensely changed. Even with the exception of 20,000 American soldiers or service[men], there live now 120,000 people in our town instead of 80,000 before. And not one house has been erected. So you can imagine the crowdedness. Wandering through the Hauptstrafe [a street name] you see especially poor refugees, peasants from the Sudeten, maimed soldiers, tramps a.s.o.[and so on]. And yet the face of the landscape is lovely as ever, the sun is shining—too much in this arid summer, it is true, but benevolent nevertheless,—and we poor people enjoy the moment as mankind will have done at each time.
>
> Now in chattering I forgot my thanks, felt so warmly, for the wonderful parcel. Do you know what is a "Wunderknauel"? Small girls when learning knitting get the knitting yarn wound over dozens of small gifts which unroll one or another wonderful thimg [*sic*]. So is mine, every time I get a parcel from you or another good American friend. It is not only the small quantity of our food, but the uniformity which to experience is not quite easy. Now finding chocolate or white flour or fat or meat or sugar or raisins or dried egg or dried milk—all of it is charming, promising variety of our meals. But no less I enjoyed the sewing things—we are really in need of everything and glad for every friendly gift. Very nice were the paper napkins, a luxury, because paper is a very rare matter. I suppose it is difficult to understand our situation for all living in better circumstances. Nevertheless, I am well aware of the changes, your country too has undergone, and I appreciate from this point of view also what my friends are doing for me. And I am glad that I am allowed to count you among them. [39]

Thea Hoffmann wrote:

> October 7, 1947. . . .How unfortunate that you could not be here today, when the post brought your terribly nice letter and at the same time the package card for the retrieval of your charitable gifts! We both cheered loudly and the opening of the package was a real celebration. . . . So we thank you from our hearts for all the beautiful things, which will help us to get through the dreaded winter. The splendid rice represents a really great fortune, since we haven't been getting any potatoes for weeks, and will only receive a small quantity for the entire winter, since the entire harvest has been [unreadable] due to the months long drought, only in a few places in Germany could a normal harvest be brought in. Vegetables also, we've had to do without since the early summer, for the same reasons. Good neighbors shared their fallen fruits with us once in a while, with this we had to made do and it went fairly well. The best, our dear and fine friends have provided for us and, like a squirrel, I have prepared for the long winter months. . . .
>
> You ask so sweetly about the small things that we are in need of. We very much lack shoelaces (ties), black and brown for men's boots, short for men's loafers; I can no longer wear suede loafers, because I don't have shoe ties in beige or light in beige or light-brown color. Also short, white ties for light summer shoes, I lack. And one doesn't have rags to clean the floor with! But it all must go on after all. Once the larger economic situation improves, then it will get better for us as well. Let us wait patiently and hope that it comes soon!—The main thing is that my husband is doing decent, that he can work and lecture, so life for us is wonderful and rich.[40]

After the war, the University of Heidelberg wanted to hire professors who had not collaborated with the Nazi regime. Ernst Hoffmann and Marie

Baum were in the first group of professors hired. John Riedl remained in Germany through 1953 to work with the military as a civilian. He did not follow through on his plan to help Liddell publish her work at Marquette or anywhere else.[41]

Millions of men returned to jobs filled by women during the war. Women tucked their wartime memories into scrapbooks and set them aside. Most returned to lower paying women's jobs or left the workforce. Still, some women, especially those who had careers before the war, continued their careers. Mildred McAfee Horton had taken a leave of absence as President of Wellesley College to be the Director of the WAVES. After the war, she returned to Wellesley. Jacqueline Cochran was the most famous American female aviator when she took over leadership of WASPS. After the war, she continued her aviation career. In 1952, she was the first woman to break the sound barrier.

After the war, millions of men wanted to enroll in higher education using the newly created G.I. Bill. In summer 1946, the University of Florida (UF) received over 8,200 applications for the 6,000 slots for the upcoming year. There was pressure to enroll men at FSCW. However, the Buckman Bill of 1905 specified that UF could only enroll men and FSCW could only enroll women. Besides, FSCW was already crowded. Its enrollment had grown almost 50 percent during the previous five years, making it the second largest state women's college in the country.[42]

The solution for the 1946–1947 school year was the creation on the FSCW campus of the Tallahassee Branch of the University of Florida (TBUF) with a maximum of 1,000 students allowed. The only connection TBUF had with UF was the name, so chosen to circumvent the law. FSCW administered TBUF; FSCW professors taught TBUF students.[43]

FSCW knew they could not hold the TBUF men to rigid standards. The TBUF men freely drove cars on campus and smoked whenever and wherever they wanted to do so. They dated whomever they wanted to date with no restrictions. Consequently, the restrictions on female students suddenly changed. With the permission of parents, they could now bring a car to campus and drive it. They still could not smoke everywhere, but the number of designated smoking places increased. Conversations between men and women students longer than ten minutes were no longer considered a date, and dating restrictions were retained only for freshmen women.[44]

On May 15, 1947, Florida passed a law that renamed FSCW as Florida State University (FSU) and made both FSU and UF coeducational schools for White students. Since FSCW ceased to exist on that date, the June 1947 graduates of FSCW would have their diplomas issued by FSU. The diplomas, however, had already been printed with the name of Florida State College for Women. It was too late to order new diplomas. The printer solved the problem by adding the phrase "issued by Florida State University." Thus, the 1947 graduates formed the last graduating class of FSCW and the first graduating class of FSU. The FSU years had begun.[45]

Florida State University (1947-1958)

"I especially enjoyed having boys in my classes now that we now [have] coeducation. I went to school with boys and it seems more natural that way," said Anna Forbes Liddell when interviewed by a *Florida Flambeau* (campus newspaper) reporter in 1948. Liddell and the reporter sat in wicker rockers on the sun porch that spanned the back of her home. Sprawled at their feet was a sleek, black alley cat, named Rhett Butler, who had adopted Liddell three years before. The reporter and Liddell lit cigarettes. She answered his questions with spirals of cigarette smoke circling her head. She said, "I'd rather study than anything else and I'd rather, converse than study. In fact, if I didn't have to teach I think I'd just give parties and study." As for teaching, she said that she preferred teaching general education courses instead of courses that train a student for a profession, since the general course focused on the individual while the professional course focused on the profession. She thought people stressed over money too much, because money cannot buy happiness. She explained why teaching was never boring: "Contrary to what so many people think, teaching the same subject every year isn't the same. The students are different and that makes all the difference in the world."[1]

The reporter summed up his impression of Liddell, who was fifty-six at the time of the interview:

I was amazed by her energy, vivacity, and youth. She manages her not so small house herself, works overtime teaching now that FSU has grown to such large proportions, belongs to 10 different associations and societies for which she writes an occasional paper, is vice-president of the women's auxiliary of the Episcopal church and still has plenty of time for students who drop into her office or congregate at her home for a pleasant visit and discussion of some philosophical question.[2]

Much changed when Florida State College for Women became Florida State University. Professors' salaries were increased to match those at the University of Florida. There were new courses, new rules, and new traditions. A football team dressed in garnet and gold took to the field against Stetson University in the first October of the FSU era. Seven thousand fans cheered for the FSU team in its 14-6 loss to Stetson.[3]

If FSU were to meet the enrollment demand, it would need more dormitories, more classrooms, more parking spaces, and more professors. Liddell hired six additional professors in the Department of Philosophy and Religion for the 1948–1949 school year.[4] The administrative responsibilities of Department Chair of Philosophy and Religion took much of Liddell's time. In 1951, she stepped down as Chair. She wanted to focus on teaching, studying, getting her translation of Cusanus's major work published, and, of course, partying.

* * *

On February 22, 1947, Liddell replied to a letter from Marquette University Press, Her response, in part, follows:

Early this month you wrote me that my translation of *de Docta Ignorantia* by Nicholas of Cusa is being kept on file by Mr. Charles Riedl [John

> Riedl's brother]. You asked me what disposition I want to make of it.
>
> First, I should like to know whether the Marquette University Press still expects to publish it provided, of course, that the translation has been adequately edited. I was most happy to have it included in your series, and naturally enough, have made no sort of effort to place [it] anywhere else. I assumed that as soon as you resumed publication, my translation would appear. In fact, I had been informed by Professor Riedl that mine was next in line on the series. He had said that he would himself check the manuscript for correction. That is why, as I explained before, I let it go to him is such a crude state. . . .The translation represents a good deal of work on my part. Naturally, I should be disappointed if it is not published or if I have to begin now making other arrangements about it. I should have written you much earlier, but having been informed by Professor Riedl that everything was being delayed on account of the war, I had supposed that there was nothing for me to do but wait until I had heard from you.[5]

Charles Riedl returned her manuscript. Since Marquette University Press was no longer interested, she sought other publishers. In fall 1949, Liddell received a letter from Giogio de Santillana, philosophy professor at the Massachusetts Institute of Technology. He asked whether she had any English translations of Nicolas of Cusa's work that could be included in his book, *Philosophy of Science*, which was to be published by the University of Chicago Press.[6] She sent him her translation of *Holy Days*, a sermon, and told him the history of her translation of *De Docta Ignorantia*. with Marquette University Press. She wrote:

> The manuscript was eventually returned to me. It still needs final revision. I could do this in a few weeks, but I still feel the need of checking it through with a Latin scholar. The difficulty has been that

Nicholas wrote at a time when the language had become so corrupt that most Latin scholars, used as they are to classical standards, find Nicholas baffling, and do not want to tackle him. (I mean, most of the latinists of my acquaintance.) Professor Hoffmann, withfwhom [*sic*] I was closely associated in Heidelberg for some months, was quite satisfied with my work, but unfortunately his knowledge of English was limited. I know that what I have done is basically right, but I do not want to be guilty of the small errors which can spoil a work.

You are entirely right in supposing that I am most interested in any good opportunity to have my translation published. It represents years of work, and the difficulties of bringing it to print have been most discouraging. Our own Classics Department here has grown during this last year. If I had an immediate hope of publication, I believe I could induce one of my own colleagues to work with me. I hope you will write me further.[7]

Since no other correspondence between Santillana and Liddell has been found, it is likely that he did not follow up with obtaining her translation.

Liddell gave a copy of her manuscript to Ernst Hoffmann in the summer of 1951. His reply follows:

Two decades have past, since you came to Heidelberg for the first time to study the philosophy of Cusanus. And now I have your manuscript of the *Docta ignorantia* in hand and I see how your former studies have developed and matured. You are one of those people who, once you follow him, will never be unfaithful to Cusanus. Because you have recognized his extra-temporal grandness and the authenticity of his thought. He represents the conclusion of the classic philosophy in the Christian consciousness of the medieval period and at the same time, he is a critic of the rationality, which in this respect constitutes the

> foundation of modern thought. . . .To translate Cusanus into a modern language is very difficult, perhaps even more difficult than to edit him. So far, I have only been able to check a few chapters of the first book of your translation, but divergences between your and my conception could not be discerned. I sincerely hope that your translation will be printed and will also aid to prepare a site for the Cusanus studies in America.[8]

Ernst Hoffmann died on January 28, 1952. He never recovered his health after the war. Although he could only sit up for a few hours each day in the years before his death, he continued his research and his weekly Cusanus seminar in his home. In a memorial article for the *Journal of Philosophy,* Liddell noted Hoffmann's enthusiasm for his studies right up until his death, his influence on the resurgence of the interest in the writings of Nicholas of Cusa, his powerful intellect and insights, and his personal characteristics of kindliness, sympathy, and gentle sense of humor.[9]

Continuing her work on her translation, Liddell began collaboration with a Latin scholar at Belmont College in North Carolina. She contacted the publication departments of the American Philosophical Association, the Ford Foundation, and the Saint Louis University Press. They all declined the manuscript.[10] In 1954, Fr. Germain Heron scooped Liddell by publishing an English translation of *De Docta Ignorantia.*[11] Liddell continued to seek a publisher for her translation.

* * *

Throughout the Florida State University years, Liddell attended conferences, wrote journal articles, and presented papers at professional conferences. She went to most of the annual meetings of the Southern Society for Philosophy and Psychology (SSPP) and the Society for the Philosophy of Religion. In 1948, the Society for the Philosophy of Religion recognized her scholarship and leadership when they elected her President of the Society. In 1954 she presented "Time and the Doctrine of Predestination" to the Southern Society for Philosophy of Religion. In 1958, the SSPP named her an Honorary Life Member.[12]

Liddell attended the World Congress of Philosophy in Amsterdam in 1948[13] During the 1950s, Liddell presented two papers at the World Congress of Philosophy: "The Metaphysical Significance of the Doctrine of the Trinity in the Philosophy of Nicholas of Cusa," in Brussels in 1953, and "Man and Nature in the Philosophy of Nicholas of Cusa," in Venice in 1958.[14]

Liddell studied the relationship among philosophy, religion, and science from her undergraduate college days through her professional writings in the 1950s. A continuity in her point of view is present throughout her career. She first studied these topics under the tutelages of James Creighton and Horace Williams. Her PhD dissertation proposed that Hegel's concept of Absolute Spirit was a synthesis of the concepts of Kant and Spinoza. Later, she synthesized Nicholas of Cusa's mystic understanding of the Christian trinity with her Hegelian, Kantian, and Spinozan knowledge base. Threads of pantheism and mysticism infuse her writings. So, was she a Hegelian, Kantian, Spinozan or Cusan? A Christian or pantheist? A scholar or mystic? Yes to all, because she synthesized these philosophies and methods to form her unique understanding. Liddell did not arrive at her mature views with a sudden insight that completely changed her worldview in an instant, like Paul on the road to Damascus. Rather, her understanding was a gradual unfolding that demonstrated Hegel's ideas of continual process and the synthesis of truths, which seem contradictory, to arrive at a more complete truth.

Liddell noted that Nicholas of Cusa's first mystic intuition was that he knew nothing. Then he sensed that he could learn. When Liddell read that he pondered, "How long is long?" she thought of her college philosophy classes where the students debated "How high is up?" What she learned of philosophy as an undergraduate was consistent with Cusanus's intuition and reasoning. Liddell stated that the first level of thinking is imagination, which seems like a word game. Then follows higher levels of thinking. After that come pure intellectualism, which reveals pure truth.[15] Although Liddell does not mention it in her writings, Horace Williams expressed a similar progression. He stated that there were three levels of students: those who lived in the world of facts, those who had advanced to the world of knowledge, and those who could rise to the level of wisdom.

Early in her career, Liddell differentiated between the truths that scientists learned and philosophers learned. Influenced by Nicholas of Cusa, Liddell later wrote about the unity of the truths learned by science and religion. Nicholas of Cusa found in his own life a unity between theology and science. Summing up Cusanus's view, Liddell wrote:

> The physical universe is not merely God's Creation. It is God as Existence. It is not therefore to be interpreted symbolically in terms of moral purpose and value, it is what it is, to be studied for its own sake. Knowledge of the universe is Knowledge of God. Natural science is theology. . . .Far from being antagonistic toward science, Christianity, according to Nicholas, makes science necessary, establishes its truth, and the scientist is as dedicated to the service of God as is the priest or friar.[16]

In the same paper, Liddell noted that Cusanus's assertions about science were bold since in his day, the Catholic Church was hostile toward science.

Concerning the relationship of God and the universe, Liddell wrote, "Since God is the infinite unity, which comprises all things, everything exists in God, bears his image. The physical universe is not a product of divine power separate from its creator." However, she asserted that God and the universe are not identical. God is infinite, whereas the universe is finite. If God did not exist, then the universe would not exist; however, if the universe did not exist, then God would still exist. She wrote about harmony, unity, and the interconnectedness. She wrote, "Harmony unifies the whole so that all events are interrelated, all things inter-dependent, but any single object or event, regarded alone is accidental, contingent. According to Nicholas it would seem that anything might happen, but whatever did happen the universe would remain in equilibrium."[17]

In an article about philosophical mysticism and science published in *The Personalist*, Liddell asserted that science and religion both use the intellect. She stated that mysticism, although criticized in modern times as unscientific and criticized in the Middle Ages as unorthodox, even heretical, has persisted throughout history. Mystic truth arising through intuition does not rely on authority and has no critical method. Mystics can be saints; Liddell asked whether mystics could be scholars as well. That mysticism does not use critical thinking does not prevent a critical analysis of its content. If a mystical experience has philosophical value, then that experience must be examined as carefully as a scientific experiment. The mystical experience that reveals psychological truth comes to those who have prepared themselves intellectually.

Liddell then connected science with mysticism. She shared a conversation she had with a chemist about the nature of reality. The chemist said, "I like to base my conclusions on something I can weigh and measure." Liddell asked her, "How do you account for the concept of weights and measures?" The chemist returned to her laboratory without replying. Liddell then explained that the scientist begins with intuition and the hope that truth can be discovered. She wrote, "Science has no end. Every achievement opens up new problems, but when the individual scientist has checked his results and they appear as verified, does he not then enjoy the mystic moment of illumination, the ineffable satisfaction of having attained the truth?"[18]

In Liddell's 1953 presentation in Brussels to the World Congress of Philosophy, she discussed Cusanus's concepts of the Trinity. Her paper was titled, "The Metaphysical Significance of the Doctrine of the Trinity in the

Philosophy of Nicholas of Cusa." Liddell knew that other Cusanus scholars may disagree with some of her interpretations of Cusanus's works. For one, Cusanus scholar Peter J. Casarella disagreed with her views expressed in the 1953 paper. However, Liddell was sure that her interpretations captured the essence of the philosophy of Nicholas of Cusa, and she had always relished scholarly debate.[19]

* * *

The 1950s was a time for wanting to return to simpler times after the previous two decades had brought the Great Depression and World War II. Married women experienced the greatest push toward domesticity since the nineteenth century. Women again got the message that their greatest happiness comes from devoting themselves solely to managing a home for her husband and children. Women married earlier, had more children, and were less likely to attend college than in the 1930s. Although a higher proportion of the population had a college education, women received only 35 percent of the bachelor's degrees in 1959–1960, compared to 40 percent in 1929–1930. Women comprised only 22 percent of the higher education professional staff, compared to 29 percent in 1931–1932.[20]

Newspaper, magazines, movies, and the new technology of television promoted traditional gender roles. Articles in women's magazines, such as the *Ladies Home Journal* and *McCall's*, mainly printed articles with domestic themes of best housekeeping practices, how to save a marriage, recipes, parenting tips, fashion, make-up application, and hair styles. In previous decades, these same magazines had printed similar domestic articles, but also included articles on culture and politics, such as the writers shaping American literature or the issues in a political election. Magazines advertisements in the 1950s depicted a happy housewife wearing heels and pearls serving a meal, prepared on her new range, to her happy husband and children. Television shows, such as *Father Knows Best* and *Leave it to*

Beaver, portrayed a traditional family with a happy housewife and a breadwinning husband. In *I Love Lucy*, when Ricky Ricardo and Fred Mertz complained about the amount of money their wives spent, the couples reversed roles. Lucy Ricardo and Ethel Mertz took jobs wrapping candies in a chocolate factory, while Ricky and Fred did the household chores, including baking a cake. Ricky and Fred's cake was a disaster, but the highlight of the episode was when Lucy and Ethel failed to keep up with the speed of the unwrapped candies coming toward them on a conveyer belt. As the conveyer belt moved faster and faster, the women frantically stuffed candies in their clothing and their mouths. Although it was a hilarious scene with a classic comedic plot, it subtly reinforced the concept that life is better when traditional roles are lived.

There were often contradictions in the message sent by media. These contradictions were signs, even in the conformist 1950s, that change was coming. The *I Love Lucy* show, which built its comedy on Lucy Ricardo's ineptitude, was one of the few television shows with scripts revolving around the actions of a woman. Lucy Ricardo wanted more from life. Her antics sprang from her trying to live a life different from the one prescribed for women by her culture. Before the 1950s, there were few female comedians or producers. Yet Lucille Ball showed, by her example, that women could succeed in those fields.

During the push for the return to traditional gender roles, the programs of the Tallahassee Branch of the American Association of University Women (AAUW) continued to include the topics of Florida education, international affairs, appreciation for the arts, and the status of women. In a 1956 panel discussion on the opportunities for women, the speakers noted that more women, including married women, worked, but few women worked in professional or technical fields. Few were in leadership positions. The panelists noted that the culture perpetuated this disparity by its message that women should be dependent upon men. Because of the culture, women were not provided opportunities for education and training for employment or they did not take advantage of opportunities offered.[21] The panelists did not discuss the disparity of opportunities between White and Black women. Better opportunities for women, however limited, were only for White women. After World War II, Black women went back to working as domestics or farm laborers. The best opportunities for Black women were as teachers in schools for Black children or in the ministry of Black churches.

The newspaper article reporting the Tallahassee AAUW panel discussion did not provide the reaction of the audience. Neither did it mention other aspects of the culture that made it more difficult for women than for men to take advantages of opportunities.

Women at this time did most of the shopping for groceries and clothes for the household, regardless whether they worked outside the home as well. Stores generally opened mid-morning and closed in the early evening on Monday through Saturday, and were closed on Sunday. That left only Saturday and a few evening hours on weekdays for working women to shop.

Getting hired was also more difficult for a woman than for a man. It was legal for a potential employer to ask a woman how many children she planned to have and to discriminate based on her answer. It was also legal not to hire a woman simply because she was of childbearing age.

When the husband and wife both worked outside the home, the husband's job was usually considered more important than the wife's. Women interrupted their careers to move to other cities for the advancement of their husband's career. Seldom did a husband quit his job to move for his wife's job opportunity. If a child or elder relative needed care in the home, it was usually the wife who left her job to take care of the family member. To interrupt a wife's employment instead of the husband's employment made economic sense since the wife's job was usually lower paying.

Liddell often spoke at meetings such as those of the Episcopal Diocese,

Beta Sigma Phi, local civic clubs, or at university events. In one speech, she stated that, as women take their place in the world in creative areas previously open only to men, they will use their creativity to preserve life.[22] Her statement showed her thinking that women and men use their creativity differently—that women, who bring life into the world, will use their creativity to nurture life. This idea is the same concept of the moral superiority of women that Liddell expressed in her *Life Magazine* essay on feminism in 1914.

* * *

During the 1950s, Anna Forbes Liddell spoke up about the threat to academic freedom that textbook bans and the censorship of professors posed. This controversy was similar to the evolution controversy that arose in the 1920s. This time, however, the subject was communism instead of the teaching of evolution. There was much concern in the country about the growth of communism after World War II when the Soviet Union and the United States began the Cold War. In 1945, the House Committee on Un-American Activities (HUAC) became a permanent standing committee until its dissolution in 1975. It had been a special committee from 1938 to 1944. The committee investigated people and organizations suspected of being subversive to the US government. Prior to World II, it investigated suspected fascist and communist organizations and people. During the war, the committee investigated Japanese Americans and defended the internment of Japanese Americans in camps. After WWII, the committee declined to investigate the Ku Klux Klan because it was an American organization. From the end of WWII through the 1950s, the committee focused on the suspected infiltration of communists into the US government and institutions. The HUAC's most famous investigation was of Alger Hiss.[23]

Based only on suspicions, people investigated by the HUAC could be fined and imprisoned. They often lost friendships and jobs. In 1947, an investigation of the Hollywood motion picture industry resulted in a blacklist of 300 motion picture screenwriters, producers, directors, and actors, including Charlie Chaplin, Orson Welles, and Paul Robeson. Many of those blacklisted could never reestablish their careers. In the 1960s, the committee under the chairmanship of Edwin Willis investigated the Ku Klux Klan. Other groups investigated in the 1960s were the Yippies and Vietnam War protesters.

The activities of the HUAC in the 1950s are often confused with those of Senate committees headed by Senator Joseph McCarthy. In 1953, McCarthy, as chair of the Committee on Government Operations, launched investigations into governmental employees suspected of being subversive to the United States. He interrogated witnesses before his committee by bullying and intimidating them. Without sufficient proof, over 2,000 governmental employees lost their jobs. McCarthy, next, turned to investigating army personnel. Since his committee hearings were televised, the public could see for themselves the type of interrogation he used. McCarthy's public support waned. His influence further diminished when the journalist Edward R. Murrow made McCarthy's aggressive interrogations the subject of his television program "See It Now."[24]

HUAC and the McCarthy Committee worked in tandem to investigate suspected communist infiltration. Focusing on unfounded conspiracy theories, these investigations exacerbated the popular fear of communism. The US State Department responded to the pressure from these committees by banning books written by pro-communists and other controversial persons from overseas American libraries. Some libraries burned the banned books.

The HUAC also investigated the activities of college and university students, professors, and staff. It demanded the membership lists of student organizations. Many higher education institutions eliminated student organizations that were in any way affiliated with communism. As a result, many students, professors, and staff at colleges and universities became afraid to speak freely or to write their opinions or to join organizations.[25]

In 1953, Assistant Professor John Reynolds of the University of Florida was brought before the HUAC. When the chairman asked Reynolds whether he had ever been a member of the Communist Party, Reynolds refused to answer the question based on his constitutional right not to answer a question that might incriminate him. He further stated, "I believe that this kind of investigation is detrimental to American education, and, that is a second reason for my refusal to answer. I think that, it will, undoubtedly, if continued, lead to an end to free investigation by teachers and students."[26] Reynolds's stance created an uproar in Florida. Some say he was fired from his job, although the official explanation was that he resigned. Forty-three Florida college professors answered questions posed by *Tampa Tribune* reporters on Reynold's case, on academic freedom, and on the banning of books.

Most professors responded to the reporters that Reynolds should have answered the question; a few said that, although he had the legal right not to answer, he had a moral responsibility to do so. Liddell responded with a minority view. She said:

> According to all the accounts which I read in the press, the sole source of my information, the professor at the University of Florida who was dismissed, exercised his legal rights in refusing to say whether or not he was or had ever been a member of the Communist Party. Without more knowledge of his reasons and motives, I cannot say whether or not he was ethically right.[27]

When asked to define academic freedom, the professors agreed that academic freedom was the right to teach truth, even to discuss communism, but that it did not include teaching propaganda for any cause. Liddell replied, "Liberal education is intended to impart accurate information, and to develop logical thinking. Academic freedom is freedom to perform these functions without directing the process toward the achievement of specifically defined predetermined ends. Academic freedom is freedom to participate, as administrator, teacher, or student in the process of a liberal education."[28]

The professors unanimously replied that banning of books violated academic freedom. A few held, however, that communist propaganda should not be archived in overseas American libraries. Liddell replied:

> Book-burning seems to me a dramatic but futile gesture. Certainly, it was so at the time of the Inquisition. "Elimination of all books and other literature dealing with Communism" is a very broad statement. Would this necessitate eliminating the Bible because it says (Acts 21-44) that the Christians had all things in common?
>
> One of the most important functions of the educator is the selection of books for study. The good educator makes wise use of the books he selects. The properly educated person is not liable to become the victim of propaganda. The fact that a book has been banned is all too likely to arouse curiosity about it and inculcate a strong desire to read it. Consequently, the burning of a book defeats its own intention. . . .
>
> I hold that persons worthy of being teachers are capable of selecting the books they need to use and of determining the use to be made of them. If they are not capable of this, they should not be teachers. If they are, it is essential to their academic freedom that they be permitted to do so.[29]

Not only did Liddell support academic freedom for professors, she supported the right of every citizen to criticize their institutions and governments. In an undated unpublished paper called "Freedom and

Society," she wrote, "It is both the right and the duty of each person to support the institutions of his society but it is equally his right and duty to examine and criticise [*sic*] them and to concern himself actively in making and keeping them adequate to secure the freedom of all."[30]

* * *

In 1954, the US Supreme Court ruled in the case *Brown vs the Board of Education* that racially segregated schools were not equal. The Tallahassee Branch of the American Association of University Women responded by asking Paul Odum, Florida's assistant attorney general, to speak at a meeting. Odum presented the work of the interracial Florida committee tasked with overseeing desegregation. The committee had surveyed Florida citizens through questionnaires and interviews. White people who were surveyed overwhelming urged for desegregation to proceed cautiously and slowly to prevent disruption of Florida education. Odum, himself, felt that if desegregation proceeded too quickly that it might end public education in Florida. Most Black citizens who were surveyed wanted a faster desegregation.[31]

The AAUW itself was grappling with race. For years, Black women with a college education joined at the national level as members-at-large, but often were not welcome in local branches, especially in the South. In 1949, the national AAUW modified its bylaws to clarify that educational status was the only criteria for joining at all levels. It, however, did not push branches to integrate. It would not be until the 1970s when the AAUW became integrated at all levels.[32]

After the state of Florida failed to move quickly with the desegregation of Florida's public schools, activists filed several lawsuits to force the state to enroll Black students in White public schools from the elementary level through graduate and law school. The courts ruled in favor of the plaintiffs. In 1958, George Starke, a US Air Force veteran, was the first Black student to enroll in the University of Florida Law School. In 1959, four Black students enrolled in Miami's Orchard Villa Elementary School. The school had 200 White students in the previous school year, but when the four Black students arrived in fall 1959, there were only eight other students enrolled in the school, because the other white students had left the public school system. Orchard Villa Elementary School eventually became a majority Black school. It would be five more years before Florida public schools were appreciably desegregated. In 1962, Maxwell Courtney was the first Black student to enroll as an undergraduate at Florida State University.

During the time of desegregation of Florida schools, LeRoy Collins was the thirty-third Governor of Florida, serving from 1955 to 1961. In his 1954 and 1956 gubernatorial campaigns, Collins had pledged to maintain segregation of schools. He defended segregation on legal grounds, not because he thought it was morally right. Before the end of his term in 1961, Collins publicly declared that he was the governor of all Floridians, regardless of race, economic class, or political influence. He stated that segregation in public places was morally wrong. He added that it was wrong for a department store to refuse Black people access to one section of a store while accepting their money in another section of the store.[33]

Liddell kept up her friendship with LeRoy and Mary Call Collins. She often went to the Governor's mansion to see them. We know of at least one time (and there were likely more) when she dropped by the Governor's mansion without an invitation to introduce her out-of-town relatives to Leroy and Mary Call Collins.[34]

* * *

It was during the 1950s that Anna Forbes Liddell and George Milton developed a deep friendship. Milton became a well-known artist in Tallahassee, but at the time Liddell and Milton met in 1952, he was an undergraduate student at FSU. He never took a course from Liddell, but he knew her reputation. He described their first meeting:

> It was in the summer, when I was on my way to a 7:00 a.m. class. She was mellifluously taking her four feet eleven inches to an early class, wearing a mustard colored, cotton print dress. A little flat top, wide brimmed straw hat sat securely on her head, and she was eating a banana that blended beautifully with her costume. We exchanged a friendly 'good morning' after which she offered me a bite of her banana.[35]

Milton did not interact with Liddell again until the spring 1956, after a campus performance of the Nellie-Bond Dickinsen's Theatre Dance Group. He had made Dickinsen some paper eyelashes that she wore in her solo act. Milton reminisced:

> After the performance, Anna Forbes told Nellie-Bond that if she had some eyelashes like the paper ones, she felt sure she could hold her class's attention for many lectures. Nellie-Bond passed the word on to me and I immediately sent Anna Forbes a pair of paper eyelashes through the campus mail with the request that for payment I be furnished with two box seat tickets for her first lecture when she wore the eyelashes. I immediately had a thank you note telling me that as soon as she could locate a lecture hall with box seats, the tickets would be forthcoming.

Milton continued:

> Our next meeting in person was during the late Spring of 1958, just prior to her leaving for the International Congress of Philosophy, where she read a paper at that meeting in Venice. She called on my mother, (we lived in the same neighborhood) and after several Aunt Rose comforts (a drink made with rum and wine) we were friends forever! Then several weeks later she came by and graciously offered us her

> lovely little house for the summer as she and her dear mother were to be away until fall. Well, ever since she returned from Europe, our friendship has become faster and more furiously thick. [36]

Milton asked Liddell to give him the poems that she had written over the years. She did so and added new poems she wrote based on his questions about her life. He pasted these poems into a standard spiral-bound college notebook. The pages were not numbered. He decorated the brown cardboard cover with a drawing of red tassels. *Tassels* was the nickname Milton called Liddell. He wrote the following as the dedication to the collection:

> The privilege of dedicating this collection of poems by Anna Forbes Liddell should rightfully be hers, but inasmuch as *Tassels* is too busy trying to fish out the olive from her martini glass, the collector will make the dedication. This collection is dedicated to Clifton Van Brunt Lewis, a student of Anna Forbes Liddell, and who is also my *Patron Saint*—and a lover of all mankind.[37]

Florida State University (1959-1962)

In 1959, Florida State University faculty honored Anna Forbes Liddell when they selected her as the Robert O. Lawton Distinguished Professor, which is the highest honor that the faculty can bestow on a colleague. Her colleagues wrote:

> As a gifted teacher she is unsurpassed. She has the rare ability to communicate the most abstract philosophical ideas in such a way that students can make them their own at their level of thought and experience. Her aim is to teach them to 'philosophize' *themselves*, that is, to give them enough background to think significantly for themselves about the important issues of philosophy. Her many, many students over many years express the warmest appreciation for the intellectual fire, the inspiration, and the friendship she has given them.[1]

One of the students that Liddell taught was James Soles, who earned bachelor's and master's degrees from FSU and a doctorate in government from the University of Virginia. Soles became the Chair of the Department of Political Science at the University of Delaware. In his speech at the 1993 New Student Convocation at the University of Delaware, he recounted:

> Dr. Anna Forbes Liddell. . .in her course on the Greek philosophers taught us equally well that we alone have the power to examine our lives and make choices of how we shall live them. And she would say, time and time again, summing up profound philosophical truth in her own grand way: "Don't let your love go wrong." Question. Question. Question. Accept nothing. Question.[2]

Liddell did not tell students what to do or to think, but questioned them in a way that planted seeds of thought. She brought photographs and artifacts from her many travels into the classroom to bring the past into the present. Sometimes, she read a poem she had written and asked her students to reflect on its meaning.[3]

Students dropped by her campus office just to talk. And she invited students to come to her house for philosophical discussion at a time when professors rarely interacted with students outside the classroom. She wrote:

> I've got too many children to keep them in a shoe.
> More girls, more boys, more ev'ry year.
> They bring to me their problems for I know what to do:
> LISTEN. (And they tell me things their mothers never hear).[4]

Students remembered how Liddell helped them in times of trouble. When a graduate student needed money, Liddell took a brown paper grocery sack and went around the faculty members' offices, asking for donations.[5] Tann Hunt recalled a time when Liddell interceded on her behalf with a library clerk. Hunt, a medical and family law attorney for many years in Tallahassee, earned a BA in 1957, a PhD in 1972, and a JD in 1982, all from Florida State University. In 1956, she was a young married undergraduate student. She checked out two reserved books from the FSU library. The rule for reserved books was that they had to be returned by 8 a.m. the next morning with 25 cents charged for each hour late. The evening she checked out the books, she and her husband received a phone call for them to come to Pensacola immediately because her father-in-law was seriously ill. They left that night and did not return for several days. Hunt expected that the library staff would make an exception for the late book fines because of the family emergency, but she was very wrong. When she returned the books and explained the emergency, the unpleasant clerk at the library desk snapped that there were no exceptions. Hunt recounted:

> I would have asked once again for an exception, but I was on the verge of tears. Out of nowhere came a voice, "Take the books back and forget the fine." I turned halfway around and saw nothing. The voice, I discovered came from a very short woman. I recognized her immediately as someone I had seen before only from a distance but had heard about in tones bordering on veneration. The voice belonged to Dr. Anna Forbes Liddell, professor of philosophy. It was clearly a demonstration that size and might don't make it right; right makes right. I have never forgotten her kindness.[6]

Decades after graduation, Liddell's former students remembered the effect she had on them. At their fiftieth class reunion in 2006, Ruth Stewart and Virginia Mickler reminisced about Liddell. Stewart said, "I was always stimulated by her lectures and when I left class, I felt my brain had been stretched! She encouraged us to continue to study for MA degree." Mickler remembered:

> She really had a ball of fire personality. . . .She seemed to be interested in all of her students. And we were not hesitant to ask questions you know. She always listened. She knew her subject. . . .I just remember I tried to take good notes, and she said so much it was difficult. It was difficult to do justice to the note taking so I could study properly for the exam that I knew was coming.[7]

It is important for young people to see adults who look like them living successful lives. No matter how many times adults tell young people that they can achieve whatever they dream, those words do not mean as much as seeing adults who look like them living their dream. The example that Liddell set inspired young women to have their own dreams and follow them.

One student Liddell affected by example was Tricia Browne-Ferrigno, who was a first generation college coed. She had not dreamed of a career in academia until she studied with Liddell in a sophomore humanities course. Liddell was the inspiration for the life Browne-Ferrigno eventually led—a career as a university professor.[8] At the end of the course, when the nineteen-year-old Browne-Ferrigno told Liddell of her dream, the conversation went like this:

> "I want to do what you do," said Browne-Ferrigno.
> "What? Be a college professor?" replied Liddell.
> "Yes," Browne-Ferrigno answered.
> Liddell bluntly snapped her reply, "Well, do it!"[9]

* * *

By 1960, Anna Forbes Liddell was discouraged. Only her mother was living from that generation of the family, and she had not yet gotten her translation published. She confessed to George Milton her feelings in this poem:

> My friend is ill, my mother old.
> From house to campus, to church and back
> Week after week I follow the track.
> Morning and night I kneel and pray,
> For the patience and courage to meet a new day
> And the tale of my life is told.

The gay, wild thing you pretend to see
Moving as free as a breeze that blows,
Scattering fragments of joy as she goes,
Silken tassels from whiring skirt,
The dancing doll who parties and flirts—
I *like* her George—but she isn't me.[10]

Liddell did not name her ill friend in the poem. It likely was Bess Brevard. They had been friends since 1926 when Liddell first came to Tallahassee. Although Liddell thought Milton had an erroneous impression of her, she confessed that she still liked to party. She wrote:

My cheeks are lined, my hair is grey.
A woman my age should be glad to stay
At home to rest when her work is done.
I want to go out and have some fun.[11]

* * *

Anna Forbes Liddell mourned Rawley Myers's death for years. Just when she thought she had finished grieving, suddenly her sorrow would break through, such as when she saw a theater production of Noel Coward's *Private Lives.* The play, about a tumultuous relationship where the man and woman could not live together without arguing, but could not live apart because of their love, brought up memories of Myers. She cried because they could never again *fight.* She would give up ten years of peaceful life for one brief hour of *fighting* with Rawley.[12]

Right after Myer's death in 1930, Liddell felt his presence daily, but finally his memory begin to fade. In 1933, she wrote this partial draft of a poem to Myers:

It used to be that every day
Had oh so many things to say!

Each time I watched a flower grow
I felt, somehow that you must know.

The teasing winds were more than air;
Your rumpling fingers mussed my hair.

The sky reached down wide arms of blue
To hold me in the thought of you.

In every moving leaf I heard
The murmur of your whispered word.

But now—somehow—you are not there.
(And why)? Do I no longer care?[13]

Still, Liddell never forgot Myers. Over the years, every trip she took, every honor she received, and every significant event in her life, she longed to share with him and wondered what he would have said. She wrote a poem to him after she received the Lawton Distinguished Teaching Award. The poem alludes to the custom at the time for a woman to be known with her husband's first and last name after marriage. If she had married Rawley Myers, her accomplishments would not have been reported as those of Anna Forbes Liddell Myers, but as Mrs. Rawley Myers. She wrote:

"A married woman" you said, "is an S
Tacked on to her husband's name.
You ought to win your own success

Your own degree of fame."

They chose me *Professor of the Year*,
But you weren't there that night
To say to me, "My little dear,
You see now, I was right."[14]

Thirty years after Rawley Myers's death, Liddell finally came to acceptance. She wrote:

Resurrection

Inspired and inspiring words that the apostle said
Of the spiritual body of the resurrected dead.
Majestically beautiful, and faith must hold them true.
They did not help me, darling, the day men buried you.

Your spirit incorruptible seemed anything but near.
And oh, your body in the flesh had been so very dear.
Your lips, your hands, your firm strong arms in depth of lonely pain.

I put away your picture. It tortured me to see
The paper image of your eyes that could not look at me.
God knows how long I walked in fog, how long I played a part
Before I learned to build a life around an empty heart.

In blessed wonderment I find after so many years,
Your voice, your features come to mind and bring no flood of tears.
I can recall the joy we shared, without a stab of pain.
Your loving Spirit, darling, has filled my heart again.[15]

* * *

On September 20, 1960, WFSU-TV began educational television programming in a small studio on campus. The station produced a low-power black and white signal that only partially covered Tallahassee. By today's standards, this is primitive, but it was a healthy beginning.[16]

Roy Flynn, the director of WFSU-TV, and Tommy Wright, in charge of the station's educational programming, wanted only the best professors to showcase this new educational medium. They selected Anna Forbes Liddell to teach the first credit course in basic humanities for the station. They knew her lecture would be well organized and stimulating. But there was a problem. Flynn went to Richard Puckett, the station's art director and studio supervisor in his first job out of college, and said, "Dick, we're going to put Forbes on camera. She's just a mess. And you have got to do something with her."[17] Flynn was talking about Liddell's appearance, which would detract from her message.

The first day Liddell showed up in Puckett's studio, she wore a matronly gray dress with small flowers printed all over it. He looked at her image through the camera and it was bad. He thought, "How am I going to talk to this old lady." After all, he was twenty-six and she was a sixty-eight-year-old distinguished professor. He wondered what they could have in common. Although old in age, Liddell was young in heart and liked to be around young people. She quickly set him at ease. Soon they were talking like age peers.[18] Puckett explained to Liddell that clothing needed to be simple and solid-colored, not patterned for the camera. She told him to come over and pick out from her closet what she should wear. Puckett went to her house. After looking at everything in her closet, he shook his head and exclaimed, "Oh—I don't know. There is nothing here."[19] It was hard to find professional looking clothing for someone so petite. From then on, Bertha Cook who had a dress shop on the corner of College and Duval streets would bring back solid colored suits for Liddell when she went to market. This solved the clothing problem.

Puckett, next, had to tackle Liddell's hair and face. He reminisced in 2005:

> I had never done hair and I haven't to this day done hair, but, God, I have got to do something because it is a total mess. And so I started working with it and we had two restroom dressing rooms in the art department and so everyone walked through where you were working constantly. And so we sat in front of the mirror and I went and bought a lot of different kinds of make-up and of course, working with the gray scale, you had to get things that would, instead of red lipstick, the lips would just be dull. You had to work it out. And then check her out and look at it.[20]

Liddell enjoyed the new experience of educational television. She said, "At the age of sixty-eight I thought I had enjoyed every good experience as a teacher. Now, through teaching on TV, I have discovered a whole new dimension. It's exhilarating to get a new perspective. It's challenging. It's also hard work." She continued, "We're all learning about TV. We all started green at the beginning of the semester and now we toss television terms around like old pros. And what's more, we know what we're talking about." About having her appearance changed by Flynn and Puckett, she said, "Never did I think I would submit to such indignity at the hands of little boys. They make me look like a worldly grandmother in a home-permanent commercial. I like it." And expressing her wit, she exclaimed, "Teleprompters are lovely things. You get so dependent upon them to tell you what to say that after a while you have difficulty in saying 'good morning' unless it's in print in front of you." She continued, "I used to think it was vulgar to be noticed too much by the public. Now I find myself fighting an urge to demonstrate cake-mixes on TV."[21]

It took Liddell at least eight hours to prepare the material for the half-hour lecture. A lecture on TV had to be structured differently than one in a lecture hall. Liddell said, "Werner Vagt helped me visualize the course without making a spectacle of it. I don't specially [*sic*] mind making a spectacle of myself, but course content should be treated with respect."[22]

When Liddell got to the TV studio, there were two hours of preparation with Puckett for her make-up and hair. Liddell's lecture was in mid-morning and she arrived at the studio just as she had gotten out of bed with hair all wild and her face just washed with no make-up. She would say, "I'm ready," and Puckett would reply, "Heck, yeah, fix me." She dressed for the taping in her solid-colored suit. Puckett placed a covering over her so her clothing would not be messed up, and he *fixed* her.[23]

Liddell smoked cigarettes while Puckett was doing her hair and makeup. They sat in a fog of smoke while he worked and she told him stories about growing up in Charlotte, her parents, and Rawley Myers.

Often when she had a presentation to give, she scheduled it right after her television program. She would ask Puckett to give her a touch-up. She went to the presentation with hair and make-up freshly done. Puckett reminisced, "You know, she got a lot of attention. And she knew how to carry it off. And she had a very deep voice. . . .a very deep and a little bit raspy, but she knew how to project [her voice]."[24]

Richard Puckett lived in an apartment in a house that had once been a large private home. The building had a porch that spanned the entire front. One hot summer day, Puckett and his friends were sitting outside on the steps to the porch and drinking beer. He had just adopted a part Airedale female puppy, but he had not yet named her.[25]

Puckett had always loved Airedales and when a professor had an Airedale who gave birth to twelve puppies, Richard knew he wanted one. The puppies were strange looking, because, although the mother was an Airedale, the father was a Collie. Some had wiry hair, some had curly hair, and some had straight hair. Some had long legs and some had medium length legs. The puppies had various colorings. Puckett went three times to see the puppies. The first two times, the puppies all rushed to greet him; then, they all run away. On the third visit, a female puppy, the runt of the litter with a long tail that curved, did not run away but stayed. Richard knew she was the one for him.[26]

While Puckett and his friends were suggesting names for the puppy, Liddell strolled down the sidewalk toward them, eating a banana. Puckett yelled, "Hey, Dr. Liddell, come on over. Would you like to join us and have a beer?" She did so. Puckett got enough nerve to ask her, "You know, would you mind if we name the dog after you? We'll just call her Forbes." Liddell thought for a while and then replied, "Well, I've never had a namesake, but it might as well be a bitch."[27] And that is how Forbes the dog got her name.

Since Puckett's apartment was in an older wood-frame building with insufficient insulation, it was drafty and cold in the wintertime. Liddell remembered being very cold when she was young in New York City and in Ithaca, NY. She loaned Richard a lovely satin down-filled comforter to keep him warm. He was proud of the comforter and very careful with it. You could not buy such an item in Tallahassee then.

When Puckett left for work, he put his dog Forbes in the bedroom and closed the door. One day when he went home at lunch to let Forbes out for a walk, he opened his bedroom door and there were feathers everywhere and a dog who looked like a four-legged chicken. How would he find a replacement comforter in Tallahassee and how would he tell Liddell that his dog had destroyed her comforter? Finally, he got the nerve to call her. When he finished telling the story, there was a long silence. Liddell finally said, "Well, what did you *think* when you named the dog Forbes?"[28]

* * *

On August 7, 1961, Anna Forbes Liddell's mother passed away in

Tallahassee at home at the age of 98. In 1962, Liddell retired after 35 years of teaching at FSCW and FSU when she reached the compulsory retirement age of 70. Named Professor Emerita of Philosophy, she kept an office on campus for several years. Retired as a full professor, she did not retire from academic life. She taught university courses part-time for several years. She also remained active in her club and church activities and hoped that with more free time in retirement, she would finally get her Cusanus translation published.[29]

Last Years (1963-1979)

In 1963, Anna Forbes Liddell and Richard Puckett gave themselves a one-hundred-year birthday party. Puckett turned twenty-nine in February. In the previous December, Liddell had her seventy-first birthday. Their ages summed to one hundred. The birthday party was held at Puckett's apartment and the guests were all of their friends. Most of the faculty and staff at the TV station were there. Bill and Catherine King, a woman named Jenny who worked at the station, and Dorothy Davison were among the guests. The dining table was laden with food, alcohol was abundant, and cigarette smoke filled the air. Liddell and several guests got quite inebriated. Jenny noticed there was too much smoke in the house, more than could come from the cigarette smokers. She ran around yelling, "Something is on fire." Dorothy Davison, sitting in the living room, was holding a lit cigarette in the air near her head. Her hair, stiff with lots of hair spray, was on fire. The fire was snuffed out and the party went on. Bill King sat on the living room floor since all the seats were filled. Liddell plopped down in his lap and opened the presents the guests had brought for her.

The next day Liddell called Puckett. She said, "Richard, How ARE you today." He replied, "I'm surprised to hear from you." She continued, "Oh, it was a lovely party. I'm so sorry that the Kings weren't there. I'm so fond of them and I wish—." Richard cut her off, "You little fool. You sat in his lap and opened your presents."[1]

* * *

The fight over desegregation of Florida's schools continued in the early 1960s. In 1962, Farris Bryant, a segregationist, followed LeRoy Collins as governor. The Tallahassee newspaper printed an editorial that praised Governor Bryant for defying a federal court order on desegregation. In response to that editorial, Liddell wrote the following letter that was printed in the *Letters to the Editor* section of the newspaper:

> I read with concern your lead editorial of June 26, 1964, "A Patriotic Move." As to whether or not Governor Bryant's refusal to obey the summons of a federal judge is to be commended, I am not qualified to offer an opinion. What disturbs me is the attitude of the editorial toward the national government, especially its courts and judges.
>
> Is it always justifiable to assume that whereas State officials are always upright and trustworthy, Federal officials, especially judges, are liable to be self-seeking, even corrupt.
>
> Am I wrong (and I sincerely hope I am) in interpreting your last paragraph as implying that the national government is potentially, sometimes even actually, hostile to the state?
>
> Is there any surer way of playing into the hands of the communists than by weakening people's confidence in the national government?
>
> Like thousands of other citizens of the state, I am not native to Florida. I confess that it was not altogether easy for a "Tar Heel Born" to decide

to change residence. Yet it was not too hard either. After all, I had merely moved to another part of the same great country. I was a citizen of the United States first, last, and always.

The State of Florida has been good to me. It gave me opportunity to make a professional career, to build and maintain a home, and now, since my retirement it provides for me generously. In return I have tried consistently through the years to be a good teacher and a good citizen.

I love Florida, but I can not [*sic*] separate the love of state from the love of country, the whole Country in which every state is an integral part.[2]

The Civil Rights Act of 1964 created the Community Relations Service to mediate community conflicts over race, color, or national origin. President Lyndon Johnson appointed LeRoy Collins as its first director. Collins negotiated with civil rights marchers and Alabama authorities to prevent violence in the second of the March 1965 Selma to Montgomery marches. In the first march, *Bloody Sunday*, Alabama state troopers attacked 600 marchers as they crossed the Edmund Pettus Bridge. Collins negotiated for the marchers in the *Turnaround Tuesday* march to be allowed to cross the bridge, pray, and then return to the other side. In the third March 1965 march from Selma, Collins walked alongside King for a portion of the route. Collins was talking about plans to avoid violence when the marchers reached Montgomery. Although Collins was a negotiator, not a marcher, newspapers printed a photograph of Collins walking beside King. When Collins ran in 1968 for a US Senate seat, his opponent Edward Gurney used the photograph in campaign ads to smear Collins. Collins lost the election and never ran for political office again. His stand on civil rights was unpopular in Florida at the time, but it later won him respect. He is considered one of Florida's greatest governors.[3]

* * *

In the 1960s, women still had not gained equal rights. A married woman could not have a credit card without permission from her husband, and she could not get a credit rating in her name alone. Single women found it difficult to rent an apartment. Newspapers still listed jobs separately as *For Men* and *For Women*. Mothers who worked found few childcare options. Men were still paid more than women when doing similar types of work. Medical schools still had quotas that limited the number of women admitted. Even if a woman had qualifications that placed her in the top tier of all applicants, she might be denied enrollment because women could make up only five percent of the incoming class. A lesser qualified man might be admitted before her, simply because he was a man.[4]

Sexual harassment and domestic violence existed, but were not considered problems that needed to be addressed. It was not until 1975 that the term *sexual harassment* was coined to describe conditions that women often faced in the workplace, such as being groped, being subjected to degrading language and jokes, or receiving demands for sex as a condition of employment. And even as late as 1964, some medical doctors considered wife beating as beneficial therapy for a husband whose masculinity had been threatened by his overbearing, assertive, and frigid wife.[5]

Such discrimination was accepted as the way it should be because most people had internalized the concept that a woman was not as worthy as a man was—that a woman should always defer to a man—that a woman could not hold a position of responsibility because she was illogical and too emotional—that a man should always speak more, speak louder, and be believed more than a woman should. A 1960s riddle showed the depth of the unconscious gender bias. The riddle goes like this: "A father and his son are injured in a car accident. When they are taken to the hospital, the son is wheeled into the operating room. The surgeon says, 'I cannot operate on this boy, because he is my son.' How can this be?" The riddle's answer that the surgeon was the boy's mother stumped most people because few people thought a surgeon could be a woman.

The first draft of the Civil Rights Act of 1964 did not include sex in the list of individual characteristics that could not be the basis of discrimination. The National Woman's Party (NWP) advocated for an amendment to the draft legislation to prohibit discrimination based on sex. The NWP was the organization founded by Alice Paul to fight for woman suffrage, and its members in 1964 were mostly the elderly original members and their relatives. Alice Paul herself was seventy-nine years old, and the NWP President, Emma Guffey Miller, was eighty-nine years old. The NWP asked Howard Smith, a congregressman from Virginia, several times to introduce an amendment that would add sex to the list of characteristics that could not be the basis of discrimination. Smith eventually agree to do so. The NWP might have selected Smith because he was an influential Southern conservative legislator who had supported an Equal Rights Amendment since1945. Smith's reasons likely were mixed. With sex added to the list, legislators could vote against the bill without being called a racist. There is some evidence that Smith did so to defeat the bill, although he insisted that he was serious about the amendment. His tone, however, when introducing it was mocking, and he did not speak in support of the amendment. The ensuring discussion included laughter at the very idea of taking sex discrimination seriously. Finally, Representative Martha Griffiths from Michigan rose to speak. She said that the laughter proved that women were considered a second-class sex. She continued to point out that without this amendment that Black men and women would have legal recourse if subjected to discrimination, whereas White women would not. The amendment passed.[6]

There was tension between the civil rights and feminist movements. Some Black activists had even opposed the sex amendment to the Civil Rights Act, because they worried that including women's rights would dilute reform efforts. Additionally, women who worked in the civil rights movement often experienced discrimination from males in the movement. This caused them to reflect on their status in society as women, exactly as the abolitionist movement in the 1800s had caused women abolitionists to take up the cause of suffrage. There was also tension between the Black and White women in the civil rights movement, because Black women often experienced racial discrimination at the hands of White women.[7]

Because many people did not take women's rights seriously at that time, sex discrimination was often considered the least important one. That was the case with the Equal Employment Opportunity Commission (EEOC) that was established by the Civil Rights Act. It considered sex discrimination as less serious than other types of discriminations. Women's rights advocates were outraged when the EEOC ruled that newspaper job advertisements separated as *For Men* and *For Women* were not discriminatory. Four months after the EEOC ruling, the National Organization of Women (NOW) was founded with 300 members and with Betty Friedan, the author of *The Feminine Mystique*, as president. NOW pushed for passage of an equal rights amendment. Various equal rights amendments had been introduced for congressional action for decades, but none of them had passed. In 1972, Congress passed the Equal Rights Amendment (ERA) to the US Constitution. This Act stated, "Equality of rights under the law shall not be denied or abridged by the United States or by any state on account of sex." Many organizations, such as the American Association of University Women, which had opposed such an amendment decades before, now supported it. The League of Women Voters, which had remained neutral for decades, supported the ERA as well.[8]

Liddell was the perfect spokesperson for women's rights when Florida considered ratification of the ERA. After women got the vote in 1920, she had thought that equal rights in all other areas would naturally happen. She likely would have thought that the ERA introduced in 1923 was unnecessary. If so, she changed her mind after fifty years passed with little progress on women's rights. Interviewed in 1973, she said, "But, even if the apparatus is already there, if it has to be spelled out twice to be convincing, then I think the ERA is needed."[9]

In April 1973, the Florida House Committee on Rights voted on whether the ERA would be sent to the House floor for a vote for ratification. Liddell, frail from her 81 years, rose from her wheelchair to speak and steadied herself. A hush fell over the audience. With a strong voice, Liddell spoke clearly to say that the arguments against the ERA were similar to those against woman suffrage over fifty years ago. The audience gave her a standing ovation when she lowered herself back into her wheelchair. The Committee voted 6–3 to send the ERA forward.[10]

The 1973 Florida Legislature did not ratify the ERA. The matter was brought up again the next year. On April 9, 1974, the Senate Rules Committee voted whether to send the ERA to the Senate floor for consideration. The scene at the meeting vote was similar to the one the year before in the House Committee meeting. All seats were filled and people stood in the back and aisles. People stood on their seats to see better. More people jammed the hallway outside. Again, the room silenced when Liddell was wheeled to the front to testify. She spoke from her wheelchair this time, and her hands shook with palsy. Yet her voice was strong. Chiding opponents of the ERA who assumed every woman has a "sweet, wonderful, protective husband," she said, "I am an old maid. I've never had a husband, not mine, nor anyone else's. I've had to do the best I could on my own." She asked lawmakers to think of their own daughters, saying, "I've never seen a father who didn't think that his daughter was every bit the equal, or maybe even a bit superior, to another man's sons." Liddell was the only speaker that day to receive a standing ovation. The Senate Committee voted ten to eight to send the amendment to the Senate floor.[11] However, the Legislature failed to ratify the amendment again that year.

In an interview after her 1974 committee presentation, Liddell noted that in every job she held, a man had preceded her and a man had followed her. In each instance, she was paid less than the man for the same work. She also said that the opponents confused equality with female identity and that their arguments were irrelevant. Women should have equality before the law. Liddell noted that there was not a shocking effect on society when the Suffrage Amendment passed. Consequently, neither would the ERA have a shocking effect. She explained, "I'm not obliged to do everything that I am legally permitted to do."[12]

The ERA needed thirty-eight states to ratify it before June 1982 for it to become law. By the deadline, only thirty-five states had ratified it. Florida was not one of those states. Additionally, four states had rescinded their ratifications. Article 5 of the US Constitution only speaks to ratification of amendments, but is silent on whether states can rescind ratification.

The nineteenth amendment to the US Constitution, which in 1920 granted women the vote, succeeded, largely because it was clear about what it would do. By contrast, the legal ramification of the ERA was never clear. People wondered what it would mean for sexual assault victims, labor protection, divorce laws, abortion laws, and many other issues.

The interest in ratification of the ERA continued. In January 2020, Virginia became the thirty-eighth state to ratify the ERA. However, this left the status of the ERA ambiguous, because the 1982 deadline had passed and because four states had rescinded their initial ratification. On February 13, 2020, the US House of Representatives voted to remove the 1982 deadline for ratification.

* * *

The American Association of University Women is the leading organization providing scholarships and fellowships for women. In the 1970s, if a local branch raised $50,000 for AAUW fellowships, the branch could name a fellowship. The funds for the named fellowship would not be limited to the endowment of $50,000, but would have access to all money available for fellowships. In 1978, the Tallahassee Branch of AAUW created the Anna Forbes Liddell American Fellowship for graduate or post-doctoral study. The branch made an initial donation of $2,500 and proceeded to raise the remaining $47,500. By bestowing this honor on Liddell, the branch members recognized her as one of the few women whose work had spanned two waves of the women's rights movement: the first wave for woman suffrage ending in 1920 and the second wave for passage of ERA generally dated from 1967 to 1982. In between the two waves, as progress in women's rights stalled before moving forward again, Liddell continued to open doors for women in higher education as a student and as a professor.

* * *

As Anna Forbes Liddell aged, her body failed her, but her mind remained sharp. At age eighty-six, she was still attending theater events on the Florida State University campus with college students. She would tell the students how the current production compared with a production she had seen fifty years before. Thus, the students gained a deeper perception of the play and the history of its production. When the FSU theater department produced *The Importance of Being Earnest* in 1978, Liddell compared its production of the Oscar Wilde play with one she had seen in London in 1925. The earlier performance was staged with the colors preferred by Wilde—all black and white with touches of purple and red.[13]

It was hard for Liddell to depend on other people when she got older. Her nieces remembered she had always been good-natured—she never fussed at them when they were children. Yet when she became dependent, she became irritable. Eva Curry remembered her aunt saying when she was mostly bedridden, "I walked all my life. I walked all over Europe. I walked to work every day which was a block away from my house and now I can't walk."[14]

Anna Forbes Liddell died on August 30, 1979, at age eighty-seven.

Remembrances and Legacy

The most recognized landmark on the Florida State University campus is the gothic-styled Westcott Building, with its magnificent fountain standing in front. The fountain, surrounded by a brick-lined plaza in the center of a courtyard, is a gathering place for students and a site for traditions, such as throwing a student into the fountain on the student's twenty-first birthday or having a graduation picture taken with the fountain and building in the background.

The Westcott Fountain, a gift from the Florida State College of Women class of 1915, was renovated in 1982 and completely rebuilt in 1988. Bernie Sliger, President of Florida State University, dedicated the 1982 renovation of the fountain to the memory of Anna Forbes Liddell. This honor recognized that Liddell was a beloved campus legend for half a century.

In 2006, the FSU Class of 1956 honored Liddell at their fiftieth year reunion by selecting her for the Dean Eyman Distinguished Service Award. This award is given by the Florida State University Emeritus Society for faculty or staff (living or deceased) who had a special relationship and commitment to students and contributed to developing the University.

In 2016, Chancellor of the University of North Carolina Carol Folt announced a new program to rename scholarships after notable firsts in

UNC history. Anna Forbes Liddell was one of the first to have a scholarship renamed for her in this new program.

After Liddell's death, the Tallahassee Branch of the American Association of University Women (AAUW) continued to raise money to endow fully the Anna Forbes Liddell Fellowship. At each December holiday party, members donated to the fellowship fund and shared stories about her. The fellowship fund grew slowly. In 2005, the amount collected was just over $50,000. However, between 1978 and 2005, the national AAUW had increased the amount needed to name a fellowship to $100,000, and the Anna Forbes Liddell Fellowship had not been grandfathered in at the lower limit of $50,000. In 2005, the Branch launched a major fellowship endowment drive and created the Anna Forbes Liddell Project. Fully endowed in 2012, the Anna Forbes Liddell Fellowship awarded its first fellowship. Now the Educational Foundation Fund of AAUW awards an Anna Forbes Liddell Fellowship annually. The fellowship assists women during the time they are writing a PhD dissertation or are conducting post-doctoral research

Anna Forbes Liddell Project members collected information about Liddell and interviewed colleagues, friends and students. Eva McBride Curry, Liddell's youngest niece, interviewed her family. Helen-Aline McBride Jackson, Curry's oldest sister, remembered when her aunt took her and her brother to Washington, DC, and New York City in 1931. She recalled that her aunt gave her a college graduation trip to Germany in 1939. She reminisced, "Well, I remember when I was a little girl that she came to the rescue of Santa Claus' reputation when on Christmas Eve we had the family party and I did not get the book satchel that I expected to get from my mother. I said that was alright because I had asked Santa Claus and he would bring me one. But lo and behold, I got the book satchel; it was there the next morning. I found out years later my aunt Anna Forbes made a mad dash to town to a drugstore before it closed and bought the book satchel." Jackson added, "When I was a student at Florida State

College for Women, she saw to it that I had very pretty clothes. I had grown up during the Depression. I often wore other people's hand-me-downs. But Anna Forbes bought me all new clothes and very pretty, stylish clothes. She put me through school. I need to list what she did. She paid for dancing school lessons; she paid for braces on my teeth; she paid for my going to St. Mary's for three years; and two years at Florida State and paid my sorority dues."[1]

Mary Anna McBride Turner, Curry's other sister, recalled:

> [Anna Forbes Liddell] was extremely considerate and thoughtful of other people. One thing I remember, in particular, when I was eight years old, I had scarlet fever. And at that time, scarlet fever was a very serious disease for a child, extremely serious, and I was sick in bed for about six weeks and every single day I got a package from Anna Forbes. It might have been pictures that she had cut out of a magazine. . .it was small things, little things, but every day I had a package to open. I'll never forget that. . . .And she liked to make everyday events kind of special occasions, like always having a pretty table set for each meal, I think. More than for somebody to put a cereal box and a milk carton on breakfast room table. No. Everything was special. Oh, my gosh, she was fun-loving; she was outgoing; she loved to travel; she loved people. She was a great party giver. She knew how to stretch a modest income. She was good-natured and, as a child, I remember she never fussed at us. She never seemed to get mad or fuss. Do you remember her ever getting mad or fussing?

Curry replied, "I don't remember her getting mad or fussing. I do remember when she took me to the World's Fair in 1939, she made the whole tour group wait while she put foot powder in my shoes, because my new shoes had worn blisters, and I was horribly embarrassed." Turner added, "Well, she was not self-conscious. I can remember days like that, but there again, she was concerned about your feet and often she was obstinate. . . .I think everybody remembers her as fun-loving, party-giving, brilliant professor, but I remember her mostly as a thoughtful, generous, considerate person."[2]

Mary Anna Dunn, Turner's daughter, said that her great-aunt had inspired her to follow her own dream. Dunn, a poet and educator, earned an EdD in Curriculum and Instruction from the University of Virginia. She is now the director of The Enrichment Alliance of Virginia.[3]

Jane Pickens Church, Vinton Liddell Pickens's oldest daughter, remembered, "She had a wonderful way of holding onto a man. She would look up—she came up about to his belt—and she would look up at him and take hold of his necktie so he could not get away and then talk to him looking up at him."[4]

In 1960, George Milton summed up his impressions of Liddell:

> I have fully decided that she is much too fabulous to describe, and that I shouldn't have even tried to say this much. However, I must go on—words fail me when I think of her in that little red dress at one of our Art Gallery openings. She looked as if she were going to make another red-hot debut at a much too youthful 67! Or, the evening she tricked me into going home from a party before she left so that she could climb up into the tree house that the hostess had recently had constructed. Anna Forbes ("Tassels" as I have named her) knew that I would try to make her act over 18, but she just has to be as young as she feels and looks even if she is a walking brain with common sense.
>
> Once I made an *Oscar* and presented to her for being the most outstanding actress on Educational Television—and if such awards were seriously given, I'm sure she would have won it. She should be given an *Oscar* for continuously giving the best performance in 'all the world is a Stage.'[5]

Judy Matthews also remembered Liddell, "There was a lot of *womanness* about her. She was so small, she wasn't the kind of person you think of as being sexy, but there was a sexuality about her. It's like she was a certain kind of woman when she was young and she stayed the same from age twenty until she died."[6]

Richard Puckett said of Liddell, "She wasn't ordinary. That's why I liked her. I don't like just ordinary people. My brothers would say, 'Don't you know anyone that's normal.' And I said, 'Yeah, I know a lot of those people but they don't fascinate me yet.'" Then he leaned forward and said, almost in a whisper:

> I found her fascinating in all areas. She didn't know a stranger and most everyone who had met her remembered her. . . .she did not always speak up when you asked her questions but she would think about it and then she'd respond and it was exactly what you wanted to hear. If it was about a problem or someone or something she could put it all together in beautiful words, words to convey what you wanted and what she wanted you to know.[7]

As a beloved professor, Liddell challenged her students to question everything, to choose their own path in life regardless of what others may think, and to take responsibility for their choices. She repeatedly told her students, "Don't let your love go wrong." By *love*, she meant love of wisdom, which is what the word philosophy means when it is broken down to its Greek roots. She told her students that wisdom is not abstract, but is the practical ability to determine what is true and to make the best choices for one's life. Her students may not have remembered the difference between nominalism and realism, but they remembered the petite professor with the captivating personality who asked them to think big.

Liddell never published her translation of *De Docta Ignorantis,* and no copy of it has been found. Only the preface and the first page were discovered in 2008 in a box in a closet at Florida State University. The box contained the contents of her office desk. Liddell may have given the manuscript to S. J. Lemoine of the University of Wisconsin for him to complete.[8] If so, he did not publish it.

Although Liddell never published her translation, her study of Nicolas of Cusa formed her mature views and provided material for her many journal articles, conference presentations, and class lectures. The American Cusanus Society was established in 1983, four years after Liddell's death. Today, there are Cusanus Societies around the world, and Cusanus's works are available in many languages, because of Anna Forbes Liddell, Ernst Hoffmann, Raymond Klibansky, and other early twentieth century scholars who brought his work out of obscurity.

What Anna Forbes Liddell accomplished during her lifetime would be outstanding for any person in any time. When one considers she began her life's journey when women could not yet vote and when there were barriers inhibiting women from breaking out of their culture-given roles, we can better appreciate her influences as a trailblazer for women and as an inspiration for both men and women. Her competence in areas previously restricted to men helped to silence those who wanted to limit higher education for women and continues today to provide evidence that individuals must be free to follow any path in life that they choose. Or, as Anna Forbes Liddell would say, "Don't let your love go wrong."

Summary of "Arabelle and Wiggellywumps"

"The Wonderful Adventures of Arabelle and Wiggellywumps in the Enchanted Garden" is a collection of four adventures published in *Holland's Magazine* in eight installment in 1920. In the first fairy tale adventure, "The First Adventure—the Coming of Wiggellywumps," Arabelle is in her grandmother's garden sitting on a plank that forms a bridge over a drainage ditch. She holds a seedpod that has fallen out of a tree when a yellowish gray cat with white markings on his paws, neck, and chest comes into the yard. Arabelle does not know this neighbor's cat, but she knows instinctively that the cat's name is Wiggellywumps. She shows the cat the seedpod and tells him that it is a canoe and that fairies ride in such seedpod canoes. She wishes that she and Wiggellywumps could ride in a seedpod together, as the fairies do. Suddenly, the cat jumps right into the seedpod. There is plenty of room, so Arabelle jumps in, as well. Not that the seedpod is so big; but that Arabelle and Wiggellywumps have become so small.

The seedpod canoe drifts down the ditch on a stream formed by water gushing out of a garden hose. Rapids speed them past the perils of slithering serpents (worms) and a fire-breathing dragon (lizard). Suddenly, an ostrich-sized Jay Bird sweeps down to capture Wiggellywumps, who looks like a four-legged caterpillar with a long tail (a reversal on cats chasing birds). Wiggellywumps jumps out of the canoe and scampers away.

While looking for the lost cat, Arabelle sees a doodle bug hole and calls the doodle bug out with the familiar rhyme, "Doodle, Doodle, Doodle, Come and get a grain of corn." Doodle comes out of his hole, expecting corn. He fusses at Arabelle for not keeping her promise.

Next, Arabelle meets Green Knight, who looks just like a June bug. Green Knight's mission is to help damsels in distress—so he agrees to help her look for Wiggellywumps. He says that he saw a strange-looking four-legged caterpillar on the other side of the forest. Since it is too far to walk, they must fly. Even though Arabelle is small, she is too heavy to fly on the back of Green Knight. A devil's-horse bug agrees to let Arabelle ride on his back. So off they go to the other side of the forest—Arabelle on devil's-horse and Green Knight flying beside them. There, they meet KatyDid, and ask her if she saw the cat. KatyDid replies, "Katy Did see her kitten." A passing grasshopper says to ignore KatyDid, since she does nothing but always says she did. The grasshopper says that KatyDid is a liar. Arabelle instructs the grasshopper that her mother said to never call anyone a liar. The devil's-horse expresses many opinions, but he always starts each opinion with the phrase, "I never like to express an opinion, but the fact of the matter is." His opinion of lying is that all liars are occasionally truthful and that everyone lies sometimes. Maybe they should believe KatyDid. If she is lying, they will not be any worse off than they are now, and, if she is telling the truth, they will find Wiggellywumps. KatyDid says that Wiggellywumps is in the catnip bed near the forest of flowers. Arabelle asks, "Is it very far away?" The devil's-horse replies that it depends: to the snail, it is far, but to the jaybird it is not far—yet the distance is the same in both cases.

The devil's-horse, with Arabelle on his back, flies to the flower forest with Green Knight, Katy, and the grasshopper. When they get to the flower forest, they encounter a thing that is like two trees that have grown together halfway up. The thing has only two branches with twigs on the end of the branches and no leaves. The grasshopper, who has encountered many of these things before, says that they have no purpose, create much damage, steal fruit from the trees, and kill insects. The devil's-horse with Arabelle on his back lands on a brown twig that has a hard, white section on top of the end of the twig. The twig shakes and they fall off the twig into a petunia flower. Arabelle knows, without being told, that the twig was not a twig, but a human finger. She looks around for her insect friends and cannot find them.

The second adventure, "Adventure Two—The Trip to China," begins after a torrential rainstorm has caused the drainage ditch in the center of the circular driveway in the front yard to back up from leaves and sticks and form a small pond. Parks-the-Gardener makes Arabelle a boat from two magnolia leaves tied together with long thorns from a mock orange tree. He ties a thread to it to keep it from floating away. Arabelle wades into the pond, pulling the boat by the thread. She stubs her toe against a rock. She pulls the rock out of the water. The smooth white stone is the prettiest rock she has ever seen. Holding it in her left palm, she places her right thumb in the center of the rock and turns her right hand around the rock, keeping her thumb in the center. When she has turned her hand as far as it can go, she sees her fingers are pointing southeast. That is how she knows, without being told, that the rock is a wishing stone. She closes her eyes and wishes for Wiggellywumps to come play. He appears on the shore. She has to pull the boat back to the shore since cats hate getting wet.

Wiggellywumps jumps into the boat and tells Arabelle to jump in. She does and they go sailing. The pond has turned into an ocean, and they travel for a long time. Arabelle sees something blue and white in the distance. It looks like the dishes her grandmother uses to serve breakfast. Wiggellywumps says the blue and white land is China. They sail to the shore, but have trouble landing since the ground is hard and slippery, like a china plate. A wave tosses the boat ashore. Men with straight hair pulled back in long pigtails surround the girl and cat. The men, dressed in blue, speak a language Arabelle does not understand. The men are friendly and serve them tea in blue teacups. After Arabelle and Wiggellywumps drink the tea, they can speak Chinese fluently. In this land, the houses look like upside-down tea cups and the people are either leaning out of the windows or sitting on the outside of the houses—Arabelle cannot tell which it is. The men in blue take the pair to see the Emperor. A flock of blue birds lands at their feet. When Wiggellywumps jumps on a bird, he hurts his paws since the bird is hard. Mad, Wiggellywumps slaps the bird, making it fall and breaking its head off. The men are angry and throw the pair into a deep pit. Arabelle and Wiggellywumps try to climb out, but the walls of the pit are slick. Hungry, Arabelle finds four gumballs in her pocket. Wiggellywumps suggest they lick the gumballs, instead of biting into them, to make them last longer. Wiggellywumps licks his paw to clean his face after eating, as cats do. The sticky goo from the gumball gets on his paw, and then his paw sticks to the floor. Arabelle and Wiggellywumps realize they can use the sticky goo to get out of the pit. With sticky hands and paws, the pair scale the slick walls of the pit and climb out.

Astonished, the blue Emperor and men think that the pair have magical powers. The Emperor gives Arabelle a huge green palace in a green land with many green servants. In this land, there are silver bridges, a silver dragon, silver birds, and hard pink and green flowers that have no scent. This time, Wiggellywumps leaves the birds alone. Arabelle sits on a silver throne while Wiggellywumps curls up on a pillow at her feet. Tired of the green land, Arabelle and Wiggellywumps want to go home, but their boat is still in the blue land. Arabelle orders her green servants to get the boat from the blue land and place it on the ocean shore in the green land. Arabelle and Wiggellywumps climb into their boat and sail away. The ocean water drains away, and a voice in the distance calls Wiggellywumps home.

The third adventure is "Adventure Three—The Terrible Forest." On a scorching afternoon, Arabelle plays with her dolls in her nursery while the adults are resting. She undresses her dolls and puts them to bed, even though it is the middle of the afternoon. She is bored and wanders around the house, but it is dark since everyone is napping. She goes outside, parting the wild cherry trees, and is frightened because it looks like she is entering a jungle. She wants Wiggellywumps's company and knows she could summon him with her wishing stone. But she can use the stone for only one wish a day. What if she needs the stone to wish away a wild beast in the jungle? When there is something special that can be used only once a day, then a person needs to use it wisely and not waste it. She thinks about how her family would miss her if she got eaten by a wild beast. But if more than one beast attacks her, then the one wish will not save her from being eaten. With that reasoning, she might as well use her one wish to summon Wiggellywumps, which she does. Suddenly, a tiger appears. Arabelle is afraid until the tiger speaks and asks if she recognizes him. The tiger is Wiggellywumps. He always turns into a tiger when he enters a jungle.

Arabelle and Wiggellywumps trek through the jungle and hear hissing sounds in the distance. A blue bird swoops down to warn them to go away because there are snakes ahead. They ignore the warning, but soon they come to the edge of an enormous chasm full of hundreds of snakes lying on top of each other on the bottom of the chasm or slithering up the sides. Arabelle says that they must go back, but the jungle closes behind her—the trees interlock their branches and the leaves fuse to form a wall that Arabelle and Wiggellywumps cannot break through. Arabelle regrets not listening to the bird's warning. They must go forward. Wiggellywumps has an idea. Arabelle is doubtful, but follows him. They climb up a tall, slender sycamore tree. As they climb higher and higher, the tree sways across the chasm until the top of the tree is on the bank on the other side of the chasm. Arabelle climbs over Wiggellywumps's back, and then Wiggellywumps jumps onto the bank; the tree springs back. The pair runs into the forest far from the chasm with the snakes.

Next, they hear a horrible sound. A giant is walking through the forest. On this hot day, he has pulled up an oak tree to use as a parasol to protect himself from the sun. The giant is about to step on the girl and the cat, so they jump away, but Wiggellywumps lands on the giant's foot. The giant mistakes Arabelle and Wiggellywumps for toys left outside in the forest. He puts them into his pocket to take home to his giant daughter, named Tiny. The giant's house looks like a blue mountain, but it is a house, painted blue, with trees growing in the window boxes and with a stone archway for a door like the opening to a cave. Tiny treats Arabelle and Wiggellywumps as dolls. She undresses them, makes them go to bed when they are not sleepy, and spanks them when she decides they are naughty. Arabelle is humiliated, but now knows how her dolls feel when she treats them the same way. She thinks that dolls should have some rights and vows to treat her dolls better when she gets home. Tired of playing with her new dolls, Tiny goes into her mother's closet and plays dress-up with a green velvet dress. The giant mother comes home and scolds Tiny for trying on the dress. With the giant mother and daughter distracted, Arabelle and Wiggellywumps slip out of the house and run as fast as they can all the way home to Arabelle's grandmother's house. A distant voice calls Wiggellywumps home. Arabelle goes inside and lets her dolls play and enjoy themselves.

The fourth adventure is *The Last Adventure—The Robbers.* A dog chases Wiggellywumps up a pear tree in Arabelle's grandmother's yard. Since everyone knows that cats easily climb up trees, but have trouble climbing down, Arabelle climbs up into the tree to help him. When she looks down, the landscape has changed. Instead of her grandmother's house, she sees a gray stone castle. Robbers live in the castle. Arabelle can see through the window that the robbers have imprisoned a beautiful princess in a glass cage. The ugly chief robber wants to marry the princess. She refuses and says she would die before she would marry him. Arabelle knows they need a knight to save the damsel in distress. Suddenly the Green Knight she had met in her first adventure appears. Arabelle says that she needs the devil's-horse also, so Green Knight summons him. Arabelle places the wishing stone in her left palm, her right thumb in the center of the stone, and turns her hand around. Then she closes her eyes and wishes for the Green Knight and the devil's-horse to be larger than she is. Suddenly, they are out of the tree on the ground. Beside the Green Knight, now larger than she is, is a winged horse. Arabelle explains her plan to rescue the damsel in distress and says that the Green Knight should marry the damsel after they rescue her. He objects, since he has spent his life rescuing damsels in distress, and none of them expected marriage. Arabelle insists that, even if the princess does not expect marriage, he still needs to ask the princess to marry him. Then, it is up to her to decide if she wants to marry him. Arabelle helps the Green Knight with the wording of the proposal, but he objects to her suggestions, since all the phrases are only partly true, such as asking if the princess would honor him by becoming his wife and making him happy. He says that those two statements could not both be true. If she honors him with marriage, it will not make him happy. Thus, Arabelle and Green Knight compromise on his asking only for the honor of her becoming his wife. With the plan developed, Arabelle and Wiggellywumps climb on the devil's-horse's back, and the Green Knight climbs onto the back of the winged horse. Although the Green Knight flew in the first adventure, his wings are now gone, and he cannot fly. As the rescue party flies towards the castle, it moves away three times faster than the rescuers are flying. Thus, they reverse direction and go around the earth, over mountains and seas, to catch the castle.

At the castle, Green Knight subdues the chief robber who is guarding the princess. The other robbers rush into the room. Wiggellywumps holds the chief robber back, while Arabelle and Green Knight chop the other robbers in half. The devil's-horse and the winged horse kick the pieces out the window. The rescue party frees the princess from the glass cage using the key to the cage on the belt of the chief robber. Then, the rescue party locks the chief robber into the glass cage.

Arabelle is now confused since she, Wiggellywumps, the devil's-horse,

Green Knight, and the winged horse all had a part in rescuing the princess. Whom, she wonders, should the princess marry? The princess agrees that they all rescued her and falls on the floor at Arabelle's feet. Since nobody helps the princess up and since the princess is uncomfortable on the floor, she just gets up herself with nobody helping her. The Green Knight reluctantly asks the princess to marry him because Arabelle said he should. The princess declines, since she is in love with the prince imprisoned in the dungeon. They all go down to the dungeon and free the prince. So, it is not true that every damsel in distress wants to marry the man who rescues her.

Arabelle asks the princess and prince if they will marry and live in the castle. The princess says yes, and she asks Arabelle to stay and live with them. The devil's-horse whispers that the princess does not mean what she says, reminding Arabelle that sometimes people say things to be polite, but they do not really mean them. The rescue party flies back home. Arabelle notices that the trip home always feels shorter and less exciting than the trip going somewhere. Back home, Wiggellywumps wishes the Green Knight and the devil's-horse back to their regular size since Arabelle had already used her wish for the day. A voice from the house calls Arabelle in from play.

The last short segment of the fairy tale is "The End of the Story." Arabelle goes outside to say goodbye to Wiggellywumps. She places the wishing stone in her left palm, her right thumb in the center of the stone, and turns her hand around. She closes her eyes and wishes for Wiggellywumps to appear. When he appears, she tells him that she is leaving on a train that night for a visit. A voice in the distance calls Wiggellywumps. He says that the person is calling him to come eat ice cream. Arabelle says that he must go, since ice cream melts quickly. He tells her to wish for him when she gets back. She promises to do so.

Liddell's Published Writings

Compiled by Richard T. Hull and Carolyn Dubard

Listed in Chronological Order

"Feminism." *Life Magazine*, 4 Jun. 1914, 1042.

"The Wonderful Adventures of Arabelle and Wiggellywumps in the Enchanted Garden," an eight part serial, Illustrated by Hugh Rankin, *Holland's Magazine*, Feb. 1920, 70, 72, Mar. 1920, 78–79, May 1920, 82–83, Jun. 1920, 78–79, Jul. 1920, 70, 72, Aug. 1920, 70–71, Sept. 1920, 86, 87, Oct. 1920, 86, 90.

"The Theory of External Relations in Neo-Realism." Master's thesis, Cornell University, 1922.

"Review of 'Religion's Place in Securing a Better World-Order,' by James H. Tufts, *Journal of Religion*, II, 2, 113–128." Summaries of Articles, *The Philosophical Review* 31, no. 4. (Jul. 1922): 423–424.

"Review of 'The Idea of Creation,' by J. S. MacKenzie, in *Hibbert Journal* 21, no. 2, 209–226." Summaries of Articles, *The Philosophical Review* 32, no. 4. (Jul. 1923): 439–440.

"The Logical Relationship of the Philosophy of Hegel to the

Philosophies of Spinoza and Kant." PhD thesis, University of North Carolina, Jun. 1924.

"Alexander's Space, Time, and Deity: A Critical Consideration." *University of North Carolina Studies in Philosophy*, no. 2, n.d. [1925].

"Sainte Beuve." *The Reviewer* 5 (1925): 87–88. Reprinted in 1967 by Johnson Reprint Corp.

"In Defense of Absolute Ethics." *The Journal of Philosophy* 27, no. 16 (31 Jul. 1930): 430–435.

"Communication with regard to the Cusanus Commission of the Heidelberg Academie der wissenschaften." Notes and News, *The Journal of Philosophy* 29, no. 20 (29 Sept. 1932): 558–560.

"The Relation of Philosophy to Religion." *The Personalist* 17 (Aug. 1936): 407–411.

"What is a Mature Morality?" *The Philosophical Review* 55, no. 3 (May 1946): 303–304.

"Philosophical Mysticism and Modern Science." *The Personalist* 22 (1951): 172–176.

"Communication: A Personal Tribute to Ernst Hoffmann (1880–1952)." *The Journal of Philosophy* 49, no. 15 (1 Jul. 1952): 505–506.

"The Significance of the Doctrine of the Incarnation in the Philosophy of Nicholas of Cusa." *Actes du XIème Congrès International de Philosophie, Bruxelles, 20–26 Août 1953* [Proceedings of the 11th International Congress of Philosophy] 11, 126–131.

"Man and Nature in the Philosophy of Nicholas of Cusa." *Atti del XII Congresso Internazionale Filosofia* [Proceedings of the 12th International Congress of Philosophy] 12, 281–284.

"Autobiographical Professional Note of Anna Forbes Liddell." *North Carolina Lives: The Tar Heel Who's Who*, ed. by William S. Powell. Hopkinsville, Kentucky: Historical Record Association, 1962.

"Review of *Nicholas of Cusa and Medieval Political Thought*, by Paul E. Sigmund. (Cambridge: Harvard University Press, 1964)." *The Journal of*

Politics 26, no. 4 (Nov. 1964): 933–934.

"Creative Spirit in Religion and in Art." *Actes du Cinquième Congrès International d'Esthétique* [Proceedings of the 5th International Congress of Aesthetics, Amsterdam, 1964], edited by Jan Aler. Amsterdam: 1964, 834–836.

"Henry Horace Williams: An Appreciation." Appendix A, *Origin of Belief: Toward a Philosophy of Life*, by Henry Horace Williams, edited by William Beidler. Chapel Hill, N.C.: University of North Carolina, 1978.

Acknowledgements

If the Tallahassee Branch of the American Association of University Women had not started the Anna Forbes Liddell (AFL) Project in 2005, this book would not have been written. The AFL Project collected information about Liddell to use in fundraising for the Anna Forbes Liddell Fellowship. This book is the fulfillment of a short book proposed by the branch. I am grateful to all the members of the branch because every member had a part in the project. The AFL Project interviewed Liddell's family and former colleagues, students, and friends over a two-year period. Nancy Benda, Jean Bryant, Eva Curry (Liddell's niece), Marian Moore, and I conducted interviews. The interviewers, in addition to Richard Hull, Jo Conte, and Patricia Green-Powell, developed the concept for the short book. Judy Etemadi transcribed the taped interviews. Ada Burnett produced a writing style guide for project writers.

William Adkins joined the Project because of his interest in Liddell's life. In the 1960s, he had Liddell as a substitute professor for one day in a course. He never forgot that day and the captivating lesson she provided. Years later, he was surprised to find three of Liddell's journals in a flea market. He eagerly bought the journals. Adkins provided the journals for use by the project.

Adkins, Hull, and I continued to search for material. Hull found a copy of Liddell's fairy tale published in *Holland's Magazine.* He also located Liddell's other writings and compiled a list of the writings (published and unpublished) and of citations of her in articles and books. In 2006, a box of Liddell's professional and personal papers were found in a closet at Florida State University. The FSU Special Collections kept most of the material to form the *Anna Forbes Liddell Papers.*

In 2012, the AFL Project abandoned the short book project because the archival material found was too extensive. The time needed to review adequately all the material and write an appropriate manuscript was more than the group wanted to do. At that point, I decided to write a full-length biography of Liddell using the collected material. Richard Hull enthusiastically endorsed my decision. His interest and encouragement were crucial to my completing the book. He encouraged me when my motivation lagged and periodically asked me how I was coming along on my book project. If I had set the project aside, his question would prompt me to work again on the project. Throughout the development of this book, he was a mentor and friend.

My early readers suffered through my initial writing attempts and provided excellent feedback, along with encouragement. They were Tara Boyter, Judy Etemadi, Richard Hull, Ann Mock, David Mock, and Amanda Woods. My early editor was Terry Williams. My final editor was Elizabeth Boepple. Both editors helped me clarify my purpose and develop my writing style. Historians David Mock and Irvin Winsboro professionally reviewed my manuscript and made recommendations for improving the historical context. Ann and David Mock continued their support as beta readers. Other beta readers were Pamela Crosby, Gene Tanner, and Linda Wright.

Rebekka White, a Florida State University (FSU) graduate student in the Department of Modern Languages and Linguistics, translated the Hoffmann letters from German to English. I am grateful to archivists Sandra Varry and Paige Downey who searched the photograph collections of the Heritage and University Archives, Florida State University Libraries, for photos of Liddell and assisted me with the process of obtaining permission to use the photographs. Arlene Bischoff gathered images from Mary Anna McBride Turner's family scrapbook. Turner is Liddell's niece.

I am grateful to Liddell's family members who shared their memories with me. I had many discussions with Eva Curry and Mary Anna Turner and great-niece Mary Anna Dunn. Anne Bentley, Liddell's great-niece, provided photographs.

Finally, I thank my husband. This book was sixteen years in the making. During this time, it was as if Anna Forbes Liddell had moved into the house with us. I thank John for his patience in listening almost daily to the many stories of Liddell and my research journey.

About the Author

Carolyn Dubard began her career in 1969, which was only seven years after Anna Forbes Liddell's retirement. She experienced firsthand the barriers that still existed for women in nontraditional fields and was grateful for the opportunities she had because of women, like Liddell, who preceded her. Dubard earned a PhD in measurement and statistics. Her models for forecasting school enrollment have been used by the state of Florida for over forty years to fund public school education.

Notes

Introduction

1. Tad Bartimus, "Dr. Anna Liddell in Second Battle for Women's Rights," *Tallahassee Democrat*, 10 Apr. 1973.

2. Ibid.

3. Ibid.

The Liddells Move South

1. Anna Forbes Liddell (AFL), *Diary & Stories of Anna Forbes Liddell*, 91–94, Mary Anna Turner private collection.

2. "The Funeral of Mr. Liddell," *Charlotte Observer*, 6 Nov. 1888; Helen Ogden Liddell (HOL), "Re Liddell Family (II)," Liddell and Pickens Family Papers, Southern Heritage Collection, Wilson Library, University of North Carolina at Chapel Hill (LPFP).

3. Vinton Liddell Pickens (VLP), "Liddells 1819–1821," LPFP; John Miller, *A Twentieth Century History of Erie County, Pennsylvania: A Narrative Account of its Historical Progress, its People, and Its Principal Interests,* Vol. I. (Chicago: The Lewis Publishing Company, 1909), Kindle edition. 690–693; Lyla Sparks, comp. *Atlantic*

Ports, Gulf Coasts, and Great Lakes Passenger Lists, Roll 6; 1820–1863 [database online], Provo, UT, USA: Ancestry.com Operations Inc., 2003; "The Funeral of Mr. Liddell," *Charlotte Observer*, 6 Nov. 1888. The Erie City Iron Works was established in 1864, when George Selden and J.H. Bliss bought out W.J.F's interest in the firm of Liddell, Selden & Bliss. The latter firm had been preceded by the New Foundry, which was the preceded by the Old Foundry.

4. James Forbes to James Liddell, date illegible, LPFP; HOL, "Re Liddell Family (II);" AFL, *Diary & Stories of Anna Forbes Liddell*, 91–92.

5. HOL, "Re Liddell Family (II);" Anna Amelia Liddell to Vinton Liddell (AFL's cousin), 30 Nov. 1913, LPFP; US Department of Commerce, Bureau of Census, *Historical Statistics of the United States, Colonial Times to 1970*, "Table: School Enrollment Rates, by Color and Sex: 1850 to 1957," 213; "A Remarkable Woman," *New-York Tribune*, 23 Sept. 1920.

6. Copy of marriage certificate, LPFP; HOL, "Re Liddell Family (II);" Miller, *A Twentieth Century History,"*693; conversion from 1864 to 2021 dollars as of 12 May 2021, https://www.measuringworth.com/dollarvaluetoday/?amount=10000&from=1864. Depere is sometimes written DePere or De Pere.

7. HOL, "Re Liddell Family (II)."

8. Barbara Miller Solomon, *In the Company of Educated Women,* (New Haven, CT: Yale University Press, 1985), Tables 1–3, 44, 63–64.

9. Ibid., 27, 49, 80–87, 95.

10. Julia Ann Lorenz Eaton, untitled note about Annie's diary, LPFP; Annie Liddell, *Diary*, Sept.–Dec. 1866, LPFP. The quote is on page 4.

11. "1866 to 1875," https://www.bucknell.edu/about-bucknell/womens-resource-center/history-of-women-at-bucknell/1866-to-1875, accessed 29 Jun. 2019. link is no longer active; Solomon, *In the Company of Educated Women*, 100–101.

12. Annie Liddell, *Diary*, 28 Sept. 1866, 5, LPFP; Annie Liddell to W.J.F. Liddell, 11 Dec. 1868 and 16 Jul. 1872, LPFP.

13. AFL, *Diary & Stories*, 88–89; VLP, "1868–1874," LPFP; Annie Liddell to W.J.F. Liddell, 22 Aug. 1872, LPFP; regarding Walter's college enrollment and expulsion, communication from Eva Curry to author, 2010. Forbes is listed in the 1872–1873 yearbook as being in the junior preparatory department of Lawrence

University in Appleton, Wisconsin. However, a letter from Annie Liddell to Forbes, 11 Nov. 1872, LPFP, for Forbes's recent move to Salt Lake City for his asthma.; W.J.F. Liddell, "Retribution," undated, LPFP.

14. HOL, "Re Liddell Family (II)."

15. HOL, "Re Liddell Family (II);" US Department of the Treasury, *Financial Panic of 1873*, https://home.treasury.gov/about/history/freedmans-bank-building/financial-panic-of-1873.

16. HOL, "Re Liddell Family (II);" "Car Building." *Wisconsin State Journal*, 25 Nov. 1871.

17. HOL, "Re Liddell Family (II);" *Green Bay Weekly Gazette*, 15 May 1875; Anna Amelia Liddell to Eva and Vinton Liddell, 11 May 1876, LPFP; Jane Liddell Battle, "Re Liddell Family (I)," LPFP.

18. The population of the township of Charlotte was 6,085 in 1870 and 10,547 in 1880, see *1880 Census: Volume 1. Statistics of the Population of the United States*, Table III, 282, https://www.2.census.gov/library/publications/decennial/1880/vol-01-population/1880_v1-11.pdf; "The Visitors to Charlotte," *Charlotte Democrat*, 24 May 1875; Evan Andrews, "Did North Carolina Issue the First Declaration of Independence?" (1 Sept. 2018), https://www.history.com/news/did-north-carolina-issue-the-first-declaration-of-independence; James Williams, "The Mecklenburg Declaration–History" (10 Jun. 2008), https://www.meckdec.org/declaration.

19. HOL, "Re Liddell Family (II)."

20. Jane Liddell Battle, "Re Liddell Family (I).

21. VLP, "Liddell 1876–1879," LPFP.

22. Frances Fielden Eppley, *The First Baptist Church of Charlotte,* (Charlotte, NC: Heritage Printers, Inc., 1981), 59, 61, 68, 116; Carrie L. McClean, *First Baptist Church, Charlotte, NC, 1832–1916*, (Charlotte, NC: Washburn Press, 1917), 52, 57–65, 116.

23. "Death Comes to Vinton Liddell," *Charlotte News*, 15 May 1915; Jane Liddell Battle, "Re Liddell Family (I);"Thomas W. Hanchett, "The Growth of Charlotte: a History," https://www.mecknc.gov/Pages/RegionalHistory.aspx, accessed 12 Feb. 2021.

24. VLP, "1876–1879;" HOL, "Re Liddell Family (II)."

25. Find a Grave, memorial page for David Jayne Hill (10 Jun. 1850–2 Mar. 1932), Find A Grave Memorial no. 115029341, https://www.findagrave.com.

26. VLP, "Liddell 1882–1884," LPFP.

27. HOL, "Re Liddell Family (II)."

28. "The Death of Mr. W.J.F. Liddell," *Charlotte Observer*, 2 Nov. 1888; "Mrs. Liddell Dies, Age 98," *Charlotte News*, 30 Nov. 1922; AFL, *Diary and Stories of Anna Forbes Liddell*, 97–98.

29. Walter Scott Liddell to Helen Ogden, 20 Sept. 1885, LPFP.

Parents Nellie and Walter

1. Walter Scott Liddell to Helen Ogden, 20 Sept. 1885, Liddell and Pickens Family Papers, Southern Heritage Collection, Wilson Library, University of North Carolina at Chapel Hill (LPFP).

2. Ibid.

3. Janet L. Coryell, and Nora Faires, *A History of Women in America*, (New York: McGraw Hill, 2012), 45–47.

4. Nancy Woloch, *Women and the American Experience: a Concise History*, 2nd edition, (Boston: McGraw Hill/Irwin, 2002), 131–132; Vinton Liddell Pickens (VLP), "1915," LPFP, for Jane not having control of her money until after her husband Vinton's death.

5. Walter Scott Liddell to Helen Ogden, 20 Sept. 1885, LPFP. Ogden's questions to him were referenced indirectly.

6. Ibid., 4 Jan. 1886 (2), LPFP. There were two letters dated 4 Jan. 1886 in the transcribed collection. This letter is probably the one dated incorrectly. The correct date is likely a different day in January 1886.

7. Helen Ogden Liddell (HOL), "Re Liddell Family (II)," LPFP; Walter Scott Liddell to Helen Ogden, 4 Jan. 1886 (1), LPFP.

8. HOL, "Re Liddell Family (II)."

9. AFL, *Diary & Stories of Anna Forbes Liddell*, 85–94, Mary Anna Turner private collection.

10. HOL, "Re Liddell Family (II);" for AFL's sister Helen's birth date, *see* AFL,

Journal, 2:136, William Adkins private collection.

11. "The Death of Mr. W.J.F. Liddell, "*Charlotte Observer*, 2 Nov. 1888; *Charlotte Observer*, 1 Jan. 1886, for Robert McDowell's death notice; HOL, "Re Liddell Family (II)."

12. AFL, *Diary & Stories*, 151–153; Eva Curry to her cousins, 20 Dec. 2006, Eva Curry private collection.

13. "Addressed, Professors Confess," *Florida Flambeau*, 16 Jan. 1948.

14. "The Oasis Shriners History," http://www.oasisshriners.org/Our%20History.htm, accessed 29 Jul. 2019; link is no longer active; "The Widows' Fund," *Evening Chronicle*, 5 Dec. 1913; "Shriners Leave for Raleigh Meet Begins Tomorrow," *Charlotte News*, 22 May 1916; "Masonic," *Charlotte Observer*, 3 Dec. 1922. Later, when the Omar Temple was established, the Widows' Fund became a combined effort of the Oasis and Omar Temples, and the name changed to the Widows' Fund of Oasis and Omar Temples. At first, members of the Fund paid a fee upon application and were assessed $1.10 whenever a member died. The ten cents was used for administrative costs, and the one dollar was sent to the widow within twenty-four hours. As the number of members increased, the amount sent to the widow increased. Eventually, the plan assessed a small monthly fee, and the widow received a fixed amount of $1,500.

15. AFL, *Journal,* 2:3–4, 86, 104, 185.

16. AFL said, "My father is a Southerner, I am a Southerner, but my mother is a Yankee," family story told by Mary Anna Turner to author in 2012; for picnic, *see* VLP, "Liddell 1876–1879," LPFP; Louise Thompson Murrill, "Historical Sketch of YWCA of the City of Charlotte," *Charlotte News: Young Women's Christian Association Edition*, 26 May 1914.

17. AFL, *Diary & Stories*, 137–139.

18. Ibid., 151–153. The types of fabrics come from various letters of AFL to her mother, LPFP.

19. "Miss Liddell Delights in New Fields to Conquer—And Philosophy, *Tampa Tribune*, 4 Oct. 1959.

20. AFL, *Diary & Stories*, 86, 150; AFL, *Journal,* 2:97.

21. AFL, *Diary & Stories,"* 118.

22. AFL, *Journal,* 2:73.

23. HOL. "Re Liddell Family (II);" AFL, *Diary &Stories*, 143–144.

24. Quote from AFL, *Journal,* 2:128–129; other rules in AFL, *Diary &Stories,* 149–150.

25. Mary Anna Turner, Tallahassee American Association of University Women Interview (TAAUWI) (22 Aug. 2009), Carolyn Dubard private collection.

26. Linda Harkey, "Anna Forbes Liddell," in *FSU Voices: An Informal History of 150 Years*, edited by Maxine Stern, (Tallahassee, FL: Florida State University, 2002), 50.

27. Richard Puckett, TAAUWI (20 Nov. 2005), Carolyn Dubard private collection.

28. AFL, *Journal,* 2:129–130.

29. Carrie L. McClean, *First Baptist Church, Charlotte, NC, 1832–1916*, (Charlotte: Washburn Press, 1917), 116; AFL, *Diary & Stories of Anna Forbes Liddell*, 139–140. "National known Mason Dies Here at Age of 87 after Long Illness," unsourced newspaper clipping, Anna Forbes Liddell Papers, Special Collections & Archives, Florida State University Libraries, Tallahassee, FL.

30. AFL, *Journal,* 2:10; Frances Fielden Eppley, *The First Baptist Church of Charlotte*, (Charlotte, NC: Heritage Printers, Inc., 1981), 116–117.

31. AFL to HOL, 28 Feb. 1927, LPFP.

Family's Influence

1. Anna Forbes Liddell (AFL), *Journal,* 1:58–60, William Adkins private collection.

2. AFL, *Diary & Stories of Anna Forbes Liddell*, 113, Mary Anna Turner private collection.

3. David Hill to Eva Liddell, 13 May 1880, 19 Jan. 1881, 15 Feb. 1881, 27 Feb. 1881, 21 Mar. 1881, 8 Apr. 1881, 27 Dec. 1885, and 25 Feb. 1886, Liddell and Pickens Family Papers, Southern Heritage Collection, Wilson Library, University of North Carolina at Chapel Hill (LPFP). The quote is in the 13 May 1880 letter.

4. Vinton Liddell Pickens (VLP), "1906" and "1907," LPFP; "Death comes to Vinton Liddell," *Charlotte News*, 15 May 1915; for Vinton Liddell's business

interests, *see* "Vinton Liddell, President of Gingham Mill," *Charlotte Democrat*, 14 Apr. 1893; *Charlotte Observer*, 6 Feb. 1894; *Charlotte News*, 17 Apr. 1900.

5. Countess Olga Taveggi to Jane Hall Liddell, 10 Sept. 1914, LPFP; VLP, "Annual Notes 1914," LPFP; Helen Ogden Liddell (HOL), "Re Liddell Family (II)," LPFP.

6. "Thomas S. Franklin (1907–1909)" (2020), https://charlottenc.gov/Mayor/PastMayors/Pages/ThomasFranklin.aspx; AFL *Journal*, 2:4, 7, 15.

7. AFL, *Journal*, 2:14.

8. Ibid., 2:14–15.

9. AFL, *Diary & Stories*, 97–98.

10. Ibid., 129–134.

11. Anna Amelia Liddell to Vinton Liddell (her son), 25 Oct. 1913, LPFP.

12. Anna Amelia Liddell to Walter Liddell Hill, 23 Aug. 1896, LPFP.

13. Rory Dicker, *A History of U.S. Feminisms* (Berkeley, CA: Seal Press, 2016), 29–44.

14. AFL *Diary & Stories*, 111.

15. Ibid.103–108.

16. AFL, *Journal*, 2:79.

17. Ibid., 2:113.

18. Ibid., 2:80–81.

19. AFL, *Journal*, 2:88, 112; her imaginative scenes are inferred from her fairy tale "The Adventures of Arabelle and Wiggellywumps in the Enchanted Garden" which was autobiographical in nature, *Holland's Magazine*, 1920.

20. AFL, *Journal*, 2:66–72.

21. The first three journals are in William Adkins Private Collection; the fourth journal is in Mary Anna Turner Private Collection. The addition of notations is why her journals overlap in time. The first has its initial entry in 1903 when she was twelve with additions through 1908. The second journal starts in July 1905 and ends in February 1908. The third journal begins in 1911 and ends in 1917 when she was twenty-five. The fourth journal, likely written entirely in 1908, is entitled *Diary & Stories of Anna Forbes Liddell* and is the one that is least like a diary, regardless of the title, because it has fewer daily entries and more essays.

22. AFL, *Journal*, 1:83–84.

23. Ibid., 1:63, 94–95.

24. AFL, *Diary & Stories*, 92.

25. For Katherine Liddell's education, see unsourced newspaper clipping of obituary of Katherine Liddell, LPFP.

Coming of Age (1898–1912)

1. Charlotte Mecklenburg Library, "The Charlotte-Mecklenburg Story," https://www.cmstory.org/exhibits/turn-20th-century-life-charlotte-1900-1910-schools/south-graded-school, accessed 24 Feb. 2018; Mary Myers Dwelle, "Life was a Song on Old East Avenue," *Charlotte Observer*, 27 Jun. 1965. Mary Myers Dwelle was a contemporary of Anna Forbes Liddell and the sister of Rawley Myers, Anna Forbes's fiancé.

2. Anna Forbes Liddell (AFL), *Journal*, 1:80, William Adkins private collection.

3. Ibid.; AFL, "The Maple Tree's Story of Its Life," unpublished essay for school, 17 May 1902, Anna Forbes Liddell Papers, Special Collections & Archives, Florida State University Libraries, Tallahassee, FL (AFLP).

4. Mildred Morse McEwen, *Queens College: Yesterday & Today* (Charlotte, NC: Heritage Printers, Inc., 1980), 74; In 1914 the school's name was changed to Queens College which became Queens University in 2002.

5. North Carolina State Department of Education, "The History of Education in North Carolina" (1993), 12–13, https://files.eric.ed.gov/fulltext/ED369713.pdf.

6. AFL, *Journal*, 2:104–105.

7. Ibid., 2:142–143; Mildred Morse McEwen, *Queens College*, 74. The details of the conversation between Anna Forbes Liddell and her parents are given in her journal for her returning for her sophomore year; she did not write in her journal the summer before her first boarding year at the college; it is inferred that her parents had the same objections in the summer of 1906 that they had in summer 1907.

8. AFL, *Journal*, 2:142–143.

9. Ibid.

10. Ibid.

11. *Edelweiss (*Charlotte, NC: The Students of the Presbyterian College, printed by Ray Printing Company, 1907, 1908).

12. AFL, *Journal*, 2:119–120.

13. Ibid., 2:108–110. Quotes are on page 109.

14. Ibid., 2:88–89.

15. Ibid., 2:147–157.

16. Ibid., 2:170.

17. Ibid., 2:169–172.

18. Ibid., 2:172–173.

19. Ibid.

20. Ibid., 2: 179–180.

21. Ibid.

22. Barbara Elizabeth Lambert, "Anna Forbes" (1991), in William S. Powell, ed., *Dictionary of North Carolina Biography*, 6 vols. (Chapel Hill: University of North Carolina Press, 1996), https://www.ncpedia.org/biography/liddell-anna.

23. F.S. Freeman, Harry Caplan, and P.M. O'Leary, "Robert Morris Ogden" (1959), https://ecommons .cornell.edu/bitstream/handle/1813/18344/Ogden_Robert_Morris_1959.pdf?sequence=2&isAllowed=y.

24. AFL, *Journal*, 2:81–82.

25. Ibid., 2:83.

26. AFL, *Journal*, 1:162–164.

27. AFL, *Journal*, 2:187–188.

28. Ibid., 2:188–191.

29. AFL, *Journal*, 2:17; AFL, *Journal*, 3:8; AFL to Helen Liddell (sister), 28 Jan. 1906, LPFP.

30. AFL, *Journal*, 2: 43.

31. AFL, *Diary & Stories of Anna Forbes Liddell*, 25-28, Mary Anna Turner private collection

32. AFL, *Journal*, 2:140–141.

33. Email communication from Mary Anna Dunn to author, 21 Feb. 2020, concerning Helen's status. Kitty Cramer began her debutante time in fall 1909. When she finished her third debutante year, she did not have a marriage proposal,

or at least a proposal that she wanted to accept. Her life would have twists and turns that no one could have foreseen. She eventually married in 1915, was widowed with six children in 1930, married James Rowland Angell, (President of Yale University) in 1932, and co-founded with Francis Roth the New Haven Restaurant Institute (later named the Culinary Institute of America) in 1946. Kitty chaired the Board of Directors of the Institute until her retirement in 1966. *Gaston Gazette*, "Who Is Katharine Cramer Angell?" https://www.gastongazette.com/news/20170927/who-is-katharine-cramer-angell.

34. AFL, *Journal*, 3:8.

35. Ibid., 3:19–21.

36. Ibid., 3:24; Brenda Marks Eagles, "Daniel Augustus Tompkins," in Powell, *Dictionary of North Carolina Biography* (Chapel Hill: University of North Carolina Press, 1996), 6:42–43.

37. AFL, *Journal*, 3:24, 30.

38. "Raleigh Man Promoted," News and Observer (Raleigh, NC), 2 Apr. 1912; AFL, *Journal*, 3:30–32.

Suffrage Work (1913–1914)

1. Anna Forbes Liddell (AFL) to Jane Liddell Battle, 28 Jun. 1938, Liddell and Pickens Family Papers, Southern Heritage Collection, Wilson Library, University of North Carolina at Chapel Hill (LPFP); "Topics of the Times: Contrasting a Count with Guesses," *The New York Times,* 7 May 1912; Mary Walton, *A Woman's Crusade: Alice Paul and the Battle for the Ballot* (New York: St. Martin's Press, 2016), Kindle edition, 65.

2. Rory Dicker, *A History of U.S. Feminisms* (Berkeley, CA: Seal Press, 2016), 48; Walton, *A Woman's Crusade*, 5, 21–23, 50–52; Nancy Woloch, *Women and the American Experience: A Concise History*, 2nd ed. (New York: McGraw Hill, 2002), 141.

3. Walton, *A Woman's Crusade*, 62–65. Adelaide Grant, a federal government clerk, was brutally beaten and raped on Christmas evening 1912. Nathaniel Green was arrested and tried for the crime. He was convicted of the crime and sentenced

to death by hanging which was carried out on June 9, 1913; see Daniel Allen Hearn, *Legal Executions in Delaware, the District of Columbia, Maryland, Virginia and West Virginia: A Comprehensive Registry, 1866–1962* (Jefferson, NC: McFarland, 2015), 21.

4. Walton, *A Woman's Crusade*, 62–65; Sheridan Harvey, "Marching for the Vote: Remembering the Woman Suffrage Parade of 1913, *The Library of Congress Information Bulletin* (6 Sept. 2018), https://guides.loc.gov/american-women-essays/marching-for-the-vote.

5. Alice Janigro, "Ida B. Wells 1862–1931," https://suffrage100ma.org/ida-b-wells/, accessed 13 Feb. 2021; Walton, *A Woman's Crusade*, 62–65.

6. Harvey, "Marching for the Vote."

7. Walton, *A Woman's Crusade*, 79; Harvey, "Marching for the Vote."

8. "10,000 Marchers in Suffrage Line," *New York Times,* 4 May 1913.

9. Rima Greenberg, "Women's Rights? She's a Pioneer," *Tampa Bay Times* (St. Petersburg, FL), 1 Apr. 1973.

10. Fannie Lou Bingham, "Women Looking Back to Fight for Vote," *Charlotte News*, 3 Feb. 1935; Ida Husted Harper, ed., *The History of Woman Suffrage* (New York: Source Book Press, 1922/1970), vol. 6, chap. 32, Kindle edition; "Equal Suffrage League Formed," *Evening Chronicle*, 11 Oct. 1913. Suzanne Bynum is sometimes listed as being from Ashville and other times as being from Charlotte. She grew up in Arden, a small community near Ashville, but lived in Charlotte as a young woman.

11. Bingham, "Women Looking Back to Fight for Vote." The newspaper article was written decades after the events and was based on recollections. The date for forming the Charlotte Equal Suffrage League was printed as 1912. The actual date was 1913 based on other sources previously cited, such as Ida Husted Harper, *The History of Woman Suffrage*.

12. "Equal Suffrage League Formed," *The Evening Chronicle*, 11 Oct. 1913; "Mrs. Valentine on Equal Suffrage," *Evening Chronicle,* 3 Nov. 1913; "Equal Suffrage League Gaining Strength," *Charlotte News,* 7 Nov. 1913; untitled article, *Charlotte Observer,* 4 Nov. 1913.

13. Donald G. Matthews and Jane Sherron De Hart, *Sex, Gender, and the Politics of ERA* (New York: Oxford University Press, 1990), 8–9; "Equal Suffrage League

for North Carolina Incorporated," *Evening Chronicle* (Charlotte, NC), 28 Nov. 1913. Incorporators were Anna Forbes Liddell, Susan Bynum, Laura Reilley, Annie Abbott, M. L. Bynum, Alma Maxwell and Mary Palmer.

14. A. Elizabeth Taylor, "The Woman Suffrage Movement in North Carolina: Part I," *The North Carolina Historical Review* 38, no. 1 (Jan. 1961), 47–48; Matthews and De Hart, *Sex, Gender, and the Politics of ERA*, 7.

15. Glenda Elizabeth Gilmore, *Gender and Jim Crow: Women and the Politics of White Supremacy in North Carolina, 1896–1920* (University of North Carolina Press, 1996), 105–114.

16. Public Laws of North Carolina, 1899, Chapter 218, §§ 4–5; William S. Powell, *North Carolina through Four Centuries* (University of North Carolina Press, 1989), 435–436.

17. Elna C. Green, *Southern Strategies: Southern Women and the Woman Suffrage Question* (Chapel Hill: University of North Carolina Press: 1997), 45–55.

18. Powell, *North Carolina through Four Centuries*, 451–452; Green, *Southern Strategies*, 47–48; Gilmore, *Gender and Jim Crow*, 58–59.

19. Powell, *North Carolina through Four Centuries* 159–160; Mathews and De Hart, *Sex, Gender, and the Politics of ERA*, 195–202.

20. Anastatia Sims, *The Power of Femininity in the New South: Women's Organizations and Politics in North Carolina, 1880–1930* (Columbia, SC: University of South Carolina Press, 1997), 45–47. In 1902, seven local North Carolina clubs joined to form the North Carolina Federation of Women's Clubs (NCFWS). Other North Carolina organizations that formed statewide clubs after 1900 were the Daughters of the American Revolution and the Order of King's Daughters. These three North Carolina organizations (NCFWC, DAR, and King's Daughters) only admitted White women. North Carolina Black women formed their own local clubs and, in 1909, they formed North Carolina Federation of Colored Women's Clubs (NCFCWC). There were also Black chapters of King's Daughters and the Women's Christian Temperance Union.

21. Bingham, "Women Looking Back to Fight for Vote."

22. Communication from Mary Anna McBride Turner to author, 9 Mar. 2020.

23. AFL, *Journal*, 3:10, William Adkins private collection.

24. Ibid., 3:33–35.

25. Ibid., 3:9.

26. AFL, "Charlotte Girl" (n.d.), *Tassels*, Richard Puckett Private Collection.

27. AFL to Helen Ogden Liddell (HOL), 26 Jan. 1914, LPFP.

28. Ibid., 3 Feb. 1914; Natalie Naylor, *Women in Long Island's Past: A History of Eminent Ladies and Everyday Lives* (Charleston, SC: The History Press, 2012), 120–122.

29. John Strausbaugh, *The Village: 400 Years of Beats and Bohemians, Radicals and Rogues: A History of Greenwich Village* (Sidney, Australia: HarperCollins, 2013), Kindle edition, 99.

30. AFL to HOL, 3 Mar. 1914, LPFP.

31. Ibid.

32. Margaret Supplee Smith and Emily Herring Wilson, *North Carolina Women Making History* (Chapel Hill: University of North Carolina Press: 1999), 216; Bingham, "Suffragist Float Attracts Attention," *Charlotte Observer,* 21 May 1914; Victor Stephenson, "Story of the Suffrage Float," *Charlotte Observer,* 1 Nov. 1914.

33. Bingham, "Suffragist Float Attracts Attention;" Stephenson, "Story of the Suffrage Float."

34. AFL, "Feminism," *Life Magazine* (4 Jun. 1914), 1042.

35. Harper, *The History of Woman Suffrage* 6, chap. 32, Kindle edition; A. Elizabeth Taylor, "The Woman Suffrage Movement in North Carolina: Part I," *The North Carolina Historical Review* 38, no. 1 (Jan. 1961), 53–54.

36. "Want to Amend the Constitution," *Charlotte Observer,* 11 Nov. 1914; Harper, *The History of Woman Suffrage* 6, chap. 32, Kindle edition.

37. Ancestry.com, *U.S., World War I Draft Registration Cards, 1917–1918* [database on-line]. Provo, UT, USA: Ancestry.com Operations Inc, 2005; Don Schick, *Then & Now: Charlotte* (Charleston, SC: Arcadia Publishing, 2006), 84.

38. AFL, *Journal*, 3:37.

A Formative Time (1915–1916)

1. Anna Forbes Liddell (AFL) to Helen Ogden Liddell (HOL), 3 Feb. 1915 and 11 Feb. 1915, Liddell and Pickens Family Papers, Southern Heritage

Collection, Wilson Library, University of North Carolina at Chapel Hill (LPFP).

2. Paula Dean, *Women on the Hill: A History of Women at the University of North Carolina at Chapel Hill* (Chapel Hill: University of North Carolina at Chapel Hill, 1987), 7.

3. Ibid; no title, Coediquette, *Daily Tar Heel,* 27 Oct. 1917.

4. William D. Snider, *Light on the Hill: a History of the University of North Carolina at Chapel Hill* (Chapel Hill: University of North Carolina Press, 1992), 156.

5. Fannie Lou Bingham, "Women Looking Back to Fight for Vote." *Charlotte News,* 3 Feb. 1934.

6. AFL to HOL, 3 Feb. 1915, LPFP; "Addresses Delivered Yesterday by Equal Suffrage Leaders," *News and Observer* (Raleigh, NC), 3 Feb. 1915.

7. Ibid.

8. AFL to HOL, 3 Feb. 1915, LPFP.

9. Matthews and De Hart, *Sex, Gender, and the Politics of ERA,* 9–11.

10. Rory Dicker, *A History of U.S. Feminisms* (Berkeley, CA: Seal Press, 2016), 49.

11. "Thinks Women Should Be Allowed to Vote," *Charlotte News,* 4 Apr. 1915.

12. "Miss Liddell Delights in New Fields to Conquer—And Philosophy," *Tampa Tribune*, 4 Oct. 1959.

13. AFL to Vinton Liddell (AFL's cousin), 10 Oct. 1915, LPFP; Terry Miller, *Greenwich Village and How It Got That Way* (New York: Crown Publishers, Inc., 1990), 112–115; "The Emma Goldman Papers," *Meet Emma: Online Exhibit,* http://www.lib.berkeley.edu/goldman/MeetEmmaGoldman/index.html.

14. Miller, *Greenwich Village,* 112–115, 120–124.

15. Allen Churchill, *The Improper Bohemians: A Re-creation of Greenwich Village in Its Heyday* (New York: E.P. Dutton & Company, 1959), 39, 51, 75–76.

16. "1915: Women March for Suffrage in New York City," (23 Oct. 2014), Behind the Scenes, http://behindthescenes.nyhistory.org/1915-women-march-suffrage/; Gerald McFarland, *Inside Greenwich Village: A New York City Neighborhood, 1898–1918* (Amherst: University of Massachusetts Press, 2001), 210–226; AFL to Vinton Liddell (cousin), 10 Oct. 1915, LPFP.

17. "Miss Liddell Delights in New Fields to Conquer—And Philosophy,." *Tampa Tribune*, 4 Oct. 1959.

18. Linda Ben-Zvi, *Susan Glaspell: Her Life and Times* (New York: Oxford University Press, 2005), 150.

19. AFL to HOL, 16 Feb. 1916, LPFP; the transcriber couldn't read the date clearly on the original and guessed 1915; a question mark was added beside the year; the correct year is 1916 since AFL was in Chapel Hill in Feb. 1915 and in New York in Feb. 1916.

20. AFL, *Journal*, 3:38, William Adkins private collection; "Dr. Liddell to Speak at 'Coffee Hour'," *Tallahassee Democrat*, 24 Feb. 1960.

21. Victor Stephenson to AFL (undated), Anna Forbes Liddell Papers, Special Collections & Archives, Florida State University Libraries, Tallahassee, FL (AFLP); AFL, *Journal*, 3:38.

22. The Village Group, "Bobby Edwards, the Troubadour of Greenwich Village," http://ullagegroup.com/2011/01/14/bobby-edwards-the-troubadour-of-greenwich-village-10/; Churchill, *The Improper Bohemians*, 30.

23. John Strausbaugh, *The Village: 400 Years of Beats and Bohemians, Radicals and Rogue* (New York: HarperCollins Publishers Inc., 2013), Kindle edition, 80–81; Churchill, *The Improper Bohemians*, 34–35.

24. Robert Schulman, *Romany Marie: The Queen of Greenwich Village*, front flap of book cover, 92–93, back book cover.

25. AFL to HOL, 16 Feb. 1916, LPFP.

26. AFL to Jane Hall Liddell, 4 Mar. 1916, LPFP.

27. June Sochen, *The New Woman: Feminism in Greenwich Village, 1910–1920* (New York: Quadrangle Books, 1972), 26–45; "Dr. Liddell to Speak at 'Coffee Hour'," *Tallahassee Democrat*, 24 Feb. 1960. Liddell expressed that view in 1914 and in 1926. It is inferred that she had that view in 1916.

28. AFL, *Journal*, 3:37.

29. VLP, "Notes 1908," LPFP.

30. Hugh D. Hindman, *Child Labor: An American History* (Armonk, NY: M.E. Sharpe, 2002), 55.

31. AFL, *Journal*, 3:42.

32. Ibid., 3:44.

33. Victor Stephenson to AFL, n.d., AFLP.

34. Ibid.

35."Miss Liddell Delights in New Fields to Conquer—And Philosophy," *Tampa Tribune*, 4 Oct. 1959.

The University Of North Carolina (1916–1918)

1. Anna Forbes Liddell (AFL), Coediquette, *Daily Tar Heel*, 15 September 1917. The newspaper column has no title or byline, but the content identifies Liddell as the author.

2. Mrs. J.A. Yarbrough, "Dr. Anna Forbes Liddell," Interesting Carolina People, *Charlotte Observer*, 8 Sept. 1935. Gladys Avery was also enrolled at UNC when Liddell returned in 1916.

3. "Addressed, Professors Confess," *Florida Flambeau,* 16 Jan. 1948.

4. AFL, "Henry Horace Williams: An Appreciation," in Horace Henry Williams, *Origin of Belief: Toward a Philosophy of Life*, ed. William Beidler (Chapel Hill: University of North Carolina Press, 1978), 195.

5. Robert Watson Winston, *Horace Williams: Gadfly of Chapel Hill* (Chapel Hill: University of North Carolina Press, 1942), 111, 184; *Yakety Yak: 1918* (Chapel Hill: University of North Carolina Literary Societies and the Fraternities, 1918), 50, 108. It is unlikely that Wolfe and Liddell were in a philosophy class together, because Williams strongly discouraged freshmen and sophomores from enrolling in his classes.

6. Winston, *Horace Williams*, 70–71.

7. Ibid., 71, 90, 296.

8. Ibid., 173.

9. Ibid., 184.

10. Ibid.

11. Ibid., 57, 72.

12. Ibid., 73–74, 111.

13. Ibid., 105–106.

14. Ibid.

15. AFL, no title, Eavesdropping and Interviews, *Daily Tar Heel,* 30 Sept. 1916.

16. AFL to Helen Ogden Liddell (HOL), n.d., Liddell and Pickens Family

Papers, Southern Heritage Collection, Wilson Library, University of North Carolina at Chapel Hill (LPFP); AFL, "Henry Horace Williams in Appreciation," 199; AFL to HOL, (undated fragment), LPFP.

17. Williams, *The Education of Horace Williams*, 79.

18. AFL to HOL, 21 Oct. 1922, LPFP.

19. Winston, *Horace Williams*, 80.

20. William A. Link, "Cornelia Phillips Spencer: The Foremost Daughter of North Carolina and the Contradictions of a Nineteenth-Century Public Life," in *North Carolina Women: Their Lives and Times*, eds. Michele Gillespie and Sally G. McMillen (Athens: The University of Georgia Press, 2014), 133–149. Spencer lived from 1825 to 1908.

21. Williams, *The Education of Horace Williams*, 62.

22. Winston, *Horace Williams*, 50–51,140–141, 173; Horace Williams, *Logic for Living: Lectures of 1921–1922*, ed. Jane Ross Hammer (New York: Philosophical Library, 1951), 199–205.

23. Winston, *Horace Williams*, 139.

24. Ibid., 113.

25. Victor Stephenson to AFL, 5 Nov. 1917, Anna Forbes Liddell Papers, Special Collections & Archives, Florida State University Libraries, Tallahassee, FL (AFLP).

26. Victor Stephenson to Anna Forbes Liddell (n.d.), AFLP. From the content of the letter, Stephenson had recently moved to take a job at *The Evening Post* in New York, which dates the letter as written in 1917, because a letter from AFL to her mother dated 1 Feb. 1917 (LPFP) mentions that Stephenson had recently become employed at *The Evening Post.*

27. AFL to HOL, Mar. 1917, LPFP. Specific date not provided.

28. *Yakety Yak, 1915*; *Yakety Yak, 1917*;*Yakety Yak, 1918*;*Yakety Yak, 1919.*

29. *Yakety Yak, 1918.*

30. *Yakety Yak, 1915*; *Yakety Yak, 1917*, *Yakety Yak, 1918*; *Yakety Yak, 1919.*

31. Coediquette, *The Daily Tar Heel,* 27 Oct. 1917; the newspaper column Coediquette is untitled.

32. AFL, Coediquette, *The Daily Tar Heel*, 17 Nov. 1917, 2; although this particular newspaper column has no byline, the content makes it clear that the

author of the 17 Nov. 1917 article was Liddell and that she was not the author of the 27 Oct. 1917 article.

33. Coediquette, *The Daily Tar Heel*, 20 Oct. 1917.

34. National Center for Education Statistics, "120 Years of American Education: A Statistical Portrait," ed. Thomas D. Snyder, Table 28: Degrees conferred by institutions of higher education, by sex and level: 1868–1870 to 1989–1990, 82–83.

35. Donald G. Mathews and Jane Sherron De Hart, *Sex, Gender, and the Politics of ERA: A State and the Nation,* (New York: Oxford University Press, 1990), 11; A. Elizabeth Taylor, "The Woman Suffrage Movement in North Carolina: Part I," *The North Carolina Historical Review,* 38, no. 1 (Jan. 1961): 59–62; William J. Breen, "Southern Women in the War: The North Carolina Woman's Committee, 1917–1919," *The North Carolina Historical Review* 55, no. 3 (July 1978): 252–280; Eva Murphy, "Laura Reilley" (1994), reprinted by permission of the publisher from William S. Powell, ed., *Dictionary of North Carolina Biography*, 6 vols. (Chapel Hill: University of North Carolina Press, 1996), https://www.ncpedia.org/biography/reilley-laura-holmes. The North Carolina Women's Committee registered women for war service. It also educated women about gardening, canning, and hygiene. The Committee worked to ensure war effort financial donations did not diminish donations to orphanages, hospitals, and various charities and philanthropies. It also discouraged young women from loitering near the military camps.

36. Mary Walton, *A Woman's Crusade: Alice Paul and the Battle for the Ballot* (New York: St. Martin's Press, 2016), Kindle edition, 149–208.

37. Ibid.

38. Elizabeth Heideman, "What We Can Learn From the Women Who Passed as Men to Serve in the U.S. Army," https://time.com/3584039/lyons-rosetta-wakeman/.

39. Naval History and Heritage Command, "The Pandemic of Influenza in 1918–1919" (6 Apr. 2015), http://www.history.navy.mil/content/history/nhhc/research/library/online-reading-room/title-list-alphabetically/i/influenza/the-pandemic-of-influenza-in-1918-1919.html.

40. Molly Billings, "The Influenza Pandemic of 1918" (2005). https://virus.stanford.edu/uda/.

41. History.com editors, "Spanish Flu" (19 May 2020), https://www.history.com/topics/world-war-i/1918-flu-pandemic; J.B. Fortune, "The Open Forum," *Charlotte Observer*, 24 October 1918; Billings, "The Influenza Pandemic of 1918."

42. Naval History and Heritage Command, "A Forgotten Enemy: PHS's [Public Health Service] Fight Against the 1918 Influenza Pandemic" (6 Apr. 2015), https://www.history.navy.mil/research/library/online-reading-room/title-list-alphabetically/i/influenza/a-forgotten-enemy-phss-public-health-service-fight-against-the-1918-influenza-pandemic.html.

43. Nina Strochlic and Riley D. Champine, "How Some Cities 'Flattened the Curve' During the 1918 Flu Pandemic," National Geographic, https://www.nationalgeographic.com/history/2020/03/how-cities-flattened-curve-1918-spanish-flu-pandemic-coronavirus/.

44. History.com Editors, "Spanish Flu."

45. Tom Belton, "WWI: North Carolina and Influenza," reprinted with permission from *Tar Heel Junior Historian*, Spring 1993, Tar Heel Junior Historian Association, NC Museum of History, NCPedia, https://www.ncpedia.org/north-carolina-and-influenza; "Edward K. Graham," *The Daily Tar Heel*, 30 Oct. 1918.

Writing and Voting (1919–1920)

1. Mrs. J.A. Yarbrough, "Dr. Anna Forbes Liddell," Interesting Carolina People, *Charlotte Observer*, 8 Sept. 1935; Anna Forbes Liddell (AFL) to Helen Ogden Liddell (HOL), 26 Jan. 1919, Liddell and Pickens Family Papers, Southern Heritage Collection, Wilson Library, University of North Carolina at Chapel Hill (LPFP).

2. AFL to HOL, mid-May 1919; Victor Stephenson to AFL, 28 Dec. 1919, Anna Forbes Liddell Papers, Special Collections & Archives, Florida State University Libraries, Tallahassee, FL (AFLP). Quote is in the Stephenson letter.

3. AFL to HOL, 30 Apr. 1919 and mid-May 1919, LPFP.

4. Ibid.

5. AFL, *Journal*, 1:63, William Adkins private collection.

6. VLP, "1903", LPFP; AFL to Vinton Liddell (cousin), 20 Dec. 1903, LPFP.

7. Field Guide to Wild American Pulp Artists, *Weird Tales, The Unique Magazine*, https://www.pulpartists.com/Rankin.html.

8. Yarbrough, "Dr. Anna Forbes Liddell;" Barbara Elizabeth Lambert, "Anna Forbes Liddell" (1991), reprinted by permission of the publisher from Powell, *Dictionary of North Carolina Biography*, https://www.ncpedia.org/biography/liddell-anna.

9. Victor Stephenson to AFL, 23 Nov. 1919, AFLP.

10. Ibid., 28 Dec. 1919.

11. Leonard Rogoff, *Gertrude Weil: Jewish Progressive in the New South* (Chapel Hill: University of North Carolina Press, 2017), Kindle edition.

12. Donald G. Mathews and Jane Sherron De Hart, *Sex, Gender, and the Politics of ERA: A State and the Nation,* (New York: Oxford University Press, 1990), 12–13.

13. Ibid., 21.

14. Ibid., 21–25.

15. Ida Husted Harper, ed., *The History of Woman Suffrage*) 6 (New York: Source Book Press, 1922/1970, Chap. 22, Kindle edition.

16. Rogoff, *Gertrude Weil;* Carolyn Roff, "Tillett, Gladys Love Avery," (1996), reprinted by permission of the publisher from William S. Powell, ed., Dictionary of North Carolina Biography, 6 vols. (Chapel Hill: University of North Carolina Press, 1996), https://www.ncpedia.org/biography/tillett-gladys-love-avery; Eva Murphy, "Reilley, Laura Holmes," (1994), reprinted by permission of the publisher from William S. Powell, ed., Dictionary of North Carolina Biography, 6 vols. (Chapel Hill: University of North Carolina Press, 1996), https://www.ncpedia.org/biography/reilley-laura-holmes.

17. "Death Victim," *Charlotte Observer*, 1 Dec. 1923.

Cornell University (1921–1923)

1. United States of America, Bureau of the Census. *Fifteenth Census of the United States, 1930* (Washington, DC: National Archives and Records Administration, 1930).

2. Vinton Liddell Pickens (VLP), "Summary 1921," Liddell and Pickens Family Papers, Southern Heritage Collection, Wilson Library, University of North Carolina at Chapel Hill (LPFP).

3. Anna Forbes Liddell (AFL) to Helen Ogden Liddell (HOL), 14 Sept. 1921, LPFP.

4. Christopher Gray, "For Career Women. A Hassle-Free Haven," *The New York Times*, 1 Jul. 2012, http://www.nytimes.com/2012/07/01/realestate/streetscapes-the-martha-washington-hotel-a-hassle-free-haven.html?_r=0.

5. VLP, "Summary 1921," LPFP; AFL to HOL, 14 Sept. 1921, LPFP.

6. AFL to HOL, 27 Oct. 1922, LPFP.

7. Ibid., 5 Mar. 1922.

8. Ibid., 29 Jan. 1922.

9. Ibid., 12 Feb. 1922.

10. AFL to HOL, 4 Feb. 1922 and 10 May 1922, LPFP.

11. AFL to HOL, LPFP.

12. AFL to Walter Scott Liddell, 18 Oct. 1922, LPFP.

13. Richard T. Hull, "Biography for Pate," unpublished. Pate is the last name of a colleague of Hull.

14. G. Watts Cunningham, "In Memoriam: James Edwin Creighton," *International Journal of Ethics* 35, no. 2 (Jan. 1925): 214–215.

15. AFL to HOL, 29 Apr. 1922, LPFP.

16 Ibid., 18 Apr. 1922, 10 May 1922, 23 May 1922, and 25 May 1922, LPFP.

17. Ibid., 13 Apr. 1922, LPFP.

18. Ibid., 23 May 1922, LPFP; National Center for Education Statistics, "120 Years of American Education," 82–83.

19. AFL to HOL, 17 Feb. 1922, LPFP.

20. Ibid., 28 Feb. 1923

21. Barbara Miller Solomon, *In the Company of Educated Women* (New Haven, CT: Yale University Press, 1985), 136.

22. AFL to HOL, 29 Jan. 1922, 21 Oct. 1922 and 25 Oct. 1922, LPFP.

23. Ibid., 19 Apr. 1923.

24. James E. Creighton to AFL, 3 Apr. 1923, LPFP

25. AFL to HOL, 6 Apr. 1923, LPFP.

26. Ibid., 12 Apr. 1923.

27. Richard T. Hull, "Anna Forbes Liddell (1891–1979)," unpublished, 7 Sept. 2009.

28. AFL, Review of "Religion's Place in Securing a Better World-Order, by James Tufts, *Journal of Religion 2*, no. 2 (113–128)," in *The Philosophical Review* 31, no. 4 (Jul. 1922): 423–424; AFL, Review of "The Idea of Creation, by J. S. Mackenzie, *Hibbert Journal* 21, no. 2 (Jan. 1923): 209–226," in *The Philosophical Review* 32, no. 4 (Jul. 1923): 439–440.

29. AFL to HOL, 12 Apr. 1923, LPFP.

30. Richard T. Hull, "Biography for Pate."

31. AFL to HOL, 1 May 1923, LPFP.

Chapel Hill Again (1923–1925)

1. Vinton Liddell (Forbes Liddell's cousin) to Jane Hall Liddell Battle, 30 Sept. 1923, Liddell and Pickens Family Papers, Southern Heritage Collection, Wilson Library, University of North Carolina at Chapel Hill (LPFP).

2. Ibid.

3. Vinton Liddell (cousin) to Jane Hall Liddell Battle, 10 Nov. 1923 and 15 Oct. 1923, LPFP; Frances Gray Patton to Vinton Liddell Pickens (VLP), 30 Jun. 1967, LPFP.

4. Robert Watson Winston, *Horace Williams: Gadfly of Chapel Hill* (Chapel Hill: University of North Carolina Press, 1942), v–vii, 87, 246.

5. G. Watts Cunningham, "In Memoriam: James Edwin Creighton," *International Journal of Ethics* 35, no. 2 (Jan. 1925): 214.

6. Anna Forbes Liddell (AFL), "The Logical Relationship of the Philosophy of Hegel to the Philosophies of Spinoza and Kant," PhD Dissertation, University of North Carolina (June 1924).

7. AFL, *Alphabet of Philosophers*, Eva Curry private collection. This was widely distributed and there are copies of this poem in other collections.

8. George J. Marshall, "Hegel and the Elephant," *Philosophy of Interpretation*, https://www.bu.edu/wcp/

Papers/Inte/InteMars.htm. The quotes from John Saxe's poem, *The Blind Men and the Elephant*, come from the poem as reprinted herein.

9. AFL, "The Logical Relationship of the Philosophy of Hegel to the Philosophies of Spinoza and Kant," 93–95.

10. Ibid., 2, 89–90, 95–97.

11. Ibid., 14–15, 48–49.

12. Ibid., 50–108.

13. "Dr. Liddell Nears End of 39-Year FSU Career," *Tallahassee Democrat,* 13 May 1962.

14. AFL, "Alexander's Space, Time, and Deity: A Critical Consideration," *University of North Carolina Studies in Philosophy*, no. 2 (n.d.): 1–70.

15. Richard T. Hull, "Forbes Liddell's Philosophical Writings," unpublished (10 Jan. 2010).

16. Vinton Liddell (AFL's cousin) to Jane Hall Liddell Battle, 19 Oct. 1923, LPFP; Vinton Liddell (AFL's cousin) to Susan Hall, 30 Dec. 1923. LPFP; VLP, "Summary 1925," LPFP.

17. "Death Victim," *Charlotte Observer*, 1 Dec. 1923.

18. Nancy Woloch, *Women and the American Experience: A Concise History*, 2nd ed. (New York: McGraw Hill, 2002), 256–262.

19. Barbara Miller Solomon, *In the Company of Educated Women* (New Haven, CT: Yale University Press, 1985), 130, 137.

The Perfect Job (1925–1927)

1. *Register of Chowan College for 1925–1926*, (Murfreesboro, NC: Chowan College, 1926), 11; James I. Martin Sr., "Chowan University," *NCPedia*, 2006, https://www.ncpedia.org/chowan-college; *The Chowanoka, 1926* (Murfreesboro, NC: Senior Class of Chowan College), 21–22, 28–49; Anna Forbes Liddell (AFL) to Helen Ogden Liddell (HOL), 16 Jan. 1926, Liddell and Pickens Family Papers, Southern Heritage Collection, Wilson Library, University of North Carolina at Chapel Hill (LPFP).

2. AFL to HOL, 11 Oct. 1925, LPFP.

3. AFL, "New Conditions are Facing Women," *The Chowanian*, 6 Nov. 1925.

4. Herman H. Horne, "Standard of Conduct for the Modern Girl," *The Chowanian*, 6 Nov. 1925)

5. AFL to HOL 14 Apr. 1926, LPFP.

6. Ibid., 26 Jul. 1926; Vinton Liddell Pickens (VLP), "1926 Summary," LPFP.

7. AFL to HOL, 12 Jul. 1926, LPFP.

8. Communication from Mary Anna Dunn (great-niece of AFL) to author, 10 Aug. 2020.

9. Robin Jeanne Sellers. *Femina Perfecta: The Genesis of Florida State University* (Tallahassee, FL: Class of 1947, The FSU Foundation distributors, 1995), 133, 142.

10. Ibid., 142–143.

11. Ernest R. Sandeen, "Christian Fundamentalism: American Protest Movement" (13 Apr. 2006), https://www.britannica.com/topic/Christian-fundamentalism.

12. "Scopes Trial" (10 Jun. 2019), https://www.history.com/topics/roaring-twenties/scopes-trial.

13. William Powell, *North Carolina through Four Centuries* (Chapel Hill: University of North Carolina Press, 1989), 464–466.

14. Robert Watson Winston, *Horace Williams: Gadfly of Chapel Hill* (Chapel Hill: University of North Carolina Press, 1942), 214.

15. Powell, *North Carolina through Four Centuries*, 466.

16. Horace Williams, *The Education of Horace Williams* (Durham, NC: Published by Horace Williams, 1936), 89.

17. Winston, *Horace Williams: Gadfly of Chapel Hill*, 214.

18. Sellers, *Femina Perfecta,* 143–146, 311 note 63.

19. "Dr. Liddell Nears End of 39-Year FSU Career," *Tallahassee Democrat*, 13 May 1962.

20. Ibid.

21. Edward H. Clarke, *Sex in education, or, A fair chance for the girls* (Boston: James R. Osgood and Company, 1873), 17–18.

22. AFL to HOL, 16 Sept. 1926, LPFP.

23. *Catalogue: Florida State College for Women* (Tallahassee: Florida State College

for Women) 20:2, Jun. 1927, Heritage Protocol & University Archives, Florida State University Libraries, Tallahassee, Florida, 130–131, http://purl.flvc.org/fsu/fd/FSU_HPUA_catalog_1927_v20n2. The catalogues printed in June of a year contain the course offerings for the prior year and the announcements for the upcoming year. Thus, the Jun. 1927 catalog contains the courses offered for the 1926–1927 school year and the announcement for the 1927–1928 school year.

24. AFL to HOL, 16 Sep 1926 and 20 Sept. 1926, LPFP.

25. AFL to HOL, 4 Oct. 1926, LPFP.

26. Ibid., 27 Sept. 1926.

27. Sellers, *Femina Perfecta*, 153–154.

28. Linda Harkey, "Anna Forbes Liddell," *FSU Voices*, ed. Maxine Stern (Tallahassee, FL: Florida State University, 2002), 50.

29. AFL to HOL, 11 Oct. 1926, LPFP.

30. Ibid., 1 Nov. 1926.

31. AFL to Cornelia Pickens, 30 Oct. 1927, LPFP.

32. AFL to HOL, 3 Feb. 1927, LPFP.

33. Reed's life was portrayed by Warren Beatty in the 1981 movie *Reds*.

34. Robert Schulman, *Romany Marie: The Queen of Greenwich Village* (Louisville, KY: Butler Books, 2006), 175; "In New York," *Selma Times-Journal*, 24 Oct. 1926.

35. AFL to HOL, 11 Oct. 1926, LPFP.

36. Sellers, *Femina Perfecta*, 158–162; "Florida State College for Women Faculty List, 1927," *Tallahassee Democrat*, 14 Sept. 1927.

37. Sellers, *Femina Perfecta*, 138–139.

38. Ibid., 8–10, 39. There were only four public institutions of higher learning in Florida, each serving a different section of the population: The Institute for the Blind, Deaf and Dumb in St. Augustine, the Florida Agriculture and Mechanical College for Negroes in Tallahassee, the University of Florida in Gainesville, which only admitted White males, and the Florida State College for Women, which only admitted White females. Sellers called Florida Agriculture and Mechanical College for Negroes (FAMC) as the Florida Normal and Industrial College for Negroes. However, other sources, including the official history of FAMU at http://www.famu.edu/index.cfm?AboutFAMU&History, indicate that the name was the one used in the text.

39. Sellers, *Femina Perfecta,* 138.

40. Mary Call Collins, Tallahassee American Association of University Women Interviews (TAAUWI) (5 Mar. 2006), Carolyn Dubard private collection.

41. Stanley Marshall, "Mary Call Collins—Just Herself" (20 Jul. 2012),https://www.tallahasseemagazine.com/mary-call-darby-collins-just-herself/

42. Collins, TAAUWI.

43. "Florida State College for Women Faculty List, 1927," *Tallahassee Democrat,* 14 Sept. 1927; photograph of AFL's house, William Adkins private collection; Richard Puckett, (TAAUWI) (20 Nov. 2005). AFL to HOL, 19 Feb. 1929, 22 Feb. 1929, and 17 Sept. 1929, LPFP.

44. AFL to HOL, 15 May 1927, LPFP. Misspelling silently corrected.

45. Sellers, *Femina Perfecta*, 146. Sellers takes the quote from *Laws of Florida*, I, 1623–1624. See page 311, note 66, in Sellers.

46. Sellers, *Femina Perfecta*, 146. Sellers takes the quote from page 29 of Raymond Bellamy, "History of the Department of Sociology at FSU," unpublished manuscript (n.d.), see page 311, note 67 in Sellers.

47. Sellers, *Femina Perfecta*, 147–148.

Establishing Herself (1927–1929)

1. *Catalogue: Florida State College for Women* (Tallahassee: Florida State College for Women) 21:2, Jun. 1928, 129, Heritage Protocol & University Archives, Florida State University Libraries, Tallahassee, Florida, http://purl.flvc.org /fsu/fd/FSU_HpUAcatalog_v21n1_2; Anna Forbes Liddell (AFL) to Helen Ogden Liddell (HOL), 29 Sept. 1927, Liddell and Pickens Family Papers, Southern Heritage Collection, Wilson Library, University of North Carolina at Chapel Hill (LPFP).

2. AFL to HOL, 30 Apr. 1928 (date is incorrect), LPFP. The letter was written in 1927 instead of 1928 since the new course discussed was first provided in the 1927–1928 school year as documented by the June 1928 FSCW Catalogue.

3. AFL to HOL, 29 Sept. 1927 and 6 Mar. 1929, LPFP; AFL to Cornelia Pickens, 30 Oct. 1927, LPFP

4. "Helen Ogden Liddell's daily notes during a trip to Europe," Aug. 1928, LPFP; AFL to HOL, 9 Apr. 1929, LPFP.

5. *Catalogue: Florida State College for Women* (Tallahassee: Florida State College for Women) 22:2, Jun. 1929, 142–143, Heritage Protocol & University Archives, Florida State University Libraries, Tallahassee, Florida, http://purl.flvc.org/fsu/fd/FSU_HPUA_catalog_1929_v22n1_2.

6. AFL to HOL, 6 Mar. 1929, LPFP.

7. "Liddell Goes to Philosophy Meet Mar 28–30," *Tallahassee Democrat*, 5 Apr. 1929; AFL to HOL, 30 Mar. 1929, LPFP.

8. AFL, "C.R.," *Tassels*, Richard Puckett private collection.

9. "Local Realtor Dies of Attack," *Charlotte Observer*, 11 Oct. 1930.

10. AFL, "Dedication to R.M.," *Tassels*, Richard Puckett Private Collection.

11. Communication from Eva Curry to author, 13 Jun. 2016; AFL, "Perfect Truth" and "To R.M.," *Tassels*, Richard Puckett private collection.

12. AFL to Cornelia Pickens, 30 Oct. 1927, LPFP.

13. AFL, "You See Them Too, George," *Tassels*, Richard Puckett Private Collection.

14. Vinton Liddell Pickens (VLP), "Annual Summary 1925" and "Annual Summary 1927," LPFP; AFL to HOL, 23 Feb. 1927, 10 May 1927, 29 Sept. 1927, and 30 Nov.1927, LPFP.

15. VLP, note on a letter from W.S. Daniels to Jane Hall Liddell, 21 Jun. 1915, LPFP.

16. AFL to HOL, 14 Apr. 1932, LPFP.

17. HOL, "Re Liddell Family (II)," (LPFP).

18. "Roland Hayes an Artist," *Tallahassee Democrat*, 29 Jan. 1929.

19. AFL to HOL, 27 Jan. 1929, LPFP.

20. Ibid.

21.VLP, untitled short story (1929), LPFP. All information in paragraphs about the trip come from this short story.

22. Chi Luu, "The Legendary Language of the Appalachian 'Holler'", https://daily.jstor.org/the-legendary-language-of-the-appalachian-holler/.

A Turning Point (1930)

1. *Catalogue: Florida State College for Women* (Tallahassee: Florida State College for Women), Jun. 1930 23:2, 148, Heritage Protocol & University Archives, Florida State University Libraries, Tallahassee, Florida, http://purl.flvc.org/fsu/fd/FSU_HPUA_catalog_1930_v23n1_2.

2. Joseph Peterson, "The Twenty-Fifth Annual Meeting of the Southern Society for Philosophy and Psychology," *The American Journal of Psychology*, 42, no. 3 (July 1930), 462–463.

3. Ibid., 459–469.

4. Anna Forbes Liddell (AFL), "In Defense of Absolute Ethics," *The Journal of Philosophy* 27, no. 16 (31 Jul. 1930): 430–435.

5. The quote from Thomas Aquinas was cited by AFL as: *De potentia* 4, I—as quoted in Michel's translation of Grabmann's *Thomas Aquinas*, 37.

6. Ibid.

7. Morimichi Watanabe, "Chapter 1: An Appreciation," in *Introducing Nicholas of Cusa: A Guide to a Renaissance Man*, eds. Christopher Bellitto, Thomas Izbicki, and Gerald Christianson, (Mahwah, New Jersey: Paulist Press, 2004), 6.

8. Ibid., 8.

9. "Dr. Liddell Nears End of 39-Year FSU Career," *Tallahassee Democrat,* 13 May 1962.

10. Ibid.

11. Watanabe, "Chapter 1: An Appreciation," 16.

12. Horace Williams to AFL, 15 Feb., no year, Anna Forbes Liddell Papers, Special Collections & Archives, Florida State University Libraries, Tallahassee, FL (AFLP). The year is likely 1930 since Williams is encouraging Liddell to go to Germany for her Nicholas of Cusa project.

13. AFL to Helen Ogden Liddell (HOL), 19 Jun. 1930, Liddell and Pickens Family Papers, Southern Heritage Collection, Wilson Library, University of North Carolina at Chapel Hill (LPFP).

14. Ibid., 25 Jun. 1930.

15. Ibid., 23 Jun. 1930 and 9 Jul. 1930, LPFP.

16. Ibid., 24 Jul. 1930, LPFP.

17. Ibid., 20 Jul. 1930.

18. Ibid., 15 Aug. 1930.

19. Ibid., 17 Jul. 1930.

20. Ibid., 24 Jul. 1930.

21. Ibid., 13 Aug. 1930.

22. Ibid., 31 Jul. 1930.

23. Ibid.

24. Ibid., 13 Aug. 1930.

25. Ibid., 29 Aug. 1930. The World Congress of Philosophy was known as the International Congress of Philosophy until 1973. It currently meets every five years. Katherine Gilbert was a teaching assistant when Liddell worked on her PhD at the University of North Carolina and had preceded Liddell as the Graham-Kenan Philosophy Fellow. Gilbert's distinguished career included serving as president of American Philosophical Society. Information on Gilbert from C. Sylvester Green, "Gilbert, Katherine Everett," (1986), reprinted by permission of the publisher from William S. Powell, ed., Dictionary of North Carolina Biography, 6 vols. (Chapel Hill: University of North Carolina Press, 1996), https://www.ncpedia.org/biography/ gilbert-katherine.

26. Mrs. J.A. Yarbrough, "Dr. Anna Forbes Liddell," Interesting Carolina People, *Charlotte Observer*, 8 Sept. 1935.

27. Death Certificate of Ralinson [*sic*] Myers, Vital Statistics, State of North Carolina.

28. AFL to HOL 8 Oct. 1930, LPFP.

29. AFL, "Desolation," *Tassels*, Richard Puckett private collection.

30. AFL to HOL, 28 Oct. 1930.

31. Ibid., 24 Nov. 1930.

Rebuilding (1931–1932)

1. Horace Williams to Anna Forbes Liddell (AFL), n.d., Anna Forbes Liddell Papers, Special Collections & Archives, Florida State University Libraries, Tallahassee, FL (AFLP).

2. AFL to Jane Liddell Battle, 27 Apr. 1931, Liddell and Pickens Family Papers, Southern Heritage Collection, Wilson Library, University of North Carolina at Chapel Hill (LPFP).

3. AFL to Cornelia Pickens, 15 Feb. 1931, LPFP.

4. AFL to Helen Ogden Liddell (HOL), 11 Oct. 1925, LPFP.

5. AFL to Jane Liddell Battle, 27 Apr. 1931, LPFP.

6. Vinton Liddell Pickens (VLP), "Summary 1931," LPFP.

7. Helen Liddell McBride to VLP, 4 Jul. 1931, LPFP; Helen McBride Jackson, Tallahassee American Association of University Women Interviews (TAAUWI) (2006), Carolyn Dubard private collection

8. *Catalogue: Florida State College for Women* (Tallahassee Florida State College for Women), Jun. 1932, 25:2; Heritage Protocol & University Archives, Florida State University Libraries, Tallahassee, Florida, William H. Chafe, *The American Woman: Her Changing, Social, Economic, and Political Roles, 1920–1970* (New York: Oxford University Press, 1972), 91.

9. Ernst Hoffmann to AFL, trans. Rebekka White, AFLP.

10. AFL to HOL 16 Jan. 1932, LPFP.

11. AFL to HOL, 6 Apr. 1932, 27 Mar. 1932, and 14 May 1932, 18 May 1932, LPFP.

12. "Hitler Runs for President," The History Place: The Rise of Hitler, http://www.historyplace.com/worldwar2/riseofhitler/runs.htm.

13. Ibid.; AFL to HOL, 14 Apr. 1932, LPFP.

14. "The Republic Collapses," The History Place: The Rise of Hitler.

15. AFL to HOL, 20 Apr. 1932, LPFP.

16. Ibid., 31 May 1932.

17. "The Republic Collapses," The History Place: The Rise of Hitler.

18. Ibid.

19. Ibid. Although Hitler was Austrian, he had served in the German army in WWI.

20. Ibid.

21. Ibid.

22. AFL to HOL, 18 May 1932, LPFP.

23. Ibid., 31 May 1932 and 23 Jun. 1932.

24. Ibid., 13 Jun. 1932.

25. AFL to HOL, 8 Jul. 1932 LPFP. Albert Schweitzer Hospital was in Lambaréné, which until 1958 was situated in French Equatorial Africa, thereafter, in Gabon.

26. AFL to HOL, 5 Jul. 1932 and 8 Jul. 1932, LPFP. The quote is in the 8 Jul. 1932 letter.

27. Notes and News, *Journal of Philosophy* 29, no. 20 (29 Sept. 1932): 558–560.

28. AFL to HOL, 8 Aug. 1932 and 12 Aug. 1932, LPFP; Mrs. J.A. Yarbrough, "Dr. Anna Forbes Liddell," Interesting Carolina People, *Charlotte Observer*, 8 Sept. 1935. The quote is from Yarbrough.

29. Ernst Hoffmann to AFL, 14 Oct. 1932, trans. Rebekka White, AFLP.

30. AFL to HOL, 25 May 1932, LPFP.

31. Stanley Marshall, "Mary Call Collins—Just Herself" (Jul. 20, 2012), https://www.tallahasseemagazine.com/mary-call-darby-collins-just-herself/.

32. Ibid., Mary Call Collins, TAAUWI (5 Mar. 2006), Carolyn Dubard private collection.

Advancing (1933–1939)

1. History.com editors, "Great Depression History" (28 Feb. 2020), https://www.history.com/topics/great-depression/great-depression-history.

2. Anna Forbes Liddell (AFL) to Vinton Liddell Pickens (VLP), 8 Feb. 1933, Liddell and Pickens Family Papers, Southern Heritage Collection, Wilson Library, University of North Carolina at Chapel Hill (LPFP).

3. History.com editors, "Great Depression History."

4. AFL to VLP, 8 Feb. 1933, LPFP.

5. History.com editors, "New Deal," (27 Nov. 2019), https://www.history.com/topics/great-depression/new-deal; AFL to Vinton and Bob Pickens, 25 Jun. 1933, LPFP.

6. Erin Blakemore, "Why Many Married Women Were Banned from Working During the Great Depression," https://www.history.com/news/great-depression-

married-women-employment, accessed 1 Dec. 2020.

7. William H. Chafe, *The American Woman: Her Changing Social, Economic, and Political Roles, 1920–1970"* (New York: Oxford University Press, 1972), 58–61.

8. Ibid., 61.

9. Erin Blakemore, "Why Many Married Women Were Banned from Working During the Great Depression."

10. Janet L. Coryell and Nora Faires, *A History of Women in America* (New York: The McGraw Hill Companies, Inc., 2012), 339.

11."Black Cabinet," https://www.encyclopedia.com/economics/encyclopedias-almanacs-transcripts-and-maps/black-cabinet, accessed 1 Dec. 2020.

12. AFL to VLP, 8 Feb. 1933, LPFP.

13. AFL to Jane Liddell Battle, 26 Feb. 1933, LPFP; Robin Jeanne Sellers, *Femina Perfecta: The Genesis of Florida State University* (Tallahassee: Class of 1947, The FSU Foundation Distributors, 1995), 220.

14. AFL to Helen Ogden Liddell (HOL), 24 Apr. 1938, LPFP.

15. Ibid., 27 Mar. 1938.

16. AFL to VLP, 5 Jan. 1934, LPFP; James Gregory, "Communist Party Membership by Districts 1922–1950," https://depts.washington.edu/moves/CP_map-members.htm, accessed 3 Dec. 2020; "Great Depression: Political Movements and Social Change," https://www.britannica.com/event/Great-Depression/Political-movements-and-social-change, accessed 3 Dec. 2020; Peter H. Amann, "A 'Dog in the Nighttime' Problem: American Fascism in the 1930s, *The History Teacher* 19, no. 4 (Aug. 1986): 559–584.

17. AFL to VLP, 5 Jan. 1934, LPFP; Peter H. Amann, 559–584.

18. Seva Gunitsky, "These Are the Three Reasons Fascism Spread in 1930s America—and Might Spread Again Today" (12 Aug. 2017), *Washington Post*, https://www.washingtonpost.com/news/monkey-cage/wp/2017/08/12/these-are-the-three-reasons-that-fascism-spread-in-1930s-america-and-might-spread-aga in-today/; R.G. Price, "Fascism Part II: The Rise of American Fascism" (May 15, 2004), http://www.rationalrevolution.net/articles/rise_of_american_fascism.htm. The quotes are in the Price reference.

19. Price, "Fascism Part II."

20. Amann, "A 'Dog in the Nighttime' Problem," 559–584.

21. AFL to VLP, 5 Jan. 1934, LPFP.

22. "The Rise of Adolf Hitler: Hitler Named Chancellor" (1996), https://www.historyplace.com/worldwar2/riseofhitler/named.htm.

23. "The Rise of Adolf Hitler: The Reistag Burns" (1996), https://www.historyplace.com/worldwar2/riseofhitler/burns.htm.

24. Richard J. Evans, *The Coming of the Third Reich* (New York: The Penguin Press, 2003), 428–430.

25. Arye Carmon, "The Impact of Nazi Racial Decrees on the University of Heidelberg," SHOAH Resource Center, https://www.yadvashem.org/odot_pdf/Microsoft%20Word%20-%203253.pdf, accessed 20 Nov. 2020.

26. "Marie Baum: A Woman of the Modern Age 1874–1964," The Mendelssohns Society, http://www.mendelssohnremise.de/en/mendelssohns/biografien/marie-baum, accessed 5 Dec. 2020; "Marie Baum (1974–1964)," Enclopedia.com, https://www.encyclopedia.com/women/encyclopedias-almanacs-transcripts-and-maps/baum-marie-1874-1964, accessed 27 Nov. 2020.

27. Howard Becker and Marianne Weber, "Max Weber, Assassination, and German Guilt: An Interview with Marianne Weber," *The American Journal of Economics and Sociology* 10, no. 4 (1951), 402.

28. Ernst Hoffmann to AFL, 18 Aug. 1933, trans. Rebekka White, Anna Forbes Liddell Papers, Special Collections & Archives, Florida State University Libraries, Tallahassee, FL (AFLP).

29. Thea Hoffmann to AFL 17 Nov. 1933, trans. Rebekka White, AFLP.

30. Ernst Hoffmann to AFL, trans. Rebekka White, AFLP.

31. "The Triumph of Hitler: Night of the Long Knives" (1996), https://www.historyplace.com/worldwar2/triumph/tr-roehm.htm.

32. Ibid.

33. Ernst Hoffmann to AFL, 19 Dec. 1934 and 5 Feb. 1935, trans. Rebekka White, AFLP.

34. From the Reich, "Dispensed from Obligation" (5 Dec. 1935), enclosed in letter from Ernst and Thea Hoffmann to AFL, 17 Dec. 1934, trans. Rebekka White, AFLP.

35. Stephen P. Remy, "'We Are No Longer the University of the Liberal

Age:' The Humanities and National Socialism at Heidelberg," in *Nazi Germany and the Humanities: How German Academics Embraced Nazism*, eds. Wolfgang Bialas and Anson Rabinback (London: OneWorld Publications, 2014), 23.

36. Ernst Hoffmann to AFL, 20 Oct. 1936, trans. Rebekka White, AFLP.

37. Ibid., 20 May 1937.

38. Ibid., 16 Nov. 1938; Thea Hoffmann to AFL, 6 Feb. 1935, trans. Rebekka White, AFLP.

39. Ann D. Williams, "History of Jigsaw Puzzles," https://www.puzzlewarehouse.com/history-of-puzzles/, accessed 5 Sept. 2020.

40. AFL to Jane Liddell Battle, 26 Feb. 1933, LPFP.

41 "Dr. AF Liddell to Head Session," *Tallahassee Democrat*, 13 Apr. 1933.

42. L.H. Lanier, "Proceedings of the Twenty-Eighth Annual Meeting of the Southern Society for Philosophy and Psychology," April 14 and 15, 1933. *Psychological Bulletin* 30, no. 8 (1933): 606–607.

43. Joseph Peterson, "The Twenty-Ninth Annual Meeting of the Southern Society for Philosophy and Psychology," *The American Journal of Psychology* 46, no. 3 (Jul. 1934): 512–513.

44. AFL to Jane Liddell Battle, 5 Sept. 1934, LPFP.

45. Untitled article, *Tallahassee Democrat*, 15 Dec. 1935; "The Relation of Philosophy to Religion," *The Personalist* 17 (Aug. 1936): 407–411; Lyle H. Lanier, "The Thirty-First Annual Meeting of the Southern Society for Philosophy and Psychology, *The American Journal of Psychology* 48, no. 4 (Oct. 1936): 689; Lyle H. Lanier, "The Thirty-Second Annual Meeting of the Southern Society for Philosophy and Psychology," *The American Journal of Psychology* 49, no. 3 (Jul. 1937): 483–485.

46. Horace Williams to AFL, 9 Jan., no year, AFLP. The year is likely 1933 since the SSPP election was in 1932.

47. Horace Williams to AFL, 26 Apr., no year, AFLP.

48. Horace Williams, "The Education of Horace Williams" (Chapel Hill: published by Horace Williams, 1936), 78–79.

49. Ibid., 79.

50. Horace Williams to AFL, Nov. 1934, AFLP.

51. Ibid., n.d.

52. Sellers, *Femina Perfecta*, 236.

53. Ibid., 223.

54. Ibid., 223–225.

55. Ibid., 225–228.

56. Ibid., 222–223.

57. *Catalogue: Florida State College for Women* (Tallahassee: Florida State College for Women) 28:2, Jun. 1935, 182–183, Heritage Protocol & University Archives, Florida State University Libraries, Tallahassee, Florida, http://purl.flvc.org/fsu/fd/FSU_HPUA_catalog_1935_v28n2; Ibid., 29:2, Jun. 1936, 180–182, http://purl.flvc.org/fsu/fd/FSU_HPUA_catalog_1936_v29n2. Directed individual study courses are not included in the course counts.

58. Carolyn Gaines, Tallahassee American Association of University Women Interviews (TAAUWI) (12 Mar. 2006), Carolyn Dubard private collection.

59. Sellers, *Femina Perfecta*, 232–235.

60. "Religious Workers to Hold Meeting," *Tallahassee Democrat*, 22 Mar. 1935; "Reception Honors Dr. Liddell," *Tallahassee Democrat*, 17 Apr. 1962; "State College Y.W.C.A.'s Traditional Recognition Service Set for Tonight," *Tampa Tribune*, 28 Oct 1934; "Quillian Leads Religious Week," *Tallahassee Democrat*, 11 Feb. 1934.

61. "Mrs. J. Pasto is Guest Speaker at Episcopal Auxiliary Meet," *Tallahassee Democrat,* 8 Jan. 1946; "Lowery Speaks at Diocese Meet: Anna Forbes Liddell is Panel Speaker," *Tallahassee Democrat*, 26 Jan. 1945.

62. Linda Harkey, "Anna Forbes Liddell," *FSU Voices*, ed. Maxine Stern (Tallahassee: Florida State University, 2002), 50–51; Judy Matthews, TAAUWI, (14 Mar. 2006).

63. Judy Matthews, TAAUWI (14 Mar. 2006).

64. Harkey, "Anna Forbes Liddell," 50–51.

65. Lucy Boozer, "Glimpses and Personalities," *Tallahassee Democrat*, 5 Dec. 1939.

66. AFL to Jane Liddell Battle, 28 Jun. 1938; 3 Jul. 1938; and 10 Jul. 1939, LPFP.

67. "University Women to Raise One Million Dollar Fund," *Pensacola News Journal*, 10 Apr. 1929; "AAUW Holds First Fall Meet at Home of Mrs. Coyle

Moore," *Tallahassee Democrat*, 30 Sept. 1936.

68. *Tallahassee Democrat,* 11 Dec. 1931, for factors of current economic situation; *Tallahassee Democrat*, 17 Mar. 1932, for Rittenhouse lecture; "A.A.U.W Members in 'Get-Together'," *Tallahassee Democrat*, 23 Oct. 1932, for program on history of chamber music; "Open Meeting at College Friday," *Tallahassee Democrat*, 4 May 1933, for the Hitler regime in Germany; "Halliburton to Lecture Again at State College," *Tallahassee Democrat*, 26 Feb. 1934; "Students Invite Author to Make Address Here" *Tallahassee Democrat*, 22 Oct. 1934, for Durant lecture; "Club and Social Announcements," *Tallahassee Democrat*, 30 Jan. 1935, for the tax system of Florida; "Italian-Ethiopian Controversy to Be Subject of Forum," *Tallahassee Democrat*, 11 Oct. 1935; "Miss Zoa [*sic*] Manning Is Speaker at AAUW Forum," *Tallahassee Democrat*, 6 Dec. 1935, for rights of Florida Women; "English Will Speak at AAUW Forum," *Tallahassee Democrat*, 13 Apr. 1937; "AAUW Held Monthly Meeting Last Night," *Tallahassee Democrat*, 9 Nov. 1937, for underlying causes of the Sino-Japanese War.

69. AFL to Jane Liddell Battle, 17 Aug. 1933 and 21 Jan. 1934, LPFP; Mary Anna McBride Turner, TAAUWI (11 Mar. 2006).

70. VLP, "1937 Notes," LPFP; AFL to HOL, 17 Feb. 1938, 27 Feb. 1938, and 27 Mar. 1938, LPFP.

71. AFL to Jane Liddell Battle, 28 Jun. 1938, LPFP.

72. Mary Anna McBride Turner, TAAUWI (11 Mar. 2006).

73. Communication from Mary Anna McBride Turner to author, 9 Mar. 2020.

74. Ibid.

75. Thea Hoffmann to AFL, 15 Jul. 1939, trans. Rebekka White, AFLP; AFL to Jane Liddell Battle, 12 Aug. 1939, LPFP.

The War and Afterwards (1940–1947)

1. Anna Forbes Liddell (AFL) to Vinton Liddell Pickens (VLP), 24 Jun. 1942, Liddell and Pickens Family Papers, Southern Heritage Collection, Wilson Library, University of North Carolina at Chapel Hill (LPFP).

2. "The Great Debate," https://www.nationalww2museum.org/war/articles/great-debate, accessed 1 Dec. 2020.

3. Ibid.

4. VLP, "1940" and "1941," LPFP.

5. In 1966, when Bob and Vinton Pickens visited the Arizona Memorial in Honolulu, they saw that the Memorial had no photographs of the battleship after its two-year modernization in 1931. Thus, they sent to the Memorial their photos taken on their trip with President Herbert Hoover on the ship's 1931 inaugural cruise after its modernization. The photos were copied and returned. VLP, "Summary 1931," LPFP.

6. Allison McNearney, "Watch Terrified Men Learn to Deal with Women in the Workforce during WWII," 5 May 2019, https://www.history.com/news/women-workforce-wwii-training-video-1940s.

7. Susan Stamberg, "Female WWII Pilots: The original Fly Girls," 9 Mar. 2010, https://www.npr.org/2010/03/09/123773525/female-wwii-pilots-the-original-fly-girls.

8. Ibid.

9. Ibid.

10. Ibid.

11. "Agnes Meyer Discoll," https://www.nsa.gov/About-Us/Current-Leadership/Article-View/Article/1623020/agnes-meyer-driscoll/, accessed 1 Dec. 2020; "Genevieve Grotjan Feinstein," https://www.nsa.gov/About-Us/Current-Leadership/Article-View/Article/1621585/genevieve-grotjan-feinstein/, accessed 1 Dec. 2020.

12. "WWII History of the Army Map Service," http://easteurotopo.org/archive/history%20army%20map%20service%20wwii.html#IV.___AMS%E2%80%99s_Wartime_Map_Making_Workload; Robin Jeanne Sellers, *Femina Perfecta: The Genesis of Florida State University* (Tallahassee: Class of 1947, The FSU Foundation Distributors, 1995), 253; "Girls Who Graduated This Year Have Chosen Careers Ranging from Teaching to FBI Work" (19 Sept. 1943), *Tallahassee Democrat.* FSCW graduates who became *Military Mapping Maidens* included Mary Eleanor Bellamy, Eleanor Campbell, Helen Dahlgren, Elizabeth Davis, Elizabeth Draughn, Jimmie Fain, Ruby Herold Hutson, Lois Marchant, Eleanor Merrill, Norma Pennoyer, Elizabeth Sale, Mary Stephenson, and Ruth Trott.

13. AFL to VLP, 24 Jun. 1942, LPFP; Barbara Bess and Betty Weaver, "FSCW Faculty Answers Queries, Checks Hats and Makes Itself Useful to U.S. Service Men," *Tallahassee Democrat*, 5 Dec. 1943.

14. AFL to VLP, 24 Jun. 1942, LPFP.

15. VLP, "1940" and "1944", LPFP; HOL to Jane Liddell Battle, 14 Sept. 1944, LPFP.

16.VLP, "1942," "1943," and "1944," LPFP; HOL to Jane Liddell Battle, 3 Mar. 1942 and 14 Sept. 1944, LPFP; AFL to VLP, 24 Jun. 1942, LPFP. Pickens was head of public relations for the Services of Supply, European Theater of Operations. He often accompanied General John Lee, the commander of the Services of Supply on his military trips.

17. VLP, "1942" and "1944," LPFP.

18. Communication from Mary Anna McBride Turner to author, 9 Mar. 2020.

19. "Professor Alfred J. Hanna (1893-1978)," https://lib.rollins.edu/olin/oldsite/archives/golden/Hanna.htm, accessed 1 Dec. 2020; Alfred Jackson Hanna and Kathryn Abbey Hanna, *Napoleon III and Mexico: American Triumph over Monarchy* (Chapel Hill: University of North Carolina Press, 1971), back flap.

20. Jane Aurell Menton, *The Grove: A Florida Home through Seven Generations* (Tallahassee: Sentry Press, 1998), 49–52, 67–72.

21. AFL to VLP, 2 Feb. 1947, LPFP.

22. Ibid., 2 Feb. 1947.

23. "Florida's First Lady at War," http://www.floridamemory.com/items/show/333284. Women's Army Corps," https://www.britannica.com/topic/Womens-Army-Corps.

24. "2,220 Enrolled at University" *Tallahassee Democrat*, 19 Sept. 1943. As of the date of the article, there were 728 civilian students enrollment. The college expected additional enrollments by Sept. 25.

25. AFL to VLP, 22 Sept.1942, LPFP.

26. Sellers, *Femina Perfecta*, 255-256.

27. Ibid., 255.

28. Ibid., 252.

29. "FSCW Adds War Courses—5 Alumnae in Pacific Area", *Tallahassee*

Democrat, 20 Sept. 1942; "Many Teachers and Alumnae Serve Country," *Tallahassee Democrat*, 19 Sept. 1943.

30. "Girls Who Graduated This Year Have Chosen Careers Ranging from Teaching to FBI Work", *Tallahassee Democrat,* 19 Sept. 1943; "FSCW Alumnae Growing Fast; Many Abroad," *Tallahassee Democrat,* 19 Sept. 1943.

31. John O. Riedl to AFL, 27 Sept. 1939, Anna Forbes Liddell Papers, Special Collections & Archives, Florida State University Libraries, Tallahassee, FL (AFLP).

32. AFL to John O. Riedl, 31 Oct. 1939, AFLP.

33. John O. Riedl to AFL, 16 Jul. 1941, AFLP; AFL to John O. Riedl, 6 Nov. 1939, AFLP.

34. Ibid., 6 Nov. 1939, 26 Apr. 1940, and 13 Jun. 1941.

35. John O. Riedl to AFL, 6 Sept. 1942, AFLP.

36. Howard W. Odum, *Race and Rumors of Race: The American South in the Early Forties* (Baltimore: John Hopkins Press, 1997), 53–162, 231–234. The University of North Carolina Press published the 1943 edition.

37. Bryant Simon, "Introduction to the 1997 Edition," in Odum, *Race and Rumors of Race: The American South in the Early Forties*, vii–xxix.

38. Howard Becker and Marianne Weber, "Max Weber, Assassination, and German Guilt: An Interview with Marianne Weber," *The American Journal of Economics and Sociology* 10 no. 4 (1951): 402.

39. Marie Baum to AFL, 12.X.47, AFLP.

40. Thea Hoffmann to AFL, 8 Oct. 1947, trans. Rebekka White, AFLP. Unreadable text is due to water damage.

41. "Marie Baum (1974–1964)," https://www.encyclopedia.com/women/encyclopedias-almanacs-transcripts-and-maps/baum-marie-1874-1964; Thea Hoffmann to AFL, 8 Oct. 1947, trans. Rebekka White, AFLP; "John O. Riedl Papers, 1928–1982," Special Collections and University Archives, Marquette University, https://www.marquette.edu/library/archives/SuperC/UNIV_C-1-12sJOR2-Abstract.php; correspondence from AFL to J.L. Sullivan (22 Feb. 1947), AFLP.

42. Sellers, *Femina Perfecta*, 262–268; "College Attendance here Sets New Record," *Tallahassee Democrat,* 6 Oct. 1946.

43. Sellers, *Femina Perfecta*, 268–269.

44. Ibid., 269–273.

45. Ibid., 273–274.

Florida State University (1947–1958)

1. "Addressed, Professors Confess," *Florida Flambeau*, 16 Jan. 1948. The reporter's name is unknown since the article did not have a byline.

2. Ibid.

3. Steve Yates, "FSU Charts Course for 'Golden Era of State Education, *Tallahassee Democrat*, 3 Oct. 1947; "College Teams Meet After 43-Year Lapse," *Tallahassee Democrat*, 17 Oct. 1947.

4. Anna Forbes Liddell (AFL) to Vinton Liddell Pickens (VLP), 26 Jun. 1948, Liddell and Pickens Family Papers, Southern Heritage Collection, Wilson Library, University of North Carolina at Chapel Hill (LPFP); Yates, "FSU Charts Course;" "'47 Great Local Year Despite Lack of Titles," *Tallahassee Democrat*, 31 Dec. 1947.

5. AFL to J.L. Sullivan, 22 Feb. 1947, Anna Forbes Liddell Papers, Special Collections & Archives, Florida State University Libraries, Tallahassee, FL (AFLP).

6. Giorgio de Santillana to AFL, 15 Nov. 1949, AFLP.

7. AFL to Giorgio de Santillana, 23 Nov. 1949, AFLP.

8. Ernst Hoffmann to AFL, 5 Aug. 1951, trans. Rebekka White, AFLP.

9. AFL, "Communication: A Tribute to Ernst Hoffmann (1880–1952)," *The Journal of Philosophy* 49, no. 15 (1 Jul. 1952): 505–506.

10. AFL to Harold Larrabee, 2 Aug. 1949, AFLP; Harold Larrabee to AFL, 10 Aug. 1949, AFLP; AFL to Carl Taeusch, 27 Mar. 1951, AFLP; Dorothy Soderlund to AFL, 15 May 1953, AFLP.

11. Nicholas of Cusa, *Of Learned Ignorance by Nicolas Cusanus*, trans. Germain Heron (London: Routledge & Kegan Paul, 1954).

12. AFL to VLP, 26 Jun. 1948, LPFP; "Personals," *Tallahassee Democrat*, 29 Mar. 1948; Wilse B. Webb, "Fiftieth Annual Meeting of the Southern Society for Philosophy and Psychology, "*The American Journal of Psychology* 71 no. 4. (Dec. 1958): 793–794; "Professors Meet in City Thursday: Society for Philosophy of Religion Will Conclude Sessions Saturday," *Chattanooga Daily Times*, 28 Feb. 1954.

13. AFL to VLP, 5 Jul. 1948, LPFP; "Liddell Attends Meeting in Holland, Tours Europe," *Florida Flambeau*, 8 Oct. 1948; VLP, "1947," LPFP.

14. "35-Year Study Set for Report, "*Orlando Sentinel*, 12 Aug. 1953.

15. AFL, "Philosophical Mysticism and Modern Science," *The Personalist*, 32, Issue 2 (April 1951): 175.

16. AFL, "Man and Nature in the Philosophy of Nicholas of Cusa." *Atti del XII Congresso internazionale filosofia* (Proceedings of the 12th International Congress of Philosophy) 11, Firenze: Sansoni, 1960: 281–284.

17. Ibid.

18. AFL, "Philosophical Mysticism and Modern Science," 172–176.

19. AFL, "The Significance of the Doctrine of the Incarnation in the Philosophy of Nicholas of Cusa," in *Actes du XIème Congrès International de Philosophie, Bruxelles*, 20–26 Août 1953 (Proceedings of the 11th International Congress of Philosophy), vol. 11, ed. M. Barzin, L. De Raeymaeker, and J. Lameere (Bruxelles: Edition du Congrès, 1953): 126–131; Peter J. Casarella, "Negative Theology and Christology," in *Nicholas of Cusa on Christ and the Church: Essays in Memory of Chandler McCuskey Brooks*, ed. Gerald Christianson and Thomas M. Izbicki (Amsterdam: Brill, 1996), 283 n12; AFL, Preface to her English translation of *de Docta Ignorantia*, AFLP.

20. National Center for Education Statistics, "120 Years of American Education: A Statistical Portrait," ed. Thomas D. Snyder, Tables 26: Number and professional employees of institutions of higher education: 1869–70 to 1991, and 28: Degrees conferred by institutions of higher education, by sex and level: 1868–1870 to 1989–1990 (Washington, DC: National Center for Education Statistics, 1993).

21. "AAUW Plans Music Hour," *Tallahassee Democrat*, 5 Mar. 1951; "AAUW Study Group to Hear Frank Hanson," *Tallahassee Democrat*, 19 Oct. 1952; "AAUW Study Sessions to Cover Needs and Problems of Dependent Children," *Tallahassee Democrat*, 10 Jun. 1956; "Dr. Campbell Speaks to AAUW on Israeli-Arab Dispute," *Tallahassee Democrat*, 5 Nov. 1956; "Panel Argues Teacher Training Course Merits in AAUW Meet," *Tallahassee Democrat*, 18 Feb. 1958; "AAUW to Hear Dr. Oppenheimer," *Tallahassee Democrat*, 24 Sept. 1959; "AAUW Panel Discusses Women's Opportunities," *Tallahassee Democrat*, 13 Feb. 1956. Panelists were Christine Foster, PhD; Sara

Herndon, PhD; Ida Thompson (no PhD); and Dorothy Hoffman, PhD.

22. "Miss Smith Chosen for Soph Council at Florida State," *Tallahassee Democrat*, 23 May 1952; "Creative Thinking Discussed by Dr. Anna Forbes Liddell," *Tallahassee Democrat*, 7 Mar. 1956; "World Community Day Observance Held," *Tallahassee Democrat*, 5 Nov. 1956.

23. "HUAC," 7 Jun. 2019, https://www.history.com/topics/cold-war/huac; "House Un-American Activities Committee," New World Encyclopedia, accessed 14 Dec. 2020, https://www.newworldencyclopedia.org/entry/Special:CiteThisPage?page=House_Un-American_Activities_Committee.

24. "Joseph McCarthy," 16 May 2019, https://www.history.com/topics/cold-war/joseph-mccarthy.

25. Allison Hawkins Crume, "The Historical Development of the Student Government Association as a Student Sub-Culture at the Florida State University: 1946–1976," PhD diss., (Florida State University, 2004), 12–14, http://purl.flvc.org/fsu/fd/FSU_migr_etd-2977.

26. Herbert D. Cameron and Sam Mase, "Professors Say They're Obligated to Answer Congress Questions," *Tampa Tribune*, 7 Jun. 1953.

27. Ibid.

28. Herbert Cameron and Sam Mase, "Florida Professors Say Classroom Is No Place for Communists," *Tampa Tribune*, 5 Jul. 5, 1953.

29. Sam Mase and Herbert Cameron, "College Professors Hit 'Book Burning' by State Department," *Tampa Tribune*, July 8, 1953.

30. AFL, "Freedom and Society," undated and unpublished document, 2, AFLP.

31. "Desegregation Topic for AAUW Program," *Tallahassee Democrat*, 10 Nov. 1954.

32. Susan Levine, *Degrees of Equality: The American Association of University Women and the Challenge of Twentieth-Century Feminism* (Philadelphia, PA: Temple University Press, 1995, 120-135.

33. Martin A. Dyckman, *Floridian of His Century: The Courage of Governor LeRoy Collins* (Gainesville, FL: University Press of Florida, 2006, Kindle edition.

34. Elizabeth McBride, Tallahassee American Association of University Women Interviews (11 Mar. 2006), Carolyn Dubard private collection.

35. George Milton, untitled essay, *Tassels*, 1960, Richard Puckett private collection.

36. Ibid.

37. George Milton, dedication page, *Tassels*, 1960, Richard Puckett private collection.

Florida State University (1959–1962)

1. "Anna Forbes Liddell named FSU's '59 distinguished Professor," *Tassels*, Richard Puckett private collection.

2. "James Soles Introduces Delaware to Class of 1997," *UpDate* 13 no. 1 (2 Sept. 1993), 9. *UpDate* is a publication of the University of Delaware.

3. Tricia Browne-Ferrigno, "Achieving Work-Life Balance: Reflections of a Midlife Entrant to the Academy," in *Juggling Flaming Chain Saws: Academics in Education Try to Balance Work and Family*, eds. Joanne M. Marshall et al. (Charlotte, NC: Information Age Publishing Inc., 2012), 199; "World Community Day Observance Held," *Tallahassee Democrat*, 5 Nov. 1956.

4. Anna Forbes Liddell (AFL), "As of Now," *Tassels*, 1960, Richard Puckett private collection.

5. Karleen Gillies, story told annually in the early 1980s at the Tallahassee AAUW holiday party per memory of the author.

6. Tann Hunt, "Tann Hunt (Class of 1957)," *FSU Voices: An Informal History of 150 Years*, ed. Maxine Stearn (Tallahassee: Florida State University, 2002),102.

7. Ruth Stewart, Tallahassee American Association of University Women Interviews (TAAUWI) (2006), Carolyn Dubard private collection; Virginia Mickler, TAAUWI (2006).

8. Browne-Ferrigno, "Achieving Work-Life Balance," 199.

9. Communication from Tricia Browne Ferrigno to author (5 Jun. 2020).

10. AFL, "Honest Confession, *Tassels*, 1960.

11. AFL, "Wishful Thinking," *Tassels*, 1960.

12. AFL, note on untitled poem, *Tassels*, 1960.

13. AFL, untitled poem, Anna Forbes Liddell Papers, Special Collections & Archives, Florida State University Libraries, Tallahassee, FL (AFLP).

14. AFL, "To R.M.," *Tassels*, 1960.

15. AFL, "Resurrection," *Tassels*, 1960.

16. WFSU Public Media, WFSU's History: Television, https://wfsu.org/about/history.php.

17. Richard Puckett, TAAUWI (20 Nov. 2005).

18. Ibid.

19. Ibid.

20. Ibid.

21. AFL, "Radio–TV Insight by Dr. A. Liddell," a page pulled out of an unknown document, Richard Puckett private collection.

22. Ibid.

23. Richard Puckett, TAAUWI (20 Nov. 2005).

24. Ibid.

25. Ibid.

26. Ibid.

27. Ibid.

28. Ibid.

29. "Dr. Liddell Nears End of 39-Year FSU Career," *Tallahassee Democrat*, 13 May 1962.

Last Years (1963–1979)

1. Richard Puckett, Tallahassee American Association of University Women Interviews (TAAUWI) (20 Nov. 2005), Carolyn Dubard private collection.

2. Anna Forbes Liddell, "Concerned over Concern for State Domination," *Tallahassee Democrat*, 1 Jul. 1964.

3. Thomas R. Wagy, "Governor Leroy Collins of Florida and the Selma Crisis of 1965," *The Florida Historical Quarterly* 57, no. 4 (1979): 403-420.

4. William H. Chafe, *The Paradox of Change: American Women in the 20th Century* (New York: Oxford University Press, 1991), 222.

5. Eliana Dockterman, "Fifty Years Ago, Doctors Called Domestic Violence 'Therapy,'" 25 Sept 2014, *TIME*, https://time.com/3426225/domestic-violence-

therapy/; Rory Dicker, *A History of US Feminisms* (Berkeley, CA: Seal Press, 2016), 70–71.

6. Carl M. Brauer, "Women Activists, Southern Conservatives, and the Prohibition of Sex Discrimination in Title VII of the 1964 Civil Rights Act, "*The Journal of Southern History* 49, no. 1 (1983): 37-56.

7. Chafe, "The Paradox of Change," 194–198. For a discussion of the black activism and feminism from the 19th century through the 1970s, see Irvin D. Solomon, *Feminism and Black Activism in Contemporary America: An Ideological Assessment (Contributions in Women's Studies)* (Westport, Connecticut: Praeger, 1989).

8. Brauer, "Women Activists," 37; Dicker, *A History of U.S. Feminisms*, 60–61, 100–101.

9. Rima Greenberg, "Women's Rights? She's a Pioneer," *Tampa Bay Times* (St. Petersburg, FL), 1 Apr. 1973.

10. Tad Bartmus, "Dr. Anna Liddell in Second Battle for Women's Rights," *Tallahassee Democrat*, 10 Apr. 1973.

11. Carol Gentry, "The ERA Battle: Best Show in Town," *Tallahassee Democrat*, 10 Apr. 1974. Susan Lykes, "She fought to vote and fought for the ERA," *Tampa Times*, 10 Apr. 1974.

12. Lykes, "She fought to vote and fought for the ERA."

13. Linda Harkey, "Anna Forbes Liddell," in *FSU Voices: An Informal History of 150 Years*, ed. Maxine Stern (Tallahassee: Florida State University, 2002), 51.

14. Mary Anna McBride Turner, TAAUWI (11 Mar. 2006), in Carolyn Dubard private collection.

Remembrances and Legacy

1. Helen McBride Jackson, Tallahassee American Association of University Women Interview (TAAUWI) (11 Mar. 2006), Carolyn Dubard private collection.

2. Mary Anna McBride Turner, TAAUWI (11 Mar. 2006).

3. Communication from Mary Anna Dunn to author, 21 Aug. 2020.

4. Jane Pickens Church, TAAUWI (11 Mar. 2006).

5. George Milton, dedication page, *Tassels*, 1960, Richard Puckett private collection.

6. Linda Harkey, "Anna Forbes Liddell," in *FSU Voices*, ed. Maxine Stern (Tallahassee: Florida State University, 2002), 50.

7. Richard Puckett, TAAUWI (20 Nov. 2005).

8. "Dr. Anna Forbes Liddell (1891–1971)" (2006), *Dean Eyman Distinctive Service Award Program Bulletin*, William Adkins private collection.

Made in the USA
Columbia, SC
27 March 2022

58195114R00196